CENTRAL AFRICA.

ADVENTURES

AND

MISSIONARY LABORS

IN SEVERAL COUNTRIES IN THE

INTERIOR OF AFRICA,

FROM

1849 to 1856.

BY T. J. BOWEN

SEVENTH THOUSAND.

NEGRO UNIVERSITIES PRESS
NEW YORK

Originally published in 1857
by the Southern Baptist Publication Society

Reprinted 1969 by
Negro Universities Press
A DIVISION OF GREENWOOD PUBLISHING CORP.
NEW YORK

SBN 8371-1540-X

PRINTED IN UNITED STATES OF AMERICA

PREFACE.

In some respects, our anticipations in regard to Central Africa have been more than realized. So far as we have proceeded, we have found a good and pleasant country, and a remarkably kind people, who are desirous of being instructed. Even in those places where they at first suspected our motives, they have generally given us a cordial reception, so soon as they ascertained that our only design is to teach them a better religion than their hereditary idolatry. The design of the following pages is to give some additional information in regard to countries but little known, and to call the attention of Christians to a people, who, it seems, are ready to receive the Gospel.

The recipes in the fourth chapter are intended chiefly for colonists and missionaries, to whom they will be of sufficient value to warrant their insertion.

On several points, the information is smaller than I desired, but it was thought best to limit the work to its present size, even at the expense of facts which are worth relating. The manners and customs of the people, and the pleasing incidents which are constantly occurring in the missionary work, are frequently detailed in the monthly letters of the missionaries, which are generally published in our periodicals. I had intended to have given a list of the genera of plants, so far as known, which are common to Tropical Africa and the United States, many of which are not found in Hooker's Niger Flora; but this would be of little interest to the general reader.

Some of the etymologies given in the twenty-second chapter, and elsewhere, will appear obscure or clear in proportion as they are referred with more or less care to the known methods by which words pass from one language into another. The language, traditions and religion of the Yóruba people, are of sufficient importance to merit a more extended investigation than would be proper in a popular work.

If some judicious Christians dissent from the Author's views as to the importance of civilization and commerce to the missionary work, I trust that no one will have occasion to say that the spirit in which we are laboring in Africa, is contrary to the genius of the Gospel. We do not believe that natural causes can sanctify the heart, although we hold that civilization is essential to the permanence of the Gospel among any people. The best method of conducting missions is yet a question; and I confess that I have been mindful of that fact while penning the following pages.

CHARLESTON, S. C., February 1, 1857.

NOTE.

THE letters employed in spelling African names and words in this work, have the same sounds as in English, with the following exceptions:

g is always hard, as in *get*.

n final, in Yóruba words, is a nasal much slighter in sound than *ng*.

s is never sounded like *z*.

z in Puloh words, has the sound of *z* in *azure*.

a has two sounds, as in *far* and in *fat* ; never as in *fate*.

e has two sounds, as in *prey* and in *met* ; never as in *me*.

ɪ has two sounds, as in *machine* and in *pin* ; never as in *pine*.

u long has they sound of *oo* in *too* ; never of *u* in *mute*.

ai have the sound of *i* in *pine*.

au have the sound of *ow* in *now*.

In a few proper names, *ee, oo*, and final *y*, are sounded as in English.

Occasionally the parallel lines = are used as a substitute for "equal to," or "equivalent to."

Cf. a contraction of *conferre*, means "refer to," or "compare."

[5]

CONTENTS.

CHAPTER I.

A BRIEF REVIEW OF AFRICAN EXPLORATION AND MISSIONS.

Tropical Africa known to the ancients — Introduction of the camel — The Carthagenians — The Psylli — The Egyptians — the Romans — The Saracens — Present population of Sudan — Ancient voyages — Portuguese discoveries — The slave trade — Modern travelers — Missions — Native Christians in Central Africa — Portuguese Missions in Congo — Moravian Missionaries — Missions in Sierra Leone — Liberia — Western Africa — Central Africa. - - - - - - - - - 13

CHAPTER II.

MONROVIA AND THE LIBERIANS.

Detention in Liberia — The rainy season — Tropical vegetation — The surf — Harbors — Monrovia — Condition of the people — Treatment of natives — Influence of the colony — Civilization increasing — Statistics (in a foot note) — Dissatisfaction of immigrants. - - - - - - - - - - - 27

CHAPTER III.

NATIVE TRIBES IN LIBERIA.

Kroomen — Origin of the tribe — Polygamy — Condition of women in Guinea — Barbarism — Religion — Oaths — Recent improvement of the Kroos — The Golahs — Vies — Deys — Their houses, dress, food, etc. — Mandingoes — Their Schools — Religion — Traffic. - - - - - - - - - - 37

CHAPTER IV.

SOIL, FARMS, AND PRODUCTIONS OF LIBERIA.

Rocks of Liberia — Soil — Swamp — Farms — Rice — Indian corn — Millet — Beans — Arrow root — Yams — Cassava — Tania — Sweet potatoes — Onions — Fruits — Sugar cane — Coffee — Ginger — Pepper — Cotton — India rubber — Ground

peas —Telfaria — Castor oil — Lamp oils — The oil palm — The
butter tree.   -   -   -   -   -   -   -   -   -   - 44

CHAPTER V.
FUTURE PROSPECTS OF LIBERIA.

Colonization opposed — Its aims — Future emigration of American blacks — The natives will be civilized — Improvability of
man — Origin and progress of civilization — The present condition of Africa.   -   -   -   -   -   -   -   -   - 56

CHAPTER VI.
TRAVELS IN THE COUNTRY OF THE GOLAHS, IN 1850.

Departure to Golah — African singing — A mangrove swamp —
New Georgia — St. Paul's river — Navigation — The bush —
Roads — Pine apples — African water — Naked Negroes —
Venzwaw — Streets — Palaver house — Hindrances — Preaching — Traffic — Currency — Salt — Gaming — An affray — Music — A "half town" — Small pox — Villages — Soil — Suwy
— Mill seats — War — Forests — Wild animals — A tribal burying ground — A fine country — Gebby — An affray — Tazzua — Sama — A covetous king — Mr. Goodale's death — The
people of Sama — Godiri — Boonda — Mandingo — Mahometans — A law suit — Return to Monrovia.   -   -   -   - 67

CHAPTER VII.
VOYAGE FROM MONROVIA TO BADAGRY, IN 1850.

Parable of the sower — Departure from Monrovia — Foolish
Kroomen — El Mina — The Fantees — Rise of the coast —
Gold — Nudity — Immodesty — Causes of African degradation
— Queer marriages — Mulattoes — Curious weights — Costume
— A funeral — Cape Coast Castle — The landing — Wesleyan
Missions — " L. E. L." 's grave — Guinea worm — African hills
—Rocks — Rise of the coast — Departure for Badagry — What
Negroes need masters — Akra gardens — Negro vanity — Aguey
— Badagry.   -   -   -   -   -   -   -   -   -   - 83

CHAPTER VIII.
BADAGRY AND THE SLAVE COAST.

The people of Badagry — The Slave Coast — New " niggers"—
Fida -- The language — Slave trade — Soil — Climate — Relig-

ious ceremony — Witches — Markets — Currency — Cowries — Beggars — Old Simeon — A servant and a horse — Departure from Badagry — Burial in the air — How loads are carried — Prairies — A lagoon — A caravan — The country — Soil — Scenery — Countries on the Slave Coast — Eighteen months' detention. - - - - - - - - - - 93

CHAPTER IX.
ABBEOKUTA AND THE EGBAS.

Abbeokuta — Ogun river — Rocks — Soil — Egbá Country desolated by war — Ancient giants — Wars — Dahomies defeated — Missionaries invited to Egbá — Success — Translations — Hand of Providence. - - - - - - - - 105

CHAPTER X.
BREAKING UP OF THE SLAVE TRADE.

Evils of the slave trade — Opposition of natives to slave wars — The Dahomy army — Battle at Abbeokuta — Badagry burnt — Lagos taken by the English. - - - - - - 113

CHAPTER XI.
AN ATTEMPT TO PASS THROUGH IKETU, IN 1850.

Departure from Abbeokuta — Ibara —Aibo —An Albino — Preaching — Strictures on — Superstitious fears of white men — A fine country — Roadside market — Yériwa river — Villages — Ijale — Return to Abbeokuta — Robbers. - - - 125

CHAPTER XII.
INCIDENTS AT ABBEOKUTA, IN 1851.

The Yóruba language — A Puloh man — Egbá country — Human sacrifices — Oko - Obba — Immodesty — The idol Ifa — Visits to the farms — Slaves — Tobacco — Oro day — Devil bush. - 132

CHAPTER XIII.
VISIT TO IKETU, IN 1851.

Departure for Iketu — Dahomy refugees — A poor country — Villages — The " king's father" — Soil — Manners and customs

— Difficulties — Deposing of kings — Preaching — Mahometans rebuked — Slave market — A female captive — " Send me
your head!"— Amazons— Departure from Iketu.   -   -   - 142

CHAPTER XIV.

VISIT TO BI-OLORRUN-PELLU, IN FEBRUARY, 1852.

Messengers sent to Isehin — Invited into Yóruba — Opposition —
Aberrekodo — Eruwa — Scenery — Bi-olorrun-pellu — Whites
in Africa — A chief's Bible — Effects of preaching — Heathens
without idols — Irawaw — Traffic — Candid Mahometans — Invited to Awyaw — Farms — Animals — Hunting — The unicorn. 151

CHAPTER XV.

VISIT TO AWAYE, OKE-EFO AND IJAYE, IN 1852.

Departure for Ishakki — Awaye — Oke-Efo — Return to Awaye —
. A prince banished — Visit to Ijaye — Land given for a Mission
— Return to the coast — Embark for London.   -   -   - 167

CHAPTER XVI.

BEGINNING OF THE YORUBA MISSION.

Return to Africa — Sickness — War — Death of Missionaries —
Station at Ijaye — Erecting houses — Baptisms — Arrival of
Mr. Clark — Preaching — Exploring tour — Removal to Ogbo-
moshaw. -   -   -   -   -   -   -   -   -   -   - 179

CHAPTER XVII.

VISITS TO ILORRIN IN 1855.

Departure for Ilorrin — Opposition — The country — A village
priest — Reception at Ilorrin — Conferences — Arabs — Large
towns — Dasaba the Cruel — Past events at Ilorrin — The
Pulohs — Men with tails — A second visit to Ilorrin — New
Missionaries — Distances from Lagos.   -   -   -   - 188

CHAPTER XVIII.

A JOURNEY FROM YORUBA TO SIERRA LEONE, IN 1856.

Departure from Ogbomoshaw — Heathen notions of Providence —
A canoe voyage — Improvements at Lagos — Monrovia — Si-

erra Leone — Baptist churches there — Missionaries needed —
A school of Native Boys — Successful mission.   -   -   206

CHAPTER XIX.

GEOGRAPHY OF YORUBA.

Boundaries — Population — Towns — Surface — Mountains —
Prairies — Soil — Streams — Swamps — Springs — Water. -   217

CHAPTER XX.

SEASONS AND CLIMATE.

Rainy season — Dry season — Spring — Temperature — Winds —
The harmattan — Clouds — Mornings and evenings — The best
time to travel — Diseases of the natives — Diseases of white visitors — Fever — Dysentery — Debility — Causes of disease —
Heat — Dampness — Malaria — How to preserve health — Taking cold — Clothing — Houses — Bathing — Damp beds — Laws
of Malaria — Diet — Medicines.   -   -   -   -   -   - 226

CHAPTER XXI.

GEOLOGY, PLANTS AND ANIMALS OF YORUBA.

Rocks on the coast — Organic remains — Drift — Rocks in the
interior — Granite — Ancient sea coast — Vegetation — Trees
— Timber — The Upas — Poisons — Drugs — Climbers —
Flowers — Weeds of cultivation — Fruits — Beasts — Birds —
Reptiles — Ants.   -   -   -   -   -   -   -   -   - 252

CHAPTER XXII.

ETHNOLOGICAL FACTS AND TRADITIONS.

Origin of the name of Yóruba — Men created at Ifeh — Sixteen
Emigrants from the east — Drying up of the waters — Yórubas
once lived in Nufe — Six Yóruba tribes — Descended from
Nimrod — White Immigrants to Sudan — Affinities of the
Yóruba tongue — List of Yóruba and Puloh words. -   -   - 264

CHAPTER XXIII.

PHYSICAL, INTELLECTUAL AND MORAL CHARACTERISTICS OF THE SUDANESE.

Typical Negroes — Mulattoes — Original seats of the Negroes —
Their Migrations in Sudan — White Immigrants to Africa —

Effects of Climate — Permanence of Mulatto races — Black
men with European features — Activity of Negroes — Intellect
— Language — Laws — Religion — Common sense — Inventive
faculty — Science — Music — Letters — Poetry — Kindness —
Industry — Commerce needed — Immodesty — Covetousness —
Proverbs.   -   -   -   -   -   -   -   -   - 276

CHAPTER XXIV.

SOCIAL LIFE IN YORUBA.

Towns — Walls — Streets — Markets — Houses — Dress — Food
Amusements — Dancing — Religious Processions — Salutations
— Marriage — Polygamy — Divorce — Inheritance — Widows
— Children — Burial — Ghosts — Occupations of the people —
Farming — Traffic — Arts — Tools — Glass manufacture.   - 294

CHAPTER XXV.

RELIGION AND GOVERNMENT.

Monotheism — Idolatry — Mediators — Symbols — Sacrifices —
Priests — Three principal Idols — Obatalla — Shango — Ifa —
Government — War — Captives.   -   -   -   -   -   - 310

CHAPTER XXVI.

ON THE MEANS OF REGENERATING AFRICA.

Savages may be converted — They can not sustain the Gospel —
They must be civilized — The Divine method of dealing with
man — The former state of Africa — Its present state — What
type of civilization suits it — The duty of Missionaries — Importance of commerce — Commercial resources of Central
Africa — Industry of the people — Navigation of the Niger.   321

CHAPTER XXVII.

AN APPEAL FOR MISSIONARIES.

The great commission — Our Missions to Central Africa — Men
needed — Who should go — Our proposed line of stations —
A wagon road to be opened — Love to the souls of men, a motive — The heathens not saved — The appointed time for the
conversion of Africa — A wide field of labor — Liberality of
the churches.   -   -   -   -   -   -   -   -   - 346

CENTRAL AFRICAN MISSION.

CHAPTER I.

A BRIEF REVIEW OF AFRICAN EXPLORATION AND MISSIONS.

TROPICAL AFRICA KNOWN TO THE ANCIENTS — INTRODUCTION OF THE CAMEL — THE CARTHAGENIANS — THE PSYLLI — THE EGYPTIANS — THE ROMANS — THE SARACENS — PRESENT POPULATION OF SUDAN — ANCIENT VOYAGES — PORTUGUESE DISCOVERIES — THE SLAVE TRADE — MODERN TRAVELERS — MISSIONS — NATIVE CHRISTIANS IN CENTRAL AFRICA — PORTUGUESE MISSIONS IN CONGO — MORAVIAN MISSIONARIES — MISSIONS IN SIERRA LEONE — LIBERIA — WESTERN AFRICA — CENTRAL AFRICA.

No QUARTER of the globe is so imperfectly known as Africa. Cut off from the rest of the world by deserts and oceans, given up to the occupancy of barbarous races, and defended by a climate more terrible than armies, she has generally repelled or destroyed alike the covetous, the curious, and the benevolent intruder. Or if at any time the adventurer has been more successful, if he has made extensive explorations, and accurate observations, his information, for the most part, as if by some fatality, has not been permitted to reach us. We have good reasons for believing that some of the ancients, as also the Portuguese of the fifteenth and sixteenth centuries, were better acquainted with Africa than we are at present.

It is not easy to believe, that the camel was first introduced upon the wastes of Sahara by the Saracens. The name by which it is known to several nations of Sudan, is not derived from the Arabic. I believe that the Pulohs (Fellatahs) are the hybrid descendants of a white race, who crossed the desert from Northern Africa, (which they would hardly have done without camels,) many ages before the days of Mahomet. The exclusive policy of the Carthagenians, which led them to conceal their knowledge of distant countries, and the subsequent destruction of any records which they might have kept, may prevent us forever from ascertaining how far they were acquainted with the great desert and the regions beyond it. It is probable, however, that they, like the Egyptians, were aware of the fact, that the desert is interspersed with green oases or fertile spots, and that they were in possession of camels, or some other means by which they could reach these Elysian fields, so grateful to thirsty and weary travelers. The story that the interior of Africa was too hot to be inhabited, may have been a Carthagenian fiction, invented to deceive the people of Europe, who knew merely enough of the desert to make the report seem credible. Fezzan must have been known to the inhabitants of Northern Africa ; and it would be very strange if the people of Fezzan should be unacquainted with the line of oases which stretch at easy distances southward to Sudan. It is said that an ancient tribe, the Psylli, (or Psulloi,*) once attempted

---

* Perhaps the modern Puloh.

to migrate across the desert to the south; but that advancing into boundless plains of glowing sand, they all perished of thirst. It is very improbable that the Psylli, who had long occupied the northern borders of the desert, would attempt to cross it without being convinced that the journey was practicable; and since they passed through Fezzan, by a route which is not intolerable even to men and women on foot, it is very probable that they did not perish in the desert, but reached their destination in safety. Great as the horrors of the desert may be, they have always been overrated. There are not now, and never have been, billows or mountains of moving sand, to overwhelm armies and caravans. To satisfy himself on this point, the reader has only to examine the accounts of modern travelers. At present, there is an active trade going on between the Barbary States and Sudan; and if such a trade existed in ancient times, we can easily account for any extravagant stories about the dangers of the desert, which may have been circulated by the people of Northern Africa.

Egypt, too, must have been acquainted with Central Africa. This is attested by the ancient monuments, and no less strongly by the Egyptian arts and institutions which still flourish on the banks of the Niger. The peculiar beads or bugles which are found on the Egyptian mummies, are also dug from the earth in the Juku country, north of the Benue or Chadda, and again at Ifeh in Yóruba. These are the so-called Popoe beads, which formerly sold for their weight in gold.

After the fall of Carthage, the Romans a so became acquainted with the countries beyond the Sahara. Denham and Clapperton found Roman remains in the midst

of the desert. A Roman army is affirmed to have penetrated far into Sudan. There are several Latin words
in the Puloh language, as for instance, *loto*, to *bathe.*

On the whole, it is reasonable to suppose that the inhabitants of Northern Africa, if not the learned men of
Southern Europe, were as well acquainted with Sudan,
in ancient times, as we are at present. By whom the
routes across the desert were first discovered, and what
curious or mercantile adventurers penetrated into the
country of the blacks, cannot now be ascertained. But
enough is known to authorize the inference of much more
having been known than is ordinarily supposed.

On the arrival of the Saracens in Northern Africa,
they probably found the routes to Sudan as well known
to the Mauri or Moors, as they are at present. In the
tenth century, these hordes, like swarms of locusts, which
had spread desolation in many parts of Europe and Asia,
directed their course southward, and came down upon
the fertile table lands of Central Africa. Meeting the
Pulohs and other mulatto tribes on the upper Niger, they
conquered or dispersed them. Hausa, Kanikè (Burnu),
and several adjacent countries, submitted to the religion
and laws of the invaders, who established a number of
kingdoms, as Kuku or Burnu, Wangara, Tokrur or Sokoto, and Ghana or Ghinea (Kano), a name which a
mistake of Europeans has transferred to the western
coast. These kingdoms, though highly celebrated by
Arabian writers of that age, were of short continuance.
Amalgamation, aided by polygamy, concubinage, and
still grosser licentiousness, conquered the conquerors of
Sudan. The hybrid offspring of the Arabs, surrounded
by millions of negroes, grew up in the language, feel-

ings, and habits of the natives, with the exception of idolatry; and the famous Saracen kingdoms of Sudan quietly retrograded into semi-barbarous African tribes. The effects of the invasion, however, are still conspicuous. Most of the people are Mahometans; a knowledge 'of the written Arabic is extensively diffused; and there is an extensive mixture of Shemitic blood in the conquered tribes. Several Arabic writers of the Saracen period have left accounts of Sudan, which may be seen in the Appendix to Murray's Africa. After all, the whole amount of our information put together, is very small.

It was not only by crossing the great desert, that Europeans and Asiatics attempted to explore the wonders of the vast and ever mysterious African continent. At an early date, ships were sent to explore both the eastern and western coasts, and even to circumnavigate the peninsula. It is recorded that Necho, a king of Egypt, employed some Phenecian navigators to explore the whole coast, from the Red Sea to the Mediterranean, which they accomplished in three years. Nearly six hundred years before Christ, the Carthagenians explored the western coast, to a considerable distance; but how far, is a disputed point among modern geographers. Some believe that they did not pass the coast of Morocco, while others suppose that they went as far as Sherbro Island, near Liberia. The Bijogo Islands, a little to the south of the Gambia, seem to be pretty clearly described in their narratives. Other voyages were made in subsequent times. If Necho's explorers delineated the true shape of the continent, this knowledge was afterward lost, for ancient maps represent the coast as running eastward from Cape Palmas, and sweeping round to the Red Sea. This form would seem to prove, that the navigators of those times had gone as far as to the Gulf of Guinea, where the coast stretches eastward for a thousand miles ; but had not reached Cameroons, where it again bends to the southward.

The next adventurers in African waters, were the Por-' tuguese. Beginning their explorations of the western coast, about the middle of the fifteenth century, they pushed them forward with energy for more than fifty years, and rewarded themselves by taking possession of the country in the name of God, the pope, and the king. Their monopoly of discovery and acquisition was not long enjoyed. The Dutch and the English entered the field not only as rivals, but sometimes as enemies. The high title by which Portugal claimed her African possessions, was not able to retain them against the impious demand of arms. She still managed, however, to maintain her power on some parts of the coast, and her citizens performed at least their share in the transportation of heathen negroes to Christian countries, with a view to their conversion and salvation. No people prayed more fervently for the success of slavers, in thus plucking brands from the burning, than did the Portuguese. No people were more fully persuaded that the kidnappers were doing God service. Even within a few years past, a slaver has expressed his opinion, that he was instrumental in the salvation of more souls, than all the missionaries in Africa.

In their search after new countries to occupy, in their pious efforts to discover Prestyr John, and afterward in their vigorous prosecution of the slave trade, the Portuguese attained a more extensive knowledge of Africa than any other people. They visited countries which to this day have been seen by no other European. According to a Yóruba proverb, " There is a house in Awyaw, (Katanga) called the house of silence ; a white man died there." On inquiry, I was informed that a long time ago, two white men came from the coast to see the king at Awyaw, where one of them died. They were no doubt Portuguese, but whether they expected to find Prestyr John, in the powerful monarch of Hio, or were impelled by the baser motive of self-interest, I have not ascertained. Unfortunately, the extensive observations of the Portuguese were not made known to Europe. England knew nothing of Katanga, till the days of Lander, and to this day, we can scarcely credit the fact, which the Portuguese knew two hundred years ago, that there are many towns in the interior of Africa, from fifteen to twenty-five miles in circuit.

The slave trade was a dark affair in more respects than one ; and it has shed but little light on African geography. The curiosity of learned men and the enterprise of merchants have done a little more, but not much. In the beginning of the seventeenth century, the English sent out several expeditions to explore the coast and the rivers. One of these penetrated far into the interior, by the Gambia, and dug twelve pounds of gold. For a long time, very little was done in African exploration. At length, about the year 1790, the African Association in England, determined to send intelligent explorers into Central Africa. Their success was far less than their hopes. Ledyard, who was first appointed, died in Egypt. Lucas advanced but a short distance from the Mediterranean. Major Houghton, who attempted to reach Timbuctoo from the Gambia, was robbed by the Moors, and died in the desert. The two journeys of Mungo Park, and especially the first, produced a great sensation. He had penetrated into the country from the mouth of the Gambia, more than one thousand miles, to Silla, near Jene ; he had seen the Niger flowing eastward, and had learned more than was ever known before of the country and the people. His next journey was undertaken for the purpose of exploring the Niger, which some supposed communicated with the Nile. He committed the error of taking with him about forty men, instead of the two or three, which is the maximum allowed by the character of the country and people for a traveler. Death soon reduced their number to five, including Park, all of whom perished at Busa, on the Niger, which is scarcely three hundred miles on a direct line from Lagos. In 1822, Denham and Clapperton crossed the desert from Tripoli, and penetrated Sudan to Mandara, and Sokoto. Three years after, Clapperton and Lander went from Badagry to Sokoto, where the former fell a victim to dysentery. Since that time, various journeys have been made through different parts of Africa. Caillè succeeded in passing from the Atlantic to Timbuctoo, and thence to the Mediterranean. Lander discovered the mouth of the Niger, by descending the stream from Nufe. Laing reached Timbuctoo, but was murdered on his return. Laird and Oldfield ascended the Niger to Raba. Beecroft went a little farther. Dr. Barth has recently returned from a great tour in Sudan, and Dr. Livingston from another. In 1854, an English steamer ascended the Chadda or Benuè to the heart of the continent, and returned without the loss of a single man. After all, but little is known of Africa. Immense districts remain wholly unknown, and our scanty information concerning other parts is often inaccurate.

We turn now to enterprises of a different character—to the humble or professedly humble efforts of missionaries. It is not quite certain whether the ancient Christians did or did not carry the gospel to Central Africa. Now and then we hear a rumor of Christians in the heart of the continent, but the reports are too vague to be worthy of credit. When Denham was in Mandara, he saw a company of strangers from the south, who were said, by the Arabs, to be Christians. He refused to believe it, on account of their savage appearance. "Nevertheless," said his informants, "they are Christians." I met with a man in Yóruba, who affirmed that he had been far beyond Hausa to a country called Waiangarana, where the people are neither Mahometans nor heathens. But he was unable to tell what they believed or worshipped. At Ogbomoshaw, a strange-looking man was pointed out to me as a Christian. He said that he had heard of Isa (Jesus) in the east—nay, that he had seen him in a vision—and that the people in that country worship him. He may have been a deceiver, or he may have been in Abyssinia. I could make no sense of his story. Still it is not impossible that some of the negroes west of the Nile, may have learned something of Christianity, either from the Copts or the Abyssinians. If so, we may yet discover evidence of these ancient missions.

So far as we certainly know, the first efforts to convert the negroes, were made by the Portuguese. About the middle of the fifteenth century, that is, four hundred years ago, Bemoy, a Jaloff prince, was taken to Lisbon, entertained with bull-fights and puppet-shows, baptized, and sent back as a Catholic prince, with good hopes of reducing the Jaloffs to the dominion of the church. The commander of the vessel in which Bemoy returned to the Senegal, stabbed him to death on the coast of Africa, which put an end to the contemplated mission. Toward the close of the century, several princes and nobles of Congo were taken to Lisbon, instructed, and baptized. On their return home with several missionaries, the king and many of the nobles embraced the Catholic religion. The common people, not by hundreds, but by thousands, placed themselves under instruction, and were received into the fold, by baptism. This ceremony was duly performed according to the rites of the church, with exorcism, crossing, and tasting of salt. Among all these ceremonies, the last appears to have made the deepest impression on the minds of the wondering people; and the initiatory ordinance of the church was soon known through Congo as the "eating of salt" ceremony. Notwithstanding this natural and innocent mistake as to a name, the converts ran well according to the forms of their new religion. They appear to have been captivated and carried away by the imposing ritual of their new worship. No people could kneel and cross themselves more zealously. They were fond of processions, in which the admiring missionaries were sometimes deafened by such shouts, blowing of horns, and noises, as they had never before heard.

It was now time to convert the people from the error of their ways. The attempt to abolish polygamy produced a civil war, in which the Portuguese, and a prince, who rebelled against the king of Congo, were successful. This prince being at last established on the throne, the mission flourished and spread exceedingly. Countless numbers were baptized. The apostles themselves had not made converts more rapidly than did these people, after their fashion. All history records no instance of a people so eminently susceptible as the Congoes. There were some things, however, which still needed reforming. The converts had not yet renounced idolatry. Neither the superior ceremonies of the church, nor the urgent and repeated admonitions of their new spiritual guides, could shake their attachment to the devil-worship of their ancestors. Wearied by the obstinancy of the people, the good missionaries thought that a little physical force would give the greater efficacy to moral suasion ; and they began to apply this severer discipline of their church. The first attack was made on the gods, which the missionaries knocked down and hammered to pieces with their cudgels. The next was on the temples, which were burnt down, sometimes secretly in the night, to prevent disturbance. Some of the more stupid and obstinate of the idolatrous converts, were disciplined with whips and rods. It happened that the queen herself was unwilling to give up her beloved idol. What harm could a little addition to the gospel do? Her confessor reasoned, till reasoning was absurd, and then as a last resort, applied the extreme discipline. A few strokes of the whip enlightened her majesty's understanding so amazingly, that she heartily renounced idolatry, and submitted herself humbly to her pastor. But unfortunately, her goodness soon disappeared like the morning dew, and she related the whole circumstance to the king with so much indignation, that he espoused her cause, and renounced the friendship of the missionaries forever. From this time, the mission was obliged to struggle with difficulties, and declined apace, till it finally expired. This event was probably hastened by unexpected events in Europe. Luther's great schism occurred just at the time that the struggling Congo mission needed efficient support, not only from the religious classes, but from the strong arm of the Portuguese government.

More than a hundred years ago the Moravians sent a party of missionaries to the Gold Coast, but they were soon cut off and dispersed by the diseases of the country.

During the revolutionary war, a number of negroes in the Southern States attached themselves to the British, by whom they were first taken to Nova Scotia, and then to London. Poor, unhealthy, and rapidly diminishing in numbers, they seemed in danger of utter extinction, when it was proposed to settle them in Sierra Leone, as a colony. Evangelical Christians had already begun to feel the impulse of the missionary enterprise, which at present stands forth as a prominent feature, and a great problem in the affairs of the world. The churchmen sent missionaries to Sierra Leone, who were soon followed by Wesleyans and others. No mission of modern times has been more successful than this, as I shall show in the sequel. The American colonies called missionaries to Liberia and Cape Palmas. The Wesleyans established themselves at Cape Coast Castle, and afterwards at Badagry. At the latter place, they were joined by churchmen from Sierra Leone, and both parties advanced to Abbeokuta, about sixty miles in the interior.

In the mean time, Central Africa was occasionally mentioned as a future field for missions, but nothing was done. Not a few persons, appalled by the mortality of missionaries on the western coast, had almost concluded that white men should not be sent to that country. The natives on the coast also were considered to be, in their present degraded state, nearly or quite too low to demand immediate attention. Almost any field appeared to be preferable to Africa. The Foreign Mission Board of the newly formed Southern Baptist Convention had no white men in that country, and their colored missionaries confined their labors mostly to the colonists. The question arose, What can be done for Africa? The prospect appeared gloomy, so far as regards white laborers. Finally, it was suggested that Sudan, remote as it is, might be accessible ; that it might have, and ought to have, by reason of its elevation, a healthy climate ; and that the people were certainly superior in intelligence and morals to those on the coast. Here was a new hope. The effort might be a failure, but still the probabilities of success were sufficient to authorize, if not to demand a trial. On the 22d of February, 1849, I had the satisfaction of being appointed a missionary to Sudan. The next difficulty was to find a colleague. I traveled through several of the Southern States, and the brethren listened with interest even where they doubted ; but no one volunteered to go. After several months' delay, Hervey Goodale, who was under appointment for China, was transferred to the proposed mission in Central Africa, and soon after, Robt. F. Hill, a young colored man, was selected to accompany us.

Our instructions could not be very definite. We were expected to penetrate into Sudan, or some adjacent country, and to remain there till we should become well acquainted with the character of the climate and people. It was thought that Badagry, on the Slave Coast, might be a convenient point from which to commence our explorations, and that Igboho (Bohoo) in the north west of Yóruba, would probably be a suitable place for our first location. Should the undertaking prove to be unsuccessful or disastrous, this was what we had agreed to risk. If our hopes were realized, other missionaries would join us, and a line of stations would be formed from the coast to the remote interior.

The object of the following pages is to show what has been attempted and accomplished in pursuance of this design ; and to acquaint the public, especially those who are interested in this attempt to evangelize Central Africa, with the countries and tribes which have been seen by the writer.

CHAPTER II.

MONROVIA AND THE LIBERIANS.

DETENTION OF LIBERIA — THE RAINY SEASON — TROPICAL VEGETATION —
THE SURF — HARBORS — MONROVIA — CONDITION OF THE PEOPLE —
TREATMENT OF NATIVES — INFLUENCE OF THE PEOPLE — INFLUENCE
OF THE COLONIES — CIVILIZATION INCREASING — STATISTICS (IN A
FOOT NOTE) — DISSATISFACTION OF IMMIGRANTS.

WE sailed from Providence, R. I., on the 17th of December, 1849, and arrived at Monrovia, the capital of Liberia, on the 8th of February following. Here we were informed that the vessel in which we had come out, could not proceed to her destination, till she had made a voyage of considerable length to the windward, that is, in the direction of the great desert. This movement, together with the delay of trading at the ports to the leeward of Liberia, would prevent our reaching Badagry before the rainy season, which is generally very dangerous to travelers in the sickly climate of Africa. At this time, we were ignorant of the interesting fact, that the rains in Yóruba and the countries beyond, are never so severe as to prevent safe and comfortable traveling; and accordingly, we went ashore at Monrovia, to remain till the next dry season, unless we should find an immediate passage to Badagry. This delay was not agreeable ; but we should gain the advantage of pass-

ing through the process of acclimation, before proceeding on our journey, and might in the meantime find
abundance of missionary work to do in the colony. Our
first employment ashore was to look at every thing
within our reach, and to inquire into every thing we
could think of. It may be presumed, that we were not
inattentive observers. We were in a new country and
climate, where every beast, bird and plant bore the impress of novelty. We were surrounded by black men
in a new relation, the citizens of their own free republic,
civilized, and standing forth in strong contrast with
" the naked negro," in his primeval rudeness.

Liberia has frequently been described, sometimes
with great fairness, and sometimes with surprising de-
partures from the truth. Men of equal candor, measur-
ing the state of the colony by different standards, one
comparing it with the most flourishing countries of the
globe, and another with the barbarous States of Western Africa, have naturally differed widely in their judgment. Both parties have erred. To form a correct
judgment in regard to Liberia, we must compare it
with other newly settled countries, making due allowance for the circumstances of each case. It is not my
purpose to correct many erroneous statements, either
for or against Liberia ; but to state briefly what I saw
and heard during my stay in the country, and to express
my opinion as to what may be, or ought to be, the result
of African colonization. For this digression, I must
crave the indulgence of the reader, on the ground that
a friend of Central African Missions can scarcely fail to
feel a deep interest in the missions and colonies which
have been planted on the western coast. The colonies

of the west, and the missions of Sudan may eventually flow together and become one interest. I remember also that many of my readers may not have seen any other work on Liberia, and to them a description of the country and people by an eye witness will probably be acceptable.

One who has never been in the torrid zone can form no just conception of the exuberance, and I may say, intensity of tropical vegetation. The first thing that arrested my attention, as we entered the anchorage off Monrovia, was the dense verdure which clusters on the promontory of Mesurado. The whole view from the ship, consisting of a low monotonous beach, fringed on one side by the white foam of the surf, and on the other, by a thick-set wall-like forest; the dashing of the waves against the rocky base of the promontory, which hangs like a heavy cloud of vegetation over the sea; the half-clad and unclad natives, some pulling off to meet us in their little canoes, and others standing in groups on the beach; the absence of all marks of civilization; and the back ground of the picture fading away in the dim, smoky horizon which distinguishes the dry season—all presented a scene of mingled beauty, wildness and sombreness which accorded well with my previous conceptions of Africa. It was very natural that imagination should look forward beyond the blue smoky mountain tops which lay like clouds in the distant interior, and wonder what strange rivers, towns and people were there in the unknown countries to which we were going. Some reader may conclude that our project was about as wild as the country before us, and as visionary as our feelings when we first looked out upon the wide

continent of Africa. But if he will study our aims and
the probabilities of success, as closely as we had, he
may admit that our mission was a sober Christian work,
fully worthy of our most strenuous efforts. Monrovia
stands behind the promontory, on a peninsular ridge
between the Mesurado river and the sea. There are
two means of getting ashore from vessels in the anchorage ; one in the little round bottomed Kroo canoes,
which threaten .to capsize every moment, and would
certainly do so, should you indulge in any awkward
maneuvers ; and another in boats which glide safely
enough over the smooth rollers or long swelling waves,
and are generally able to pass though the surf on the
bar, without much danger. There are two landing
places also ; one on the beach, about a mile from the
anchorage, and the same distance from the town ; and
the other at the wharves, on the bank of the river, in
front of Monrovia. In fine weather, a boat or canoe may
be landed on the beach, and you may get ashore with
dry feet, by mounting on the shoulders of a stout Krooman. If the sea is rough, you must take a boat and
pass over the bar into the river. The water on the bar
is said to be eight or nine feet deep, and with good rowers,
there is no great danger ; but you must enjoy or suffer the
novelty of dashing through several breakers, and perhaps of being slapped in the face, or on the back, by
several white sprays before you reach the smooth water.
    Bad as the surf is at Monrovia, it is still worse at
most other places between Sherbro and Fernando Po.
There are good harbors at Goree, Bathurst and Freetown, but none at all on the Grain Coast, Ivory Coast,
Gold Coast and Slave Coast. Ships are obliged to an-

chor in the open sea, from one to five miles from the shore ; and the waves roll in so heavily upon the beach, that landing is often dangerous. Fortunately, there are no hurricanes in Africa, so that there is little danger of shipwreck. At a few places where there are rivers with several feet of water on the bar, as at Monrovia and Lagos, an increase of traffic will authorize the employment of steam lighters, which will be a great convenience.

Monrovia, which we approached by way of the river, presented a straggling, bush-grown, weather-beaten appearance, similar to some old towns in Mexico, where the sober wisdom of the people allows no useless expenditure of manual labor. The wharves were rudely constructed of stones. A few little vessels, some in the water, and some on the stocks, indicated a degree of enterprise among the people. Two or three half-filled streets of large old stores and warehouses, extended several hundred yards along the side of the water, and the hill side between these and the dwellings on the top of the ridge, was given up to weeds and bushes. My first impressions of the place were not favorable. Numbers of colonists, mostly well-dressed, met us on the wharves with smiles and cordial greetings. In ascending the bushy hill, we passed a cake shop, exactly in the style of the "cakes and beer, for sale here," to be found among old negro women in Georgia. I soon found that everything in Monrovia was as nearly a copy of similar things in America, as circumstances would permit. In general, there was only one dwelling on each of the spacious lots, and the unoccupied portions were enclosed by stone walls for gardens, or given up to the weeds and bushes. Many of the lots were still unoccupied. Want of people, and not indolence, is the true reason of the wild and straggling appearance of the town. Monrovia is a new town, or at least but thinly populated, the whole number of inhabitants not exceeding two thousand. With the same population, Freetown would present the same bush-grown appearance.

The houses in Monrovia are generally two stories high, the lower one designed for servants, store-rooms, &c., being built of stone ; and the upper one with bed-rooms, parlors, and piazzas for the family, built of wood. The furniture is similar to that used by the middle classes in America. I was pleased to see a good many valuable books and periodicals on the shelves and tables. Most of the people, in short, appear to live as comfortably as people of means commonly do at home. I have heard them accused of being too fond of dress and show, but if they were more so than other people who live in towns, I was not able to perceive it.

The public houses are a government house, president's house, jail, four churches, Methodist, Baptist, Presbyterian, and Episcopalian ; and several school-houses, one or two of which, I believe, are called colleges. A large proportion of the people are religious. Many of them, no doubt, are true Christians ; but others are too much like certain professed believers in other countries. The morals of the people generally, appeared to be much the same as our own. In one respect, however, they are said to be deficient, though not so bad, if report may be trusted, as the people of Sierra Leone, or of France. Illicit intercourse is a characteristic of Western Africa. I am told that all the schools in Liberia are supported by donations from America. This is not creditable to the people. They ought, from self respect, to do all they can to sustain their own schools and churches. If they do not stand alone, they cannot be said to stand at all. It is said again, that the young people are too much addicted to idleness. It is certainly desirable, that every young man should be trained to some useful employment, but since it is not generally done in other countries, we can hardly demand it in Liberia.

It is scarcely necessary to contradict the reiterated report that the Liberians hold slaves. Within the colony slavery is prohibited, both to emigrants and natives. I have seen a Vy man tried and fined for purchasing a girl from a native trader. In some cases, slaves have been brought down from the interior, and pawned to Liberians for debt ; but this was found to be a precarious species of collateral security, for the slave being free by law, the moment he enters the colony, may go where he chooses, without consulting either the pawnee or his master. When minors are liberated by a decision of the court, they are bound out to be civilized, and educated till the time when it is supposed they will be twenty-one years of age; and their apprenticeship being accomplished, they are citizens of the republic. Canot, the famous Portuguese slaver, who ought to know, affirms in his memoir, that Liberia has exerted an immense influence in the suppression of the slave trade.

But the Liberians cannot be justified generally in regard to the manner in which they treat the natives. Making all due allowance for social and other differences, they regard their barbarous neighbors with too much contempt. Neither do they exert themselves as they might, to improve them in civilization and religion.

It is true, that the churches and schools are open to the natives, if they choose to enter them ; but the naked and ignorant barbarians do not choose to trust themselves in among the proud and well-dressed Liberians, either to learn or to worship. I am glad that some are now making more special efforts to improve the natives, and I have no doubt that persevering, well-directed efforts will be successful.

It must not be supposed, however, that nothing has been done heretofore. The colony is said to contain about one thousand reclaimed natives, some of whom are consistent Christians. The general influence of the colony has been good. Degraded as the natives are at present, we must remember that they were far more so, twenty years ago. If they improve in the same ratio for the next twenty years, many of them will be half civilized. There have been frequent wars in Liberia, as there once were in Sierra Leone, and other colonies ; but the result of the whole has been an increase of confidence and friendship on the part of the natives. Many have placed themselves under the jurisdiction of the colony, for the sake of enjoying the just and vigorous protection of its laws. This fact is highly creditable to Liberia, and full of meaning. The Aborigines of Africa will not melt away before the emigrants, as the Indians did before the whites, in America, but being of the same race, will gradually blend into one people. Some, indeed, have surmised that the colonists may retrograde to barbarism ; but of this there is not the least danger, if we may judge from existing facts. The Liberians themselves are advancing in civilization, and the natives are rising with them.

A majority of the colonists appear to be more or less engaged in traffic. This is perfectly natural ; for there are only seven or eight thousand emigrants scattered in small settlements along the coast of four hundred miles, where they are continually presented with palm-oil, ivory and other articles of export, to tempt them from other pursuits. Liberia needs men. Place even one hundred thousand colonists there, instead of eight thousand, and there will be a demand for labor, which does not now exist, and a supply which is now impossible. After all, other pursuits are not neglected. There is a sufficient number of stone masons, bricklayers, carpenters, &c., and about one twelfth of the population are engaged in farming.*

Most of the old settlers are satisfied ; many of the new comers, especially the women, are not. They came out in ignorance of the difficulties which must be encountered in all new countries ; and were disappointed because they expected too much. Besides this, both women and men are liable to become home sick. Many

---

* I have lately received the following statistics from the best authorities, which I believe to be correct. In the whole country, which is now divided into three counties, there are:

Settlements, - - - - - -	23
Colonists, - - - - -	7,792
Half breeds [born of Colonists and natives], -	562
Liberated Africans, - - - -	954
Natives, about - - - - -	250,000
Deaths, in acclimation, about - - -	10 per cent.
Proportion of Farmers, - - -	8 per cent.
Proportion of Mechanics, - - -	5 per cent.

The statistics of Mesurado County, which includes Monrovia, are as follows :

of our own people who remove to the western country, repent it for a while, and some actually return to the older settlements. This, however, is rather a reproach to the people, than to the country which they have deserted.

Merchants, - - - - - -	18
Traders and Hawkers, - - - -	60
Sugar Mills, [others coming out], - - -	4
Steam Saw Mills, - - - - -	3
Religious Sects, - - - - - -	4
Places of Worship, - - - - -	12
Seminaries, - - - - - -	2
Day Schools, - - - - - -	9
Scholars - - - - - -	350 to 400

Proportion of people who read and write, about seven eighths of the whole.

Population of Monrovia, about - - -	2,000

CHAPTER III.

NATIVE TRIBES IN LIBERIA.

KROOMEN — ORIGIN OF THE TRIBE—POLYGAMY — CONDITION OF WOMEN IN GUINEA — BARBARISM — RELIGION — OATHS — RECENT IMPROVEMENT OF THE KROOS — THE GOLAHS — VIES — DEYS — THEIR HOUSES, DRESS, FOOD, ETC. — MANDINGOES — THEIR SCHOOLS — RELIGION — TRAFFIC.

THE Kroo people were the first natives we saw on the coast. As we approached the anchorage at Monrovia, several of them paddled off in their light canoes to meet us, and ask for work on the ship. Their only clothing was a cotton handkerchief about the loins, and even this some of them had transferred to their heads, to keep it dry till they should get aboard.

Judging from their language only, the Kroos are related to their neighbors, the Bassahs and Deys. Judged by their physical and mental characteristics, they might be considered another race. They are all woolly headed, and most of them are black ; but we occasionally meet with one who is like a Puloh, as light colored as a mulatto. They deny that these are the descendants of white men, and suppose that some of their tribe have always been of this color. So far as I could ascertain, they have no tradition as to their original location.*

---

* I have since heard that they came from the interior, where they were called Klaho.

Some of them are the most hairy and brawny men I
have seen in Africa.

The Kroos are instinctively, water men. They are
fond of working on ships, and for the sake of finding
employment, many of the men leave their country near
Cape Palmas, and build villages of huts in the suburbs
of colonial towns. They are good seamen, and generally speak English.

The greatest ambition of a Krooman, is to marry many
wives. This is said to be the chief reason why they
wander from home, and labor on ships. When a man
has earned money enough to pay the dowry and other
expenses incident to an African marriage, he returns to
his native village, takes a wife, and remains a while to
enjoy his new relation. Then he is off again to earn
more money, that he may marry another wife. The
women in this part of Africa are little better than slaves,
and they perform most of the farm work and drudgery.
When a Krooman has passed the meridian of life, he retires from service, and remains at home with his wives,
who willingly support him by their labor. He is now
what is called a "big man," and probably no distinguished merchant, politician, or scholar, in our own
country, enjoys his hard earned reputation more than he
does.

The Kroos are strongly attached to their superstitions, and even to their ignorance and barbarism. It is
said that if one of them should renounce idolatry, and
learn to read, he would be put to death by the tribe.
Some years ago, a missionary made an appointment to
preach at Krootown, in the suburbs of Monrovia. On
arriving at the place, he found the people seated on the

ground, making a noisy pow-wow over scraps of news-paper. "What are you doing?" inquired the mission-ary. "Sarvin' God, sir," was the prompt reply. More recently, a Krooman in the same village became im-pressed with the influences of the Gospel and civiliza-tion, and built himself a little cottage of boards among the palm leaf shanties of his countrymen; but he soon died, as the colonists suppose, by means of poison. Yet even the Kroos believe in one God, and only one, who is far superior to all idols. Their prayers are offered to devils, that is, idols; because, in common with other ne-groes, they regard these as the media through which God communicates protection and blessings to men. In judicial proceedings, they swear by salt, dipping their forefinger first into the salt, then pointing it to-ward the earth, then to heaven, and then putting it into the mouth.

But the changes which are working irresistibly in Africa, are affecting the Kroomen also. On my late return from the interior, I found numbers of them at Lagos, decently clad in shirts and trousers. Sitting one day at my window in Freetown, my attention was attracted by a smartly dressed Krooman, who wore a moustache, and sported a cane—an unmistakable dandy. "Who after this," said I, "will affirm that Kroomen can not be improved?" A few days after, I went down to Krootown, where I found swarms of them decently clothed. A great change seems to have come over them within a few years. Several of them are soldiers in the barracks; one is a constable in Free-town; and one is a Methodist preacher, who draws large congregations. An elderly Krooman repeated these and similar facts to me with evident pleasure, and said, "Time past Krooman was fool, now he eye open a little ; only book we want now ; we be smart man." All this probably interested me the more, because I have long predicted that the Kroos will be among the first natives of Liberia to embrace civilization, and incorporate themselves with the immigrants as citizens of the republic.

The Golah people inhabit both sides of St. Paul's river, back of Monrovia. These are the "Gula negroes," of the Southern States. They can not be referred with certainty, to any of the tribes in the same vicinity, but their language has some affinities with those on the lower Gambia, among fragmentary tribes, who probably descended from the interior. The Golahs are degraded and superstitious, and it seems to me one of the meanest tribes in Africa.

The Vy people about Grand Cape Mount, belong to the same extensive ethnical family as the Mandingoes. More than one hundred and fifty years ago, as now, they were considered superior to other tribes on this part of the coast. They are the only people in Africa who have invented an alphabet for their language. It would seem that the first navigators on this coast found them unable to count more than ten, since *hunder-dunder* and *tousan-dunder*, their terms for 100, and 1,000, and evidently borrowed from Europeans. Some of the Vies, as of other superior tribes, have renounced heathenism, and embraced the religion of Mahomet, which the more stupid tribes never do. These facts indicate the people to whom we should first offer the Gospel. I believe it is a general, if not a universal rule, that the most intelligent heathens, other things being equal, are the most easily converted from idolatry.

Of the Bassahs, Pessies, and other barbarous tribes, I obtained no definite information The Dey people who live about the mouth of St. Paul's river, numerically feeble. In language and superstition, they are related to the Kroos and Bassahs. Though somewhat improved by intercourse with the colonists, they are still savages. Their houses are circular huts, built of poles set upright, and plastered with clay. They are grossly and stupidly superstitious. Both men and women sometimes daub their faces with red and white clay, by way of ornament. Their dress is a breech-cloth and a wrapper, or sheet thrown around the body. The usual food of the country is rice, cassava and "palaver sauce,"* a stewed mixture of meat, herbs and palm-oil, seasoned with salt and red pepper. Their huts contain no furniture.

The Mandingoes, whose country lies three or four hundred miles to the north-east of Monrovia, are one of the finest tribes in Africa—tall, erect, muscular and intelligent. Their ethnological affinities extend from the neighborhood of Ashanti to the Great Desert. Like other tribes in the interior, the Mandingoes are sufficiently mixed with Caucasian blood to give them a semi-European cast of countenance, which is sometimes accompanied with a yellow or mulatto skin. They are not all Mahometans, some whole Mandingo tribes being still chiefly Pagan, but those among them who have

---

* So called because whites and negroes ate it together in palavers or councils.

embraced the religion of the false prophet, are generally more zealous, and better acquainted with the Koran, than any other negroes west of the Niger. They have schools in all their principal towns, for males only, in which the course of study is said to be seven years. Nothing is taught but the Koran; but I have no doubt that so sprightly and inquisitive a people would be eager readers of history and geography, if they had the books. All of them that I have seen are strongly opposed to intoxicating drinks, and I was told that some of them would not taste of food for which rum has been given in exchange. When introduced to one of them, in the interior, his first question was, "Do you drink rum?" They also oppose music and dancing as a heathenish practice, unfit for the worshippers of the true God. I was told of a class of devotees in the tribe, who abstain from war and traffic, and refuse to shake hands with another man's wife. Their employment is reading, prayer, and writing charms to sell to their superstitious countrymen. Some of them have manuscript copies of the Pentateuch and Psalms, all in Arabic, of course; and printed copies of the New Testament. The last is much respected; but they strenuously deny that "the prophet Jesus" is the Son of God. They have among them another little book, a dialogue or dispute between a devotee and a trader, which, from its allusions to native customs, must have been composed by one of themselves. The devotee alleges that traffic is irreligious, and that rich men are always wicked. The trader replies, that Abraham was both wealthy and righteous; and he defends traffic by urging the necessity of food and raiment. A man at Sama related to me the history of Joseph with great accuracy, except that he spoke of Rachel's grief when her son was supposed to be devoured by wild beasts. All the Mandingoes with whom I have conversed, believe that missionaries would be permitted to live and preach in their country, but they think that no Mandingo could be induced to renounce Mahometanism. They deny that the Golahs and other rude tribes are capable of being converted at all.

The Mandingoes, like the Hausas, Kanikès (Burnuese), Yórubas, and other improved tribes, are much addicted to traffic, and frequently make long journeys of months or years to distant countries. By these means, they have an extensive acquaintance with the countries, tribes, and languages of Africa, and learn something of other continents from the Arabs, and from Europeans and Americans on the sea coast.

CHAPTER IV.

SOIL, FARMS, AND PRODUCTIONS OF LIBERIA.

ROCKS OF LIBERIA — SOIL — SWAMP — FARMS — RICE — INDIAN CORN — MILLET — BEANS — ARROW ROOT — YAMS — CASSAVA — TANIA — SWEET POTATOES — ONIONS — FRUITS — SUGAR CANE — COFFEE — GINGER — PEPPER — COTTON — INDIA RUBBER — GROUND PEAS — TELFARIA — CASTOR OIL — LAMP OILS — THE OIL PALM — THE BUTTER TREE.

THE rocks at Monrovia and in the Golah country are chiefly clay stone, cemented with iron, and a very ancient amorphous trap (sometimes called "black granite,") which occasionally shows a disposition to form joints. In some places there is a small quantity of a coarse and friable sand stone, and the soil is occasionally mixed with scales of transparent mica, with now and then a bit of crystal quartz. No feldspar is visible in any of the rocks; and there is no indication of lime. Iron, which appears to be very abundant, is the only metal, unless some of the so-called iron ore is zinc.* Neither organic remains nor drift is found in this part of the country.

The soil, wherever I saw it, is generally productive, but never so exceedingly fertile as we have been taught

---

* There are specimens of rich zinc ore in the Colonization Rooms, New York, which have been received from Liberia.

to believe. It ranges from good second quality to poor, but the latter is unusual. Whether rich or poor, it is mostly of a yellowish color, which it imparts to the rivers. There is little or no swamp, except at a few points on the coast; for the country is almost universally broken and rocky, or more or less gravelly. Streams of pure water are numerous.

Liberia is too thinly occupied by immigrants, and offers too many facilities for traffic with the natives, to be an agricultural country at present. The ox and the horse, those useful auxiliaries of man in the cultivation of the soil, are scarcely ever employed in Liberia ; and I doubt whether the small and ill-fed breeds now found in the country, would be able to undergo the drudgery of farm work in a tropical climate.

The process of farming among the natives in this part of the country, is extremely simple. In the dry season, corresponding to our winter, the men cut the bushes from the land with bill-hooks, which are a kind of heavy pruning knife. In the spring, when the rains begin to fall, the women sow rice, which requires but little cultivation, because newly cleared land produces but little grass. A crop of cassava is planted for the second year, by the end of which, the grass has taken full possession of the farm, and it is abandoned for a new ground. The bushes return in full vigor after three or four years, and totally destroy the grass, which otherwise might afford rich pasturage for cattle. Indolence is the only just reason why beef, milk and butter, are not abundant in this country, where they are now almost unknown.

Unhappily the native method of farming has been too

closely followed by the Liberians. If they should cultivate the same land from year to year, it would not only
become mellow, and easily plowed, but would finally
lose its disposition to produce bushes, and would yield
a luxuriant harvest of grass every fall for horses and
cattle. In Yóruba, where there are no plows, the people cultivate the same land for many years together.
They are not to be frightened by grass. In the dry
season, when the grass is naturally less luxuriant, they
walk into their farms with their strong hoes, and turn
up the ground as deeply as many people plow, and they
never fail to raise good crops of Indian corn, millet, cow
peas, yams, &c., which are followed in the latter part of
the season by luxuriant crab-grass, for their cattle and
horses. When the land is finally exhausted, it remains
a grass field or prairie, so that the Yóruba country, all
of which has been reclaimed and abandoned again and
again, is open, airy and healthy. Even the mountains
of Sierra Leone are cultivated from year to year, and
the removal of the timber has greatly improved the
health of the country.

The productive soil and the perpetual summer of Liberia, of course adapts it to all the valuable productions
of similar countries within the tropics. Many of these
are not yet known in the colony, but might be introduced
from other countries. Among the articles already introduced or indigenous to the soil, we may notice the
following, with occasional directions how to use them.

Rice is a staple in Liberia. The quality is superior,
and the quantity may be increased to inexhaustible
stores. It grows luxuriantly on uplands, and is easy of
cultivation. In many places, there is abundance of

water power on the rocky streams for working rice mills.

Rice flour, either pounded or ground, made into dough or batter, with or without mashed plantains, and left to rise, makes good bread and pancakes.

Indian Corn is common throughout tropical Africa, where it probably existed long before the discovery of America. The Yórubas have a tradition—disfigured by superstition—that it came from the east. It was either Indian corn or millet which the Phenician navigators sowed and gathered at different places during their voyage around the continent ; for no species of wheat will produce grain on the tropical coasts of Africa. Considerable quantities of Indian corn are raised in Sierra Leone, and I have seen still better specimens in the Golah country within fifty miles of Monrovia. It would certainly be a valuable crop in Liberia, especially at a distance from the coast. In Yóruba, the best lands will produce from twenty to thirty bushels to the acre. They plant it in March and April, and a second crop in August. If put up in the shuck, it keeps tolerably free from weevils for several months. The price of corn in Yóruba varies from twenty to seventy-five cents a bushel. The Yórubas esteem this grain so much, that they have a proverb which says, "Indian corn is the chief support of man." We make free use of corn bread at our missions, grinding the corn on a steel mill, which we carried with us, because there are no mills in the country.

Corn may be prepared for food in various ways with which ourselves and the Liberians are not familiar. In Mexico they make excellent bread by boiling the corn in lye, husking it, and grinding it to a paste with water, with or without eggs and butter. The *matát*, or instrument with which the corn is ground, consists of a hard flat stone, on which the grains are laid, and a stone cylinder or roller, eight or ten inches long, and as large as one's arm, with which the corn is ground, and at the same time made into paste. Whether the bread is baked on a griddle, like buckwheat cakes, or in an oven, it is very superior and wholesome. If the Liberians would plant corn and introduce the matát, they would soon forget imported flour.

The Fantee people on the Gold Coast prepare cornbread much in the same manner as the Mexicans do, only they soak the corn in water till it sours, before they grind it.

The Yórubas grind the sour corn on a matát like the Fantees, but instead of baking it into bread, they boil it into a sour mush called *ekkaw*, as follows : Put the newly ground sour paste or wet meal into a pot of cold water, and let it soak twelve hours ; then rub it thoroughly between the hands to separate all the starch, and squeeze the bran dry in handfulls ; strain the water, and boil it to the consistence of thin mush. According to the Yórubas, this is the most wholesome food ever eaten. Diluted with warm water, it is much drunk, instead of our tea and coffee. It is also wrapped up in leaves, in balls as large as one's fist, to be sold in market. These balls are sufficiently firm to bear being carried in a basket without injury, and they will keep several days without spoiling. They are eaten with meat, palaver sauce, syrup, &c.

Several species of *millet* (sorghum) as Guinea corn,

Egyptian millet, &c., are well adapted to Liberia, and are much prized in Yóruba and Sudan. The Guinea corn is one of the best articles in the world for horses, and being easily raised, would be invaluable to Liberian farmers. The Yórubas frequently eat it in the form of *ekkaw.*

Beans and *peas* of several kinds, especially Lima beans, and black-eyed peas, flourish finely in the sunny fields of Africa.

Arrow root is a very valuable article, which grows with little trouble. To prepare it, wash the roots clean, scrape off the skin with a knife, stir the grated mass thoroughly in plenty of the clearest water, strain, let it settle, pour off the water, and dry the starch on clean white cloths. The arrow root is then ready for use or exportation. To cook it, make it into a thin paste with cold water, and pour in boiling water, stirring all the time, till it becomes a transparent mass. It is then done. If cooked with milk instead of water, it will be richer. Arrow-root flour made as above, is nice for bread and pastry, so that the poorest people in Liberia may have these articles without the expense of buying inferior wheat flour at high prices.

Yams grow best on rather sandy soil, such as may be found not far from Monrovia. They should be planted in January, in large loose hills about as far apart as sweet potatoes are, and a handful of leaves or grass should be thrown on the top of each hill, to prevent the sun from injuring the plantings. Only one yam is obtained from a hill, but that is larger than several large sweet potatoes. The vines require to be struck like beans. In Yóruba, there are several varieties of yams, some with

prickly vines, all of which are indigenous. The tropical yam is not a kind of potato, but is a totally different
plant, (dioscorea) ; two useless species of which are
found in the Southern States.

Several good things are made of the yam. *Fufu*,
which is eaten with palaver sauce, &c., is boiled yam,
peeled and pounded in a mortar, with a little water
added, till it has the consistence of wheat dough. *Elu-
baw*, which keeps for a long time, and is used to make
an excellent pudding or mush, is prepared as follows :
Peel and cut the raw yams into slices an inch thick ;
simmer the slices very slowly in a wide mouthed earthen
pot for twenty-four continuous hours ; dry them in the
sun on a scaffold, pound in a mortar, and sift.

Cassava, or cassada, grows from cuttings of the stock.
almost without cultivation. This species of the plant
has no poisonous qualities, in the roots at least ; but is
good for food both boiled and roasted, and valuable in
the raw state to fatten goats and sheep. The boiled
roots make an excellent kind of *fufu*.

To make the *farina* of commerce, grate the peeled
roots rather fine, put the mass into a bag of grass or
coarse cloth, and press it under a weight till all the
milky water is expelled, and dry it first in the sun on
cloths, and then in flat bottomed vessels, over a slow
fire, taking care to stir it to prevent burning. To cook
farina, simply stir it into boiling water. An excellent
bread is made by baking stiff farina batter, till the
crust is brown. Cassava starch is made like arrow root.
The grated mass from which the starch has been washed,
may be baked like buckwheat, and the cakes are very
pleasant and wholesome.

Tania, called *koko,* is an excellent root which grows to perfection in Africa. There are two kinds, one of which is particularly excellent.

Sweet potatoes, though not indigenous, grow like weeds wherever planted. Their flavor is much improved by keeping a month or two in a dry, airy place ; and the yellow skinned variety of America is superior to the red ones planted by the negroes.

The *onions* of Africa are found to be superior in flavor to our own. Only the small kind succeed on the coast, but large red and white ones flourish in the interior.

The *fruits* and *vegetables* of the temperate zone grow indifferently, or not at all in Africa. Apples, pears, peaches, plums, cherries, &c., are never seen. Cabbages, snap beans, garden peas, beets, mustard, lettuce, &c., &c., may or may not repay the planter, according to his skill in cultivation. The Africans have vegetables of their own, none of which would be much regarded in America.

There are many kinds of wild fruits, very few of which are worth the trouble of gathering. But the *pine apple,* which flourishes exceedingly well in the woods of Liberia, is superior to any we can procure in this country. Some botanists believe it was first brought to Africa from the western continent, and this opinion appears to be favored by the fact, that it is never seen in a wild state very far from the coast. The Yórubas call it *okpaimbo,* the white man's palm, because the plant resembles a young palm tree, and because they at least first received it from the whites. It is not found in a wild state on the Slave Coast, where the Yórubas live.

The tropical fruits which have been introduced into

Sierra Leone and Liberia, are chiefly the orange, lime, lemon, papaw, plantain, banana, mango, cashewnut, guava, granadilla, sweet sop, sour sop, avagado-pear, rose apple and tamarind. Very few of these are found in the interior, but we are trying to introduce them from the colonies. The bread fruit is becoming common at Lagos. The cocoa nut is found everywhere on the coast.

Among the articles which the soil of Liberia does or may produce for exportation, we may enumerate sugar, coffee, spices, cotton, gums, and oils, in addition to several articles above described.

Sugar cane never grows wild, as we have been informed, but is well adapted to the soil and climate especially of Liberia. Whether the free labor of that country can produce sugar as an article of commerce, is a problem which the Liberians are trying to solve by experiment. There are several sugar mills in the country, and last year, (1856,) one man planted about one hundred acres in cane. Every farmer can at least make sugar and syrup enough for his own use, as many have done in Florida.

The *coffee* of Liberia is said to be very superior, and will probably become a valuable article of export. Some have affirmed that a man who is once fairly established in the business can make five hundred dollars to six hundred dollars to the hand every year. The indigenous coffee tree is remarkable for its narrow leaves and yellowish color.

The African *ginger* is good and easily cultivated. The red pepper is scarcely equalled by any in the world. A species of black pepper, (probably a *cubebs*, though this has been doubted,) grows in the forests of Liberia, Yóruba, &c. The plant is a climbing vine, and the newly ripened berries are red. So far as I have learned, no species has been introduced from either of the Indies.

Two species of *cotton*, known to us as the sea island and upland, are cultivated in Africa ; and the staple is good, but the yield cannot be more than one-fourth of what it is on similar lands in the Southern States. There is a third species in the interior with very small pods and leaves, and of an unusually fine staple, the flowers of which are red when they first open. No kind of cotton is indigenous, but the date of its introduction into the country must be very remote. It is known by different names to different tribes or families throughout the continent. In Yóruba, cotton is planted in July, after the heaviest rains of the year have subsided. They never top the plants, though they sometimes rise to the height of ten feet.

As to *gums*, there are none of great value on the western coast ; but in some places there are considerable quantities of copal, and the Mendi country is said to afford a kind of India rubber, which is superior to any other known. It exudes from a large vine, or climber, and is thought to be abundant, though it has not yet been introduced into commerce.* Yóruba, and perhaps Liberia, produces a kind of black gum or wax, which becomes hard like wood, and is superior to any thing else for stopping leaks in canoes. A roof or

---

* Considerable quantities of another quality have been exported from Gaboon river.

coating of this material would be very durable and effectual.

Western Africa has several seeds and nuts, which are valuable for *oil*. The common *guber* or ground pea, erroneously called a nut by some, is largely exported from some parts of the coast to France and England, where it is used to make the "fine salad oil," of the shops. This traffic has caused a great increase in the industry of the natives of Bullom and other countries further north, but the benefit has not yet extended to Liberia. There is another species of it, without oil, but good for food and for feeding stock.

The *telfaria*, which is common in Yóruba, as on the eastern coast, would grow equally well in Liberia. This vigorous plant runs profusely over the tops of low trees, and bears numerous gourds or melons from one to two feet in length, which are crammed full of oily seeds as large as the end of a man's thumb. This is doubtless a valuable plant.

The *castor oil plant*, though not indigenous as some have affirmed, is frequently seen in cultivated places, and grows so well, that Liberia might supply all America with the oil. The *physic nut* (curcas purgans) produces a good lamp oil, and the seeds have been exported to France for this purpose. A valuable oil is obtained from the seed of the *benu* plant, or sesame. The Yórubas make large quantities of very fine wholesome oil from the seeds of the water melon, which is called in America the citron melon.

But the great oil producer of Africa, is the *oil palm*, which abounds on the coast, and is found occasionally on the rivers, as far in the interior as Kanikè or Burnu.

These trees grow from twenty to sixty feet in height, and resemble the date palm, but the leaves are of a brighter green color. The yellow palm oil of commerce is made from the pulp which surrounds the nut. It is much used in Africa as a pleasant and wholesome article of food. After removing the pulp from the nuts, the people in Yóruba obtain lamp oil from the kernels by roasting, pounding, and pressing. Palm oil, like cotton and tobacco, is destined to be an important item in the world's commerce ; for the demand and the supply are equally inexhaustible. This alone will be a source of perpetual revenue, especially to Liberia, and to the nations on the Bight of Benin, where the palm tree is most luxuriant.

The palm tree loves moisture, and will not flourish on the dry uplands of the interior. The soil about Ilorrin is productive, but there are no palms within twenty or thirty miles of the town. Where the palm fails from change of climate, its place is immediately supplied by the *butter tree,* the large nuts of which produce a whitish, and slightly aromatic oil, which is about as hard as butter. This oil is used in cooking and for lamps, and is said to be a valuable ointment for painful joints. In Liberia, the forests where the palms are always found, extend further than usual from the coast. It is probable there are no butter trees within one hundred or one hundred and fifty miles of Monrovia. This, however, is not to be regretted, since the palm tree is the more valuable of the two.

CHAPTER V.

FUTURE PROSPECTS OF LIBERIA.

COLONIZATION OPPOSED — ITS AIMS — FUTURE EMIGRATION OF AMERICAN
BLACKS — THE NATIVES WILL BE CIVILIZED — IMPROVABILITY OF MAN
— ORIGIN AND PROGRESS OF CIVILIZATION —THE PRESENT CONDITION
OF AFRICA.

BOTH in Europe and America there is a great diversity
of opinion in regard to the ultimate success of African
colonization. Many abolitionists regard the whole
scheme as a dishonest device of slaveholders to rid
their country of troublesome free negroes; and they
predict that the crushing of the slaveholding power, for
which they are laboring with confidence, will crush
Liberia and African missions as an offshoot of colonization; so that the waves of barbarism will flow back
upon the African continent as in former ages. Some
slaveholders look upon Liberia with a jealous eye for
other reasons. The existence of a great negro republic,
even if it were known to be possible, is not exactly in
accordance with their taste and habits of feeling. They
know, too, that some friends of colonization are anti-
slavery men; they know that slaves are frequently
liberated and sent to Liberia, where they find a comfortable home as citizens of an independent republic;
and hence they are not satisfied as to what might be
the effect of success on the minds of white people and

of negroes in America. The friends of colonization have
no fears that Liberia is to be obliterated by the crushing of the slave-power, which of course would put a
stop to emigration. They do not believe that the most
brilliant success would work any injury to the whites
or to the negroes in America, but the contrary. Their
single object and motive is to plant a great negro nation in Africa, which shall be a means of diffusing civilization and Christianity throughout the whole continent:
thus making an immense addition to the moral power
and commercial wealth of the world. As this gigantic
scheme is yet in the feeblest days of its infancy, differences of opinion as to the final result are certainly allowable, however much we may regret the unreasonable
prejudices which throw themselves in the way of success.
Considering the importance of the subject, and my own
relations to the African continent, I cannot permit this
opportunity to pass without expressing my opinion as
to the natural and probable course of events in Liberia.
It is true that great and surprising revolutions are possible, both in Europe and America, but it is not probable that anything will occur in either continent which
will overwhelm African colonization and its counter-
part, African missions.

Assuming, as we justly may, that the affairs of the
world will continue to move on, as they ever have done,
through all their changes, in obedience to the moral and
social forces which are their motive power, I feel au
thorized to entertain large hopes as to the future of the
colonization scheme now identified with Liberia. We
may define the elements of a great nation to be, first, a
numerous, virtuous, and intelligent people; second, a

wide and productive territory; and thirdly, a just and strong government. My hopes claim all these for the future Liberia, and I believe that these hopes are authorized by existing circumstances.

First, as to the *numerous people ;* I look to America and to Africa, to the emigration of American negroes, and to the civilization of African tribes.

It does not seem unreasonable to expect an extensive emigration of American blacks. Free blacks are already numerous in the United States, and their number will naturally and therefore almost inevitably increase. They are now prevented from emigrating by three causes; the hardships incident to settling in Liberia as a new country, abundance of food and employment in America, and their own prejudices against the cause of colonization. But all these hindrances to emigration will disappear. As Liberia grows older, the hardships incident to settling in all new countries will cease to exist, and there will be more food and more employment of every kind for new comers. This alone would give an impetus to emigration. But still further, the abundance of food and employment enjoyed by the free blacks in America is sure to be diminished sooner or later. Our country will at last become populous, and our peasantry, whether white or black, must experience that scarcity of food which is felt by the peasantry of all other populous countries. Then we must witness a new species of antagonism, the most uncompromising and terrible of all antagonisms, a strife for bread, which is life; and still more terrible to the free negro, because it will be a conflict of races, in which all the circumstances will be against him. Justly or unjustly, in a struggle

for food and for existence, the white race will claim
precedence, and they will enforce the claim; for ultimate sovereignty resides in the right arm of man, and
the right arm is powerful in proportion to the strength
of the will and of the intellect by which it is directed.
Even the slave, being at once the property and the family of the master, must have precedence over the free
negro, so long as the wants of the more numerous white
race will permit slavery to exist at all. I do not say
that matters will ever come to their natural extremity, but there will certainly be a powerful tendency in
that direction, so powerful that the free negro will be
obliged to yield, and to fly for the preservation of his
existence. And whither will he fly, except to Africa?
Then the land of his fathers will be his land of promise.
Then the colony which he now curses will be the bright
star of his hope. Then the opponents and traducers of
African colonization and African missions will be remembered, but not honored. The colonizationist fore-
sees the coming storm, and labors, unrequited let it be,
to provide a refuge which shall stand forth as a blessing to two races. He at least is not a purblind, self-
worshipping philosopher, whose brightest visions can
not reach the threshold of to-morrow.

But there is still another view of the case from which
we are led to expect that a great African nation will
derive its population in part from America. The God
of all the earth, without whose directing providence not
even a sparrow falls to the ground, has not located so
many Africans in America without a purpose. The
man who looks candidly and reverently upon the principles and facts of divine government, can see more

than African wars, slave-ships, and American plantations in the present relations of the white and black
races. He can see millions of civilized negroes in America, better clothed and fed, and more virtuous and happy than the analogous classes of white people in some
other countries. He can see tens and hundreds of
thousands of evangelical Christians, regenerated men
and women, among these blacks, redeemed from the
curse of sin in consequence of African slavery. And
finally, he can see African colonization and African
missions arising from this slavery, and flowing back as
a river of light and life upon the African continent.
Perhaps he will say with Jacob; "Verily God is in this
place, and I knew it not." Providence never fails for
want of means; and he will find the means to colonize
Africa. At present, before the fulness of the time, he
employs individuals to plant and nourish Liberia. As
events roll on, and the increasing number of free negroes feel the necessity of emigration, the whites will
feel it also with more and more intensity, till it becomes
a great national affair. Then the federal government,
and perhaps the legislatures of all the States, will vote
annual appropriations to aid the colored people in returning to their original seats. Such are some of Liberia's hopes from America.

Africa, too, will contribute her millions of civilized
men. While the success of colonization is yet a problem, some persons fear that the Liberians, so far from
civilizing Africa, will relapse into barbarism. But none
of these persons have considered the natural and almost
inevitable result of the various forces which are acting
in and upon Liberia. Neither have they acquainted

themselves with the more tangible argument of facts. Liberia is full of well-attended churches and schools. Sne has a good government, well administered under officers elected by the people from among themselves. She is steadily increasing in prosperity, and in everything that pertains to civilization. And she is sustained by numerous and powerful friends who would sacrifice much, from principle, to prevent her destruction.

The natives around among the colonists are barbarians, but they are men, and are capable of being elevated by the same forces that elevate others: As before stated, they are moving onward toward civilization, and this motion, which is already beginning to be remarkable, is more likely to be accelerated than retarded. Some of the superior tribes, as the Kroos and Vies, will lead the way and rise up to the estate of citizenship in the republic. Then others will follow, and yet others more and more remote from the coast, and who shall say, Thus far the influence shall go and no further ?

But we are met by the objection that the Africans are mentally and morally incapable of civilization. I have sometimes expressed the opinion, that while opponents are perplexing this question by vain arguments, there are other men who will solve the problem by doing the work. Yet it *is* a problem at present, and our efforts to civilize Africa may fail. Of this, however, I have no serious fears, provided the nations of the earth will keep sufficiently quiet to permit the continuance of our labors. Let it be granted that the dark races are constitutionally inferior to the white ; and again, that education, however long continued in successive generations, cannot improve the brain and nervous system, or the innate faculties of a race,* still the believers in a future African civilization, cannot act so absurdly as not to fall back on the following admitted truths :

1. That man is everywhere capable of improvement. The most enlightened races were once barbarians, as the Greeks, Germans, French and English; and the most degraded races, as the Hottentots and the negroes of Guinea, are now making advances toward civilization. At Freetown, Elmina, Cape Coast Castle and Akra, the natives are so much improved that they dress respectably, and live in comfortable stone houses. The natives at any other point on the coast, or in the interior, are equally capable of being improved.

2. The limit of man's improvability has never been ascertained. I can easily conceive that England and America might be now considered almost barbarous, compared with the highest moral, intellectual and social excellence of which a nation of our own race is capable. We may admit, and I think justly, that the negroes will never be equal to the whites, where the two races enjoy equal opportunities ; for the white race, everywhere, under all circumstances, is endowed with characteristics which are not found in the negroes, or in any other dark race. But this does not require us to conclude that the negro any more than the white man has reached his maximum of improvement. There might be negro nations fully as much civilized as we are at present, and there might at the same time be white nations as barbarous as the ancient Germans.

---

* This has never been proved, and it is certainly opposed by numerous facts.

Our own civilization is not purely the result of our own superior moral and intellectual powers. America, England, Germany, etc., depended for their civilization on Greece and Rome ; Greece and Rome derived theirs from the valleys of the Euphrates and the Nile ; and Egypt and Assyria were civilized of necessity, for the reason that millions of people were crowded together in fertile valleys surrounded by extensive deserts. The physical geography of the globe has been the great civilizer of man. If the deserts of Asia and Africa had not existed, and if there had been no Mediterranean sea, and no gloomy forests and rugged mountains on the north of the Grecian and Italian peninsulas, the civilized kingdoms of Europe and the grand republic of North America could not have existed.* On the other hand, physical geography has blighted Africa with the curse of barbarism. Her immense northern deserts arose as an impassable barrier to that current of eastern civilization which has overflowed Europe and America ; her climate has precluded the possibility of extensive conquest by Europeans, and her wide fertile interior has given unbounded scope to that barbarism which requires nothing but food and animal gratification.

Still further, the physical geography of the globe has established the civilization which it called into existence. Europe could not soon, if ever, have originated civiliza-

---

* The Manchus, a white race, who civilized China, were themselves driven into civilization by their position on fertile spots in the Great Asiatic Desert. Want of room to expand by emigration forced the Manchu civilization upon the prolific Mongolians of China, a race of men who probably have never made any great discovery or invention.

tion, but no part of the globe was so well adapted to
receive it, as it existed, when it was growing old, and
was likely to die a natural death in Egypt and Assyria.
Europe, herself divided by seas and mountains, perpetu-
ally shaken by the conflicts of races, and crushed by a
weight of abominable antiquities, could never have
developed and perfected the civilization which she had
received and preserved. America was discovered just
in the right time to save Europe and the world, just at
a time when it was demanded by the conflict of opinions,
feelings and interests, which then, as now, was substantially a conflict of different European races. More
than a thousand years of successive conquests running
and returning in all directions throughout Europe, had
scattered all races through all countries. But the features, feelings and habits of different families in almost every town, showed that the old races, though
mechanically intermixed, were not to a great extent *che-
mically* blended. In other parts of Europe no less than
in England, there was a class of men of similar features and character because they belonged to the same
ethnical family, who were distinguished by an intense
feeling of personal independence, which revealed itself
in a demand for civil and religious liberty. Similarity
of feeling and character led thousands of this race to
America,* where the physical geography of a vast

---

* There are many Americans of other races, and accordingly they
have other countenances and other feelings. It is not climate and
circumstances which have given a national face and character to the
American people. They are more nearly an original ethnical race
than most other white nations, and hence the national features and

region almost necessitates the existence of a nation of greater integral extent, and more powerful in the control of mankind in general, than any nation that ever has existed or ever can exist while the seas, continents, deserts, mountains and rivers of the globe retain their present form.

To this nation, the appointed arbiter of earth, God has brought the barbarous negro race, and from this country he is leading them back, civilized and christianized, to Africa. In the mean. time, African barbarism has run its course, and is growing old and decrepid. The savage exuberance of the soil has passed away, and the character of the people has necessarily changed. Almost every where they are congregated in towns, some of which are of immense size. Throughout half the continent, they are civilized on their own basis, to a degree which surprises every one who becomes acquainted with the fact. They cannot retrograde now, for that would be contrary to the geographical, moral and social causes which are moving them forward. Just at this time, precisely when needed, precisely when the people see their necessities and long for assistance, the allied causes of African colonization and African missions, backed by America, by christendom, and by the irresistible demands of modern commerce, pledge themselves to the redemption of Africa. Now we look again at the physical geography of that continent. Her first condition of isolation and savage fertility, inevitably produced its result, but these circumstances are gone

---

national character which exist every where, and has ever existed since the States were colonies.

forever, beyond the possibility of restoration. Steam unites her to the rest of the world, and four thousand years of cultivation have effectually denuded her of forests.* The next condition of her physical geography to be noticed, is seen in her great rivers, piercing to the heart of the continent, and in the immense undulating plains, whose innumerable streams and fertile soil, infallibly indicate the uses of her great rivers.

Let us now turn to feeble Liberia, and ask if there is not hope ? Where shall we fix her future boundary ? In this case, the extensive fertile territory, which is one condition of her greatness, is so extensive that we can not venture to claim a fourth part of it even for a great nation. As to the just and strong government which is necessary to her success, we have no reason to fear. She has begun well by modeling her government after the great exemplar for the nations, the constitution of the United States. When despotism shall have perished in Europe, which it is sure to do, we need not fear its existence in our own Liberia. That African colonization and missions may meet with reverses, or at least with serious difficulties, as all human affairs must do, I freely admit, but it seems to me that their perpetuation and their ultimate triumph are guaranteed by moral and social causes, which are as irresistible as the physical laws of nature.

---

* The forests of Guinea are a small portion of the continent; the rest is prairie, the result of cultivation.

CHAPTER VI.

TRAVELS IN THE COUNTRY OF THE GOLAHS, IN 1850.

DEPARTURE TO GOLAH — AFRICAN SINGING — A MANGROVE SWAMP — NEW GEORGIA — ST. PAUL'S RIVER — NAVIGATION — THE BUSH — ROADS — PINE APPLES — AFRICAN WATER — NAKED NEGROES — VONZWAW — STREETS — PALAVER HOUSE — HINDRANCES — PREACHING — TRAFFIC — CURRENCY — SALT — GAMING — AN AFFRAY — MUSIC — A " HALF TOWN "— SMALL POX —VILLAGES — SOIL — SUWY— MILL SEATS —WAR — FORESTS — WILD ANIMALS — A TRIBAL BURYING GROUND — A FINE COUNTRY — GEBBY — AN AFFRAY — TAZZUA — SAMA — A COVET- OUS KING — MR. GOODALE'S DEATH — THE PEOPLE OF SAMA — GODIRI — BOONDA — MANDINGO — MAHOMETANS — A LAW SUIT — RETURN TO MONROVIA.

Soon after landing at Monrovia, we were told of Bo Pora, a large Golah town, one hundred and fifty miles in the interior, governed by a civilized native, called King Boatswain, who had wished for missionaries to come and teach his people. Mr. Goodale was anxious to visit this town, believing that a mission there might be more useful than in Central Africa, which was too distant to communicate with Liberia, and perhaps not more healthy than Bo Pora. My own intention had been to study the Puloh or Fellatah language, as spoken on the Niger. Should the Gospel be established among these people, who are known to be the most intelligent and energetic tribe south of the Desert, they might become active missionaries, and subdue more nations by the Word, than they have by the sword. It seemed better to visit Sierra Leone in search of Puloh interpreters, than to penetrate the Golah bush, where we should find no natives superior to those on the coast, whom we had already determined to pass by, for the purpose of preaching to the more civilized people of Sudan. I was assured, however, that we should find Pulohs at Bo Pora; and that we might pass on, if we pleased, by a much frequented route from Bo Pora to the Niger. These considerations, together with my reluctance to let Mr. Goodale go alone before he was acclimated, induced me to visit the country of the Golahs. If not satisfied with Bo Pora or the country beyond it, I would return in the fall, and Mr. Goodale would probably pursue the same course.

Prudence might have dictated that we should remain at the Cape (as they call Monrovia), till we had passed through the ordeal of acclimation, but we did not believe that the fever would be more dangerous at Bo Pora than here; and it seemed preferable to prosecute our labors as long as our health should continue. We accordingly resolved to proceed immediately to the interior, and since no horses could be purchased in Liberia, we were content to perform the journey on foot.

Five days after landing at Monrovia, we departed in high spirits for Bo Pora, happily ignorant of the future. Our course lay up Stockton Creek, eight miles to the St. Paul's river. Soon after leaving the wharf, we were amused by an animated race between our boat and a canoe. The rowers sang lustily all the time, precisely in the same tone and manner that is common among our southern negroes around the corn pile. The corn song was imported from Guinea.

A mile or two from Monrovia, we entered a dismal mangrove swamp, which emits sickening odors. The mangrove never grows in places which are not visited occasionally by salt water. It is said to afford excellent fire wood, and the bark is valuable for tanning. In some places we observed slender hedges of palm leaves running along the margin of the creek, to entrap the fish when the tide rises.

On the right bank of the creek, about five miles from Monrovia, is a neat village called New Georgia, principally inhabited by Congoes, and other natives re-captured from slave-ships. The place has every appearance of being extremely sickly, and I was told that most of the first settlers were dead, though the young people born there enjoyed good health. There was no reason in selecting this place for a settlement, when the country abounds in elevated, dry, and healthy situations.

We found the St. Paul's a majestic river, flowing in a strong current of yellow water, about eight hundred yards wide. Several black rocks arose here and there, in the stream, as if they would say, "no navigation." Unfortunately none of the rivers in Liberia are navigable for more than thirty or forty miles. I think, however, that an occasional short canal at the rapids, would render the St. Paul's navigable far into the interior; and the day will come when such canals will be required and opened to relieve this country of its surplus produce. We rowed across the river into a little cove, whence we ascended the bank to a very extensive plain, which is never overflowed. Here we met with a colonist who informed us that old King Boatswain was dead,

and that Lansanna, his successor, had removed the seat
of government from Bo Pora to Sama, six miles nearer
Monrovia.

From our landing-place to a Dey village called Vonzwaw, we had a walk of five miles through "the bush,"
along a path as rugged and tortuous as the ways of
the stupid natives who made it. To have bought an
ass at Monrovia, as I intended to have done, if he had
been three feet high, would have been entirely useless,
for nobody could ride in such a path as this. I permitted the party to pass on before me, that I might enjoy
a solitary stroll in the first African forest I had ever
entered. In addition to the impenetrable jungle of trees,
vines and bushes, the ground in many places was com-
pletely coated with the rough swordlike leaves of the
pine apple. Not a breath of air mitigated the over-
powering heat, though the sea-breeze was sporting
with the rustling leaves in the tree tops above me. I
was soon bathed in perspiration, and disagreeably
thirsty. After passing the dry beds of several brooks,
I at last arrived at a clear stream, in which the water
was so warm as to be almost loathsome. There is no
cool water in Africa. About a mile from the village, I
met several specimens of "the naked negro panting on
the line," of whom we have read with so much interest
in childhood. Their dress was a breech-cloth, and they
were armed with bows and spears, which are seldom
absent from the hands of men in this savage country.
No one knows here at what turn of the path he may
meet with a hungry leopard, or a boa constrictor twenty
feet in length. A little further on, I heard some people
singing merrily at their work in a farm, which approach-

ed within a few yards of the road, but was scarcely visible, owing to the density of "the bush."

Vonzwaw, the first native town we had seen, consisted of perhaps one hundred circular huts, built of upright poles, plastered with mud and thatched with palm leaf. The bush, thick as a jungle, though the land is everywhere firm and dry, hugged it about on all sides close up to the houses. The streets were nothing but very narrow alleys, running at random in all directions, and intersecting at every possible angle. By some means I reached the "palaver house," a cleanly swept open shed, where disputes are settled ; and here I found Mr. Goodale conversing with Kyboka, the chief, who spoke rather good English.

According to custom in every part of Africa, it is not allowable for a white man to visit any town or country without sending messengers to obtain permission of the chief. This custom may be disagreeable to the impatient traveler, but no one should disregard it ; for if you intrude yourself into a country without an invitation, you may be treated as an intruder ; but if you send to the king and he invites you to come, you are then "the king's stranger," and both he and his people are bound by the sacred laws of hospitality, to treat you with courtesy. In our case, ignorance of African usages might have permitted us to visit Lansanna without invitation, and I suspect that the consequences might have been disastrous ; but we found it impossible to employ "carriers" or luggage-bearers at Vonzwaw, and we were obliged to send forward, not only for permission to come, but for men to carry our baggage. This detained us at Vonzwaw seventeen days.

Mr. Goodale, who was full of zeal, returned to Monrovia to preach on Sunday, while I remained in the village and delivered my first message to the heathens of Africa. Only one woman was present. The half-naked men sat around with their swords, bows and spears in their hands, and paid good attention to my interpreter. On the following Sunday we both preached to a congregation of Deys, Vies and Mandingoes, and other strangers from the interior.

Vonzwaw is a considerable resort of traders from Sama, Bo Pora, and other places, who bring down ivory, cam wood, rice, palm oil, country cloths, cows and ponies, and sometimes a little gold, to barter with the colonists for calico, rum, tobacco, salt, and other articles for the interior markets. An ox or a cow (both of which are called bullocks* on the coast,) was worth from eight to ten dollars, and a horse about sixty dollars. On this part of the coast the natives have no currency, not even cowries; but I am told that small iron bars are used by the Mendi tribe, and some others a few days' journey further to the windward.† We procured fowls and rice from the natives for calico, cotton handkerchiefs and leaf tobacco. The negroes on the coast manufacture salt by boiling sea water, and put it up in slender cases of palm leaves, which are

---

* Last year a traveler was presented with some milk by a native, who declared it was "bullock milk for true."

† Iron money is used in Kanikè (Burnu), and the late expedition up the Chadda or Benue, found people whose currency consisted of diminutive iron hoes. Cowries, very neatly made of gold, have been found in the Egyptian tombs, and they, like the real shells, may have been money.

called sticks of salt. Slaves, bullocks, horses, and other costly chattels, are valued at so many *sticks*, so that salt is a kind of currency.

In the better regulated country of Yóruba, gaming is said to be prohibited by law; but no such restriction is known among the barbarians on St. Paul's river. One day the chief, Kyboka, and a Mandingo played very freely by casting five cowries from the hand—the probable original of "five corns." The chief was loser, and I was told that he finally staked his young and favorite wife. Had the Mandingo won her, it is likely enough that he would have lived with her for a few weeks or months, and then have exchanged her for a couple of bullocks or a lot of rice. But the same man would have suffered severe hunger, as I once knew a Mahometan to do, before he would have eaten meat that had been butchered by a heathen. The whites are not the only people who can strain out a gnat and swallow a camel.

During our stay at Vonzwaw, the traders from the interior got up a grand affray with the villagers. No weapons were used, and the negroes are ignorant of boxing; but the combatants kicked and jerked each other about, with a great uproar, till the towns-people thought they were beaten, and took refuge in their houses. A runner was despatched for Kyboka, who was five miles distant at the beach, superintending his salt boilers. On his arrival, he stormed and blustered as if greatly offended, saying that such conduct would spoil the name of his town. After slipping into the bush for a draught of wine at the palm trees,* he sat

---

* The best palm wine is the juice of the tree, from the nuts of

down in the palaver house and called the offenders before him. Each party was fined thirty sticks of salt,
and the strangers were forbidden to gather any more
palm nuts in the vicinity of Vonzwaw. I suspected
that he had been meditating this prohibition before, for
the protection of home industry, and was not sorry to
find a good excuse for enforcing it.

About the 1st of March, our carriers arrived from
Sama, and entered the village with a grand flourish
of music, performed on drums and cows' horns. The
party consisted of about thirty men, clad in breech-
cloths, excepting two or three leaders, who wore the
patrician dress of an African shirt without sleeves.
They brought us a sheep as a present from the king,
which we butchered and distributed, to the great satisfaction of all concerned. We now ascertained that
Sama is only four days' journey, instead of one hundred
and fifty miles, from Monrovia; but we found the
marches rather long, and judged that the whole distance is eighty-five miles. The average of courses appeared to be N. N. E.; and we learned that Sama is
nearer to Grand Cape Mount, than to Monrovia. The
whole way lies through the bush, which they told us extended to the Boonda country, five days (one hundred
miles) further, where it gives place to grassy plains or
prairies. Thence the natives are acquainted with several countries, as far north as to Sangarro.

On the 3d of March we bid a joyful adieu to Vonzwaw,

which they make oil. Another species of palm, erroneously called
bamboo, in English, yields stronger wine, but inferior in flavor. The
color of palm wine resembles that of milky water.

and plunged into the bush, when to return we could scarcely conjecture. Half a mile brought us to a cluster of shabby huts, which Beymba, the king's interpreter, informed us was a "half town," (dependent village) of Vonzwaw. In one of the huts which stood apart from the rest, there was a woman who was sick with small pox, a disease which is much more feared in this country than in Yóruba. Four miles further (by our time and supposed rate,) brought us to a minute Dey village, called Quypo, which might or might not boast a population of twenty souls. The agricultural resources of the place, so far as visible, consisted of a few stalks of red pepper, inferior to none in the world. Seven miles more, still through a houseless and farmless forest, brought us to a Golah town twice as large as Quypo, which they told us was Boomba. Here was a farm of perhaps twenty acres. On descending the hill from Boomba, we discovered a beautiful sandy stream thirty feet wide ; and from this place forward the streams, hitherto sluggish and weedy, are clear and rapid. The bush, also, was not quite so dense, and the soil, though equally fertile, was more sandy, and thus better adapted to cultivation. After walking eleven miles further, we arrived at a Golah town, named Suwy, which we thought was rather larger than Vonzwaw, and by this time it was night. The fertile country about Suwy abounds in fine timber, and during the two days which we rested there, I saw several fine mill-seats on the bold rocky stream which flows by the town. This was the driest part of the year.

Some years ago, two Liberians who had been sent to this town on a government message, were murdered.

Being more than thirty miles from Monrovia, the simple Golahs supposed that the colonists would not venture to march through the bush and attack them. But in this they were mistaken. Very unexpectedly they found their town confronted by the Liberians, who, instead of yelling and dancing at a safe distance, in native style, assaulted the stockade with guns and axes, and soon laid the village in ashes. This prompt un-African mode of settling "palavers" affrighted all the natives in the surrounding country. The people of Suwy agreed to terms and rebuilt their town, but without surrounding it with a stockade, which they probably believed would be a useless waste of labor.

After leaving Suwy, we traveled twenty-five miles through an unbroken forest to Gebby. The soil is rather good, the trees majestic, and the country well watered by streams flowing eastward into the St. Paul's. Beymba told us frightful tales about the leopards in this forest, which he said had eaten fully twenty men within the knowledge of the people. The other large animals are elephants and a kind of buffalo, which the people of Sierra Leone rather aptly term "the jackass cow," on account of its peculiar shape and long ears. The lion, which loves the sandy borders of the desert, is never seen in the damp and dark forests of Guinea. In the evening we were a considerable time ascending a mountain in a shower of rain. Not far from this is a high hill, on the top of which they have long been ac customed to bury the kings of Golah. At the northern foot of the hill which we had just climbed, is a village of three shanties, called Gebby. The St. Paul's is near at hand, and a stream, thirty feet wide, flows by the village, to mingle its clear waters with the yellow river. There is another Gebby, on an island of the same name in the river, and two others, two and four miles distant, on the Sama road. All these Gebbies could scarcely muster a population of four hundred souls, and there are no other inhabitants in this section, though the land is fertile, and the country appeared to be the most pleasant of any we had yet seen. We passed on to the next Gebby, and spent the night in the hut of a Golah who had been brought up at Monrovia, but he appeared to be none the less a barbarian for all that. It is very hard for such a man to sustain his slight degree of civilization when he returns to reside among his countrymen, but I thought that he might at least have benefited his town by introducing some of the good fruits which he had loved to eat in the colony.

Before bed-time, our carriers raised a row with the villagers, in which one man was slightly cut with a knife or spear. Our usually quiet friend, Beymba, who was a Mahometan, came running for his sword, saying, "We can beat these Golahs, and take all their fowls and goats." In former times the threat would have been to sell them for slaves; but there is no slave trade in and about Liberia now, and slaves were then selling among the natives of the interior for about twelve dollars a piece. Many a lazy fellow hopes to see a return to former customs; and one said to me, "The queen of England will die by and by, and then we shall sell slaves."

We arrived at Gebby on Saturday, and desired to remain there the following day, but our carriers refused on account of last night's quarrel. They said there was a friendly village not far off, where we could rest and

procure provisions, and we agreed to go. After march-
ing twenty miles, through gloomy forests and over
several steep rocky hills, we arrived at Tazzua, the
friendly village which they pretended was almost close
at hand. Tazzua consisted of some half dozen huts, one
of which we obtained from a widow woman for ourselves and baggage. Next morning when I paid the
bill she threw her arms round my neck, and gave me a
cordial embrace, as a substitute for plain " Thank you."

Monday morning, the 6th of March, we entered Sama,
amid the firing of guns, and the acclamations of several
hundred people. Pressing through half naked crowds,
and winding through intricate alleys, we reached the
palaver house, where we were kindly received by
king Lansanna, who bade us welcome to his town, and
presently furnished us with a comfortable hut for our
home. Sama, which was a town of perhaps one thousand
inhabitants, and surrounded by a high and strong stockade, was situated in a very dense bush, on flat, heavy
land, with a muddy little stream and steep mountains,
close by on the west. I was grieved to see it have every
appearance of a very sickly locality.

On the day following our arrival we prepared what
we considered to be a sufficient present to the king for
sending his slaves to bring our baggage from Vonzwaw.
It consisted of a cheap American saddle, some uncut
pieces of calico, a lot of tobacco, and a few other articles, amounting in all to about forty dollars. He looked
at the present with indifference, and, after some talk
with his people, very coolly informed us that he must
have three hundred dollars' worth of goods. We assured him that everything in our possession was not

worth so much, and that we were obliged to keep our
cloth and tobacco to purchase food ; but he would not
be satisfied, even in a grumbling way, without a large
addition to our first offer. This affair, so briefly described, cost us a long "palaver," or, in plain words, a squab-
ble, and left us in no very good humor.

We had brought four American boys with us from
Monrovia, as servants and students. Mr. Goodale
thought best to begin a mission at this place, and opened
a school with six scholars, including a Golah boy, who
could speak English, and one of the Vy tribe, who desired to learn. He also obtained a grant of land from
the king, for a farm, and began preparations to sow
rice. I agreed to assist him so long as I should remain,
which would not be long, for I found no Pulohs at Sama,
and nothing remained but to proceed to the Niger, or
return to the coast, and sail for Badagry. In the meantime, as it would be several months before the close of
the rains, I proposed to study the Vy language, and to
preach as much as possible, through an interpreter.
Our first and last public discourses were on Sunday
after our arrival at Sama. Mr. Goodale was taken sick
on the same day, and in spite of our utmost care and
attention died about a month after. His zeal continued
unabated to the last. Not choosing to bury him in the
heathen grave-yard, we prepared his grave under a tree
on the Monrovia road, only a few yards without the
gate of the town. Almost every one knows what it is
to mourn the death of a friend, but there are not many
who can fully appreciate the sorrow and loneliness of a
man who buries his beloved and only companion in the
wilds of Africa.

I soon discovered that Lansanna would not permit me to carry any of my remaining goods to the interior. Much less could I think of sending to Monrovia for what we had left there to be forwarded if we should need it. I therefore determined to return to the coast and resume my journey to Badagry. But I must not dismiss Sama without giving the reader a little more information.

The population of Sama is a mixture of Golahs, Pessies, Vies and several other tribes. They live in circular huts, without furniture or anything else that pertains to civilization. Their principal food is rice and palaver sauce, made of herbs and palm oil. Their domestic animals are goats, sheep, dogs and fowls. Only the king has a few cows. They plant no yams, and but little corn and cotton, and have no fruits except limes and plantains. There were two or three blacksmiths in the town who had three little furnaces in the gates, and wrought knives and spear heads on a stone anvil. The women spin cotton on a distaff, and the men weave cloth six inches wide, in a little loom, constructed on the same principle as ours. Altogether, the people are good-for-nothing, contented savages, who spend most of their time in lounging about, as if to eat and sleep and talk were the chief end of man. Beymba assured me that some of the tribes further in the interior were still more degraded. After my return to Monrovia, some of the colonists affirmed that all the people in the country to which I had been, were cannibals.

The Mandingoes at Sama, and especially an intelligent old man, who had been at London and Liverpool as a sailor, told me several things about the interior of the

country. Three days' journey from Sama, the Mandingoes have built a considerable town called Gódiri, which
serves as a resting place for traders as they pass through
the barbarous tribes who inhabit the forests. Two days
further, is the open and grassy country of Boonda, which
supplies horses and cattle for the Liberia and Sierra
Leone markets. It is still four or five days' journey to
the Mandingo country, which lies on the head waters of
the St. Paul's and extends eastward to the Yolla Ba
(Big River) or Niger. Some of the mountains in that
region are "higher than the clouds," but it seems that
they are disposed in detached groups, and not in continuous ridges.

All the interior traders being Mahometans, are indi-
rectly missionaries of the false prophet, and their influence is beginning to be felt even among the rude tribes
of Guinea. A good many Vy people and a few Golahs
professed to be converts to the faith. Lansanna was a
native of the interior, and though a residence of fifty-
three years among the heathen, had rather impaired his
devotion to Mahomet, he still condemned idolatry, and
required his idolatrous subjects to obey some parts of
the "Mandingo law," particularly in the settlement of
palavers. A law suit which occurred at Sama, during
my stay, may serve as an index to the changes which
are silently going on even here under the Mandingo
traders. A man had lent a slave to his friend who was
going to Vonzwaw. As fugitive slaves are free in the
colony, the man thought fit to run away and take refuge
in Monrovia. The action was brought by the lender, to
recover the price of the slave from the borrower. Each
party paid equal fees in advance. The case was tried

by nine jurors, witnesses were examined, and speeches made, and the king, who sat as judge, pronounced sentence according to the verdict of the jury.

The various difficulties and adventures which I passed through before I could regain the coast—how the negroes appeared determined to have the remnant of my goods, —how I was bullied and threatened by Lansanna, and a personage called the Golah king, who was chief of all the Golahs in Sama,—how I had to quarrel and almost fight for seven days, before I could obtain permission to leave the town,—how the surly Golahs on the road almost starved me as I returned through their country, —how I visited Gebby Island, and found the eastern branch of the river beyond it more than a quarter of a mile wide—how my carriers tore open my packages and robbed me of several dozen knives and my bottle of Cologne water ; and how I finally arrived at Monrovia, hungry, weary, and glad, about nine o'clock at night— all this need not be related. After some delay at Monrovia, during which I visited Grand Cape Mount, and Gallinas river, I finally sailed for Cape Coast Castle, about the 20th of June, 1850.

CHAPTER VII.

VOYAGE FROM MONROVIA TO BADAGRY, IN 1850.

PARABLE OF THE SOWER — DEPARTURE FROM MONROVIA — FOOLISH KROO-
MEN — EL MINA — THE FANTEES — RISE OF THE COAST — GOLD — NUDITY
— IMMODESTY — CAUSES OF AFRICAN DEGRADATION — QUEER MARRIAGES
— MULATTOES — CURIOUS   WEIGHTS — COSTUME — A FUNERAL — CAPE
COAST CASTLE — THE LANDING — WESLEYAN MISSIONS — " L. E. L." 'S
GRAVE — GUINEA WORM — AFRICAN   HILLS — ROCKS — RISE OF THE
COAST — DEPARTURE FOR BADAGRY — WHAT NEGROES NEED MASTERS —
AKRA GARDENS —NEGRO VANITY — AGUEY — BADAGRY.

THE parable of the sower may be applied to countries ;
for a whole community may be composed of wayside or
thorny-ground hearers.   Conquest, colonization, or some
other stringent means, must be employed to raise the
people of Guinea to humanity, before the Gospel can
elevate them to Christianity.   No chemist will produce
a result contrary to the laws of matter, and no missionary will have success contrary to the laws of the human
mind.   This is taught in the Saviour's parable.   Some
persons believe that schools are the means to prepare
the people for Christianity ; but schools can not create
the wants to drive men into civilization ; and they could
not supply these wants if already created.   Desires to
stimulate, labor to supply, and the strong arm of law to
direct and restrain, are indispensable to the improvement
of any barbarous nation.   If there had been no people
in Africa superior to those of Guinea, I might have been

content to pass my days here, engaged in the lowest departments of preparatory labors ; but when I knew that the intellectual and social state of the Central Africans, already demanded the Gospel and a higher degree of civilization, it appeared to me unreasonable to neglect them for the sake of premature labors in Guinea. With these feelings, I bade a joyful adieu to Monrovia, and sailed for Badagry, whence I expected to penetrate into the interior.

As we sailed with a light breeze down the Kroo coast, three Kroomen boarded us and hauled their little canoe on deck. They were admonished to leave the vessel, because we should sail by Cape Palmas, in the night, but the hope of receiving another drink of rum next morning, was too strong for their reason, and they persisted in remaining. At daybreak they found themselves fifty miles from home, on the coast of a hostile country. Although the captain proposed to keep them on board till we should meet another vessel, they preferred to return in their canoe, and were supplied with bread and water for the voyage.

A short and pleasant run brought us to the town of El Mina, (the mine) which was settled by the Portuguese, in 1481. It now belongs to the Dutch. True to the stolid policy peculiar to themselves, they defend this little colony of ten thousand souls by two heavy and expensive forts or castles, into one of which no foreigner might enter—and are so jealous of their rights, that missionaries are not permitted to live in El Mina. In one of the forts they had a large public school, in which the negro children are obliged to learn

Dutch, although English is the commercial language of the whole coast, and all the natives are anxious to learn it.

The Fantee people, who are the most civilized of all native tribes, live at El Mina, Cape Coast Castle, and other towns in this region. Even the houses of the natives on this coast are well built of stone, and this, with the European residences, and the extensive castles, presents a civilized appearance which one is hardly prepared to see in Africa.

El Mina has no harbor, but a slight indentation of the shore makes a better landing place than is usual on the surf-beaten coast, between Freetown and Fernando Po. Boats enter a small stream which comes down through the midst of the town, and pass under a bridge to a stone wharf. A broad and beautifully shaded street runs eastward from the wharf, parallel with the sea. Here are the European residences, and the chief seat of business. We passed along this street through swarms of market women, and stopped at a commodious hotel kept by a Fantee.

After viewing the lower castle, which rises from the edge of the water, and is surrounded by a deep ditch, cut in the sand stone, I went up the beach westward, to examine a small unoccupied fortress, which appeared to be very old. The only door into the building is considerably above the ground, so that the occupants were obliged to enter it by means of a ladder. On a careful examination of this place, I strongly suspected that the land had risen several feet since the erection of the redoubt, and I have since become convinced that this part of the coast is still rising. On the beach, between the redoubt and the town, were numbers of women, some washing gold from the sand in the edge of the surf, others bathing and others walking about in nature's simplest attire, perfectly undisturbed by the presence of any one who might be passing. Scenes like this are witnessed on every part of the coast The partially civilized tribes of Sudan, are more or less mixed with Caucasian blood, and their modesty is in exact proportion to the degree of intermixture. The females in the blacker Sudan tribes, are always clothed, it is true, but they see no impropriety in leaving the upper part of the body uncovered. The whiter Pulohs are clad from head to foot. The degradation of the Guinea tribes has not resulted from intercourse with unprincipled Europeans ; for the same race, the unmixed negro, is even more degraded in the centre of the continent.*

But the conduct of most Europeans on the coast, is not calculated to make the negroes better. At El Mina, they introduced me to a sleek Fantee lassie, as " the wife" of Captain ——, who has a wife in Massachusetts. Most captains or merchants have one or more of these "wives." There are two ways of marrying in such cases, which are technically termed " by the week," and " by the run." A wife by the week, is free at the end of the term. The latter kind of wives are tenants at will, who may be dismissed, or may leave at any time. The mulattoes on this coast are generally weakly in body, and frequently worthy to be regarded as the meanest of mankind. Their laziness and dishonesty, is

---

* See Crowther's or Hutchinson's Journal of the late expedition up the Chadda.

partly the result of the manner in which they are brought
up, and partly, perhaps, a heritage from their white fathers. Whether whites, blacks, or mulattoes, the present position of the people is almost beyond the reach of
the Gospel. Within the last twenty years, two forward
and self-conceited men, who were sent from Europe as
missionaries, have found their level among the heathen.

The principal exports from this part of the coast, are
gold and ivory. Nearly all the gold is brought from
mines in the interior, the location of which is not known.
The small quantity washed from the sea sands on the
coast, is sold to the trade women, who weigh it with
little red seeds instead of weights. The natives of
Kumasi, make larger weights of brass. A set of these
which a trader offered for sale, consisted of rude little
figures, representing the industrial pursuits of the country. One represented a man climbing a palm tree, to
gather the nuts. Another was a man carrying a barrel,
perhaps a keg of powder or of rum, on his head.

Nothing attracted my attention more than the hair of
the Fantee women. It was eight or ten inches long,
well moistened with pomatum, procured from the Dutch
traders, and combed straight, so as to have exactly the
appearance of wool in samples, ready for exhibition.
Their dress consisted of a calico wrapper fastened
round the waist, and reaching nearly to the ground,
with another wrapper, often dispensed with, thrown
over the shoulders. Enormous bustles, which project
about a foot, are universal on the Gold Coast, though I
have not seen them in any other part of the country.

During my stay at El Mina I witnessed the funeral of
a wealthy Dutch mulatto. The corpse was laid out in

a large upper room of his fine dwelling, and surrounded by several women as chief mourners. About noon, a large procession formed at the house, and followed the corpse, not to the grave, as I supposed they would do, but to the lower castle and back again. Immediately behind the corpse were a number of women " skillful in weeping," who kept up a noisy lamentation. Then followed the officers of the castles and several others, perhaps merchants, palefaced Dutchmen with long swords and red whiskers; and finally a promiscuous rabble of men, women and children, one among them bearing a huge red umbrella, adorned with fringe or tassels. One negro bore an immense speaking trumpet on his head, and another who walked behind him applied his mouth to the nozzle occasionally, and bawled out something, I suppose in honor of the deceased.

Cape Coast Castle, which belongs to the English, is in plain view of El Mina, the distance being about nine miles. The towns are very similar, in regard to houses and inhabitants, but the former has only one castle. The landing at Cape Coast is dangerous, owing to the violence of the surf. It is effected in large flat-bottomed canoes, well manned by Fantee rowers. As they approach the shore, they make every exertion to poise the canoe on the back of a wave, so as to ride in upon the beach before the surf breaks, which might fill their craft with water. Cape Coast (originally Cabo Corso) like most other towns in these parts, was founded by the Portuguese.

Here I left the brig in which I had come from Monrovia, and went ashore to wait for a passage for Badagry. At first I stopped at a tolerably good hotel, kept by a native,

but was soon invited to reside in the family of Rev. T.
B. Freeman, the superintendent of the Wesleyan missions. These missions, which were commenced in 1835,
consist at present of several stations on the Gold and
Slave Coasts, and have penetrated into the interior of Kumasi, the capital of Ashantee, and to Abbeokuta, the capital of Egbá. They number several hundred converts.

I remained at Cape Coast about three weeks. In
walking over the castle one day, they showed me the
grave of the gifted, but unhappy Miss Landon (the
poetess " L. E. L.") She married a government officer,
and died here on the coast of Africa.

In the hospital I saw several natives laid up with
Guinea worm. The natives attribute this disease to bad
water, as do those of Yóruba, and of some districts on
the Red Sea. They say it prevents attacks of fever.

The hills about Cape Coast are mostly circular, and
graded down to the base, so that the numerous little
valleys which wind among them are nearly level. Isolated hills or patches, and short chains of mountains are
a general feature in Africa. A man could pass throughout the continent to Egypt at many points, without
climbing a single mountain, though he might see many
peaks during his journey.

The rocks here, as at El Mina, are red sand stone, sometimes becoming slaty, but apparently destitute of organic remains. A few hundred yards east of the castle,
there is a hill which projects into the sea, composed of
alternate layers of harder and softer gneiss. The constant dashing of the waves has washed away the softer
portion, to some depth, leaving the former in projecting
ledges. These ledges rise from the water's edge to a

height considerably above the present level of the sea, thus proving the gradual rise of the coast. Similar and very conclusive evidence of the same fact is seen in the sand stone bluffs at Akra.

About the middle of July I obtained passage to Bada- gry on a small schooner loaded with brown sugar, which " steamed" so much that the fumes banished us from the cabin. Unsafe as it might be to sleep on the dew- drenched deck, it seemed to me less dangerous than to remain all night in the palpable vapors of damp sugar. Our captain was a kind-hearted old Scotchman, who was not ashamed to confess how himself and the crew had prayed together when they were in danger of being lost in a hurricane. I have seldom met with an irreli- gious man who had the moral courage to admit that he had been frightened into prayer. We had several pas- sengers on the crowded deck, among whom were a drunken merchant of Akra, a Brazilian slaver of the Slave Coast, and a pleasant intelligent man who held the rank of colonial surgeon of Cape Coast. In speak- ing of the dishonesty and indolence of the natives, I re- marked that they ought to have masters, in obedience to the demands of natural justice. He replied, "That is true, but in these days it would not do to say so." I appreciated the remark. The world is governed by fashion, and in these days it is fashionable to regard human rights abstractly from all human relations.— Every candid and reflecting man knows that such rights are a positive nonentity. The colonial surgeon knew it, but was too prudent to avow his conviction, lest he should be accused of favoring the slave trade. But the just deserts of a lazy, thievish negro, or white man, is one question, and our authority to inflict the merited punishment, is another. Many a man deserves to be caned, but we have no right to cane him.

During our stay at Akra, I went ashore to visit the gardens. I found them like those at El Mina and Cape Coast, much inferior to my expectations. The natives here speak a different language from that of the Fantees. Their degree of civilization is about the same, most of their houses being built of stone, and the two tribes are about equal in their thievish propensities, and want of every ennobling quality. The Wesleyan mission at Akra is not flourishing. A German mission at Akrapong, fifty miles in the interior, is said to be more successful.

My host at Akra was a Mr. Bruce. Though a jet black negro, whose ancestors, for aught I know, had not been bleached by amalgamation since the days of Cush, his name was Bruce, and he must needs send all the way to Scotland for the Bruce coat of arms, which he keeps hung up in his parlor, as if he, like the Abyssinian traveler, were descended from Scotia's kings. Vanity, next to covetousness, is the strongest passion of Africans. To dress and swagger is as natural to them as breathing. In Sierra Leone, native boys are christened with English names, and frequently with great ones, as Edward Bickersteth, or Jabez Bunting. Sometimes, however, the godfathers pick up a name at random. It chanced that one boy was called Thomas Macauley instead of John Smith. He now sports the name of Thomas Babington Macauley; the additional name being an after-thought of his own. I had a servant once who used to write his name on scraps of

paper, "Samuel Charles Jones, Esq." Native assistants
in missions are more apt to grow in consequence than
in grace and knowledge ; but I have met with several
noble exceptions.

Our next stopping place was at Aguey, a most barbarous town in the Popo country, with two "factories"
(trading-houses,) one for the slave trade, and one for
lawful commerce. Here the slaves left us, as the doctor
had done at Akra. As there was no hotel at Aguey, I
stopped at the English factory, where I appeared to be
received as a welcome visitor by the lonely superintendent. The entire nudity which I have already mentioned
appeared to be more shameless and cordial than ever in
this darkest part of Africa. But here also it is confined
to one sex. I have never seen so horrible a place as
Aguey, or one which I remember with so much indignation.

At last we arrived at Badagry on the 5th of August,
nearly eight months after I had sailed from the United
States. Next day I took leave of the good old captain,
and soon had the satisfaction to find myself safely
through the roaring surf, on firm land, no more to resume my voyage. A flat, treeless prairie extends from
the beach three-quarters of a mile to the river Ossa,
which is seven hundred yards wide, and runs parallel
with the coast for forty or fifty miles till it flows into
the sea at Lagos. The banks are covered with papyrus,
which at a short distance resembles the young pine.
Immediately beyond the river is the vile old town of
Badagry ; and twenty days' journey more or less, would
bring me to Igboho (Bohoo) where I had purposed to
make the first experiment in the Central African mission.

CHAPTER VIII.

BADAGRY AND THE SLAVE COAST.

THE PEOPLE OF BADAGRY — THE SLAVE COAST — "NEW NIGGERS" —
FIDA — THE LANGUAGE — SLAVE TRADE — SOIL — CLIMATE — RELIGIOUS
CEREMONY — WITCHES — MARKETS — CURRENCY — COWRIES — BEGGARS
— OLD SIMEON — A SERVANT AND A HORSE — DEPARTURE FROM BADA-
GRY — BURIAL IN THE AIR — HOW LOADS ARE CARRIED — PRAIRIES —
A LAGOON — A CARAVAN — THE COUNTRY — SOIL — SCENERY — COUN-
TRIES ON THE SLAVE COAST — EIGHTEEN MONTHS' DETENTION.

BADAGRY contained about ten thousand inhabitants.
The houses were built of bamboo, (foot stems of white
palm leaves,) and the yard fences were of the same material.   The streets were narrow and intricate lanes, as
in all other native towns, whether on the coast or in
the interior.   Many of the people were scape-gallows
villains, who had fled from other countries.   One of
the English missionaries, who had been residing for
some time in the place, remarked that their cup of ini-
quity was full, and the people were ripe for destruction.*
About a year and a half after this, Badagry was burnt
down, in a cut throat affray among its own citizens.

This part of Africa is called the Slave Coast, because
it afforded the most intelligent, docile and industrious
negroes for the American plantations.   I am sorry to

---

* See Lander's account of this place, in 1832.

add, that these good "niggers" were the almost civilized inhabitants of Yóruba, Nufe, Hausa, and other countries in Sudan, the very people to whom I had gone forth as a missionary. They, at least, according to the inflexible laws of nature, deserved a better fate than slavery ; for if rights and relations are the just results of properties, (or character, which they undoubtedly are,) these people had a right to remain unmolested in their native land. Every planter who is forty years old, knows the great difference in the character of "new niggers." The short, stubby, silly fellows often brought into the slave markets, were chiefly from Congo, south of the line, where all the people (imported to America) have an affinity to the Hottentots. The " Gulla niggers," were from Golah country on the St. Paul's river, where they still vegetate, about the meanest of the human race, and amply worthy of the cotton field. The "Eboe nigger," was from a fine open country, above the delta of the Niger, and not from the delta itself, as we have commonly supposed.* At home he was a noble, high-minded and half civilized man, who beautified his fine country with well cultivated farms and shady villages. In America he was trusty, intelligent and industrious, but remarkable for an absolutely indomitable spirit, to which even the master must yield, when the Eboe was aroused, unless he should choose to shoot down the best slave on his plantation. No wonder : for the Eboes in common with the Sudanese, have undergone a strong Caucasian innervation, which is evidenced by the fact that some of them are nearly white. The rest of the

---

* There is a village, but no country or tribe, called Eboe.

" Guinea niggers," brought to our country, were principally the hateful Popoes, the shrewd but thievish Fantees, and others like them.

Several old writers (as Bosman, one hundred and fifty years ago) give a glowing description of a country west of Badagry, called Fida—whence the name Whydah. The country in this region is still exceedingly beautiful, but the power and glory of the Fida kingdom, if it ever existed, is not remembered by the natives. Bosman, a Dutchman, declined to give any specimens of the barbarous language in these parts, being more intent on buying slaves for half-civilized colonists than to gratify the curiosity of enlightened men. This was natural to Bosman, and to the sensual age in which he lived, when even some of the dignitaries of the church derived large revenues from the slave trade. At present, the prevailing language on this coast is the Yóruba, which has almost supplanted the Popo, by the silent and gradual progress of immigration from the interior. In vain do we inquire whether the encroachments of a superior race were already extensive in the days of Bosman.

A few miles above Badagry, on the same river (Ossa), is a still larger town called Ajasheh (which means broken by war). At this point, the river is nine miles from the sea, at Porto Novo, Domingo's slave station, a name which Europeans apply to Ajasheh. In 1850, Ajasheh, Whydah, and nearly all the Slave Coast, led by Gezo, king of Dahomy, and Kosokkoh, the usurper at Lagos or Eko, were in favor of the slave trade, and opposed to lawful commerce and missionaries. Only Abbeokuta, a large town sixty miles in the interior, and a minority at Badagry, were opposed to the slave trade, as contrary to the best interests of the country. I was informed that Gezo and Kosokkoh were concocting a plan to destroy Abbeokuta and subdue Badagry, so as to expel the English merchants and missionaries, and restore the slave trade, as in former days. The ill success of these attempts will be noticed in a subsequent chapter.

The soil on this part of the Slave Coast, which some travelers have pronounced exceedingly fertile, is often decidedly poor. No intelligent farmer could be deceived by the barren sandy soil at Badagry. Weeds and grasses, unfit for man or beast, are stimulated to luxuriance by heat and moisture, but the crops of Indian corn, peas, potatoes, &c., which depend upon soil as well as climate, are indifferent. Geologically speaking, the land on this part of the coast is little else than the sand of the "drift period," the coarser materials being deposited far in the interior.

The streams about Badagry are nothing but narrow lines of swamp, owing to the dead level of the surface. Such a country cannot be healthy. Two or three missionaries had recently died at Badagry, and the European merchants had suffered still more severely. I was told that six young men had died in a single year in one factory, the victims of rum, debauchery and fever.

During the eight days that I remained at Badagry, I rambled through every part of the town and the adjacent farms. In one of the streets I saw a dog, which had been sacrificed, and suspended to the boughs of a tree, in honor of some mangy órisha (idol). Sacrifices and processions, with noisy uproar and beating of drums, appear to be a precious amusement to the people. Christian converts in every part of Africa still retain their innate love of noise and gesticulation. Rare scenes are sometimes witnessed in the Methodist meetings on some parts of the coast. The sober Episcopalian converts are greatly delighted with the "service." To kneel a little, and to stand a little, by turns, to chaunt the doxology, and repeat the Lord's Prayer in concert, to bow the knee mechanically whenever they repeat the name of Jesus in the creed, to exclaim "Good Lord deliver us," in solemn set tones, twenty times successively, in the responses of the litany—all this has a strong hold on the hearts of the people, because it is congenial to their natural feelings. The Baptist converts can scarcely be restrained from attaching supernatural efficacy to the act of solemn immersion in water.

In addition to their other superstitions, it appears that the good citizens of Badagry were sorely annoyed by witches, who were in the habit of destroying people, especially fat ones, by sucking their blood while asleep. Sometimes an old hag of a heathen confesses the charge, and courageously resigns herself to the penalty of death. How the people stare at a veritable witch! Hearing a great uproar one day, I inquired "What's the matter?" "Oh, they have caught a witch, and are going to kill her."

I was fond of going to see the market, which was crowded every evening with thousands of people, including many from interior towns, busily and noisily engaged in buying and selling cloth, rum, tobacco, gunpowder, salt, yams, Indian corn, goats, sheep, fowls, and a long list of other articles, some from Europe and America, and others from the depths of the continent. The currency on the Slave Coast, and far interior to Hausa and Burnu, is a little shell as large as the end of one's finger, called a cowry, (cyprea moneta). They are not found in Western Africa, but are brought by Europeans from India and Zanzibar, and given to the natives for palm oil and other productions of the country. Forty cowries are called a "string," fifty strings or two thousand cowries, are a "head," and ten heads are a "bag." It is usual to value two thousand cowries at one dollar, which is twenty to the cent, but of late they are generally cheaper on the coast. I am told that the intrinsic value of good cowries in Europe, where they are used in the arts, is about equal to their current value in Africa. The iron money of Lycurgus was not more cumbersome than cowries, the net weight of ten dollars' worth, (20,000 shells) being from fifty to seventy pounds. The common price of a fowl is from 200 to 250 shells ; of a sheep, from 4000 to 6000 ; of a horse, from 60,000 to 120,000, and other things in proportion. When building our houses, we are obliged to keep a man to count the cowries every evening for the laborers. Silver and gold are not current here, because the merchants on the coast, who import the cowries, will take nothing but shells or palm oil for the cloth, guns, tobacco, rum, &c., which they sell to the natives. Neither is it possible to pay for provisions and labor in goods of any kind, barter being unknown, and cowries demanded for everything.

The people of Badagry having a poor soil, and a sufficient traffic to prevent their starving, were not much addicted to labor. Even fishing, which is vigorously prosecuted by the tribes on the Gold, Ivory, and Grain Coasts, is confined here to the sluggish Ossa river. No Badagrian would think of launching a canoe into the open sea. The town swarmed with thieves and drunkards, whose only object in life was sensual gratification. Nowhere else had I met with so many impudent and shameless beggars. When a missionary attempted to preach to a crowd in the streets or market, it was very common for some of them to reply by laying their hands on their stomachs, and saying, "White man, I am hungry!" Soon after my arrival, a fellow introduced himself as the "American chief," who was to receive presents from all American visitors. Another was called the "English chief," another the "French chief," &c. These greedy chiefs are no longer able to rob men as they did the Landers, because there is now a strong minority of the people opposed to such conduct, but if they had been left to themselves, no missionary could have passed through Badagry, without leaving a large part of his property.

One of my first cares on entering Badagry, was to inquire the way to Bohoo, for this was the place to which I had started, and no other town in Africa would satisfy my desires. Every body, whether missionaries, merchants, or natives, assured me that the road to Bohoo had been closed for a long time by the Yóruba wars, and that Abbeokuta, sixty miles to the N.E. of Badagry, was the only place in the interior to which I could possibly go. I was unwilling to pass through Abbeokuta, because it lay considerably east of my route; and I had still less desire to stop there, because I supposed it was nothing more than other towns in Guinea, of which I had seen a sufficient number. In America, I had read a pleasing account of "old Simeon," a convert in the Wesleyan mission at Badagry; and on inquiry, the missionaries informed me that he was a native of Bohoo, and had begged them to go and preach to his countrymen. Of course I paid him a visit. The venerable old man was delighted to hear that I had left home to preach the Gospel in his native city, and declared his readiness to go with me, but added that I would find it impossible to go at present.

Losing all hope of doing better, I resolved to visit Abbeokuta, and there renew my efforts to reach Bohoo. My preparations for departure were commenced by employing for a servant, a stout awkward Egbá youth, who spoke English. His wages as fixed by himself, were $1.50 per month; "poor pay, poor preach." Eight men were required to carry my baggage, and my boy Sam soon engaged them at one dollar apiece for the journey. My next exploit was to purchase a horse from a mulatto school-master, in one of the missions, for $40. His color was bay, his height eleven hands, and his name was Cæsar. The seller recommended him as "a powerful animal," and "a war-horse," which had "been in battle." On the second day of my journey, Cæsar fell lame, and Samuel Charles Jones, Esq., drove him behind me to Abbeokuta. On arriving there, I had the satisfaction to learn, that if the horse was worthless, the price was unusual; sound ponies of that size being valued at $20. Poor Cæsar lingered a while, and died of the journey.

All things being ready, I bid farewell to Badagry, on

the 14th of August, and departed on my second attempt to reach the interior of Africa. Half a mile from the town, we saw a corpse tied up in mats, and suspended horizontally between two stakes, four or five feet from the ground. In this manner they dispose of slaves who die, while in pawn for debt, so that the master, on coming down from the interior, may know that his slave has not been sold by the creditor. Two or three miles further on, we passed near the farm of the infamous Adulè, (Lander's Adooley,) who had been dead for several years. All along the road, we met numbers of men, women and children going to the Badagry market, with palm-oil, corn, yams, fowls, fire-wood, &c., which they carried in heavy loads on their heads, according to the universal custom of this country; though the Golahs, and others in that region, carry burdens on their backs. About six miles' walk through beautifully interspersed woods and prairies, brought us to Mo, or Imowo lagoon, which is half a mile wide, and so deep in the rainy season, that the people are not able to ford it. Here we found a caravan of several hundred men and women, who made the woods ring with their noisy chat and laughter, while waiting for a few canoes to convey them over the water. After a while, a nearly naked fellow, in a very small canoe, slipped out from the trees and bushes which fill the lagoon, and paddled up to the landing, with several large calabashes full of palm wine, which he retailed to the noisy travelers. Every canoe which returned from the other side of the water, was met at some distance from the bank, by numbers of people, who put in their loads and dragged it to the shore to get in themselves, so that all the begging and bawling we could do, was not sufficient to procure a passage for myself and horse, till it was too dark to go at all.

Early next morning we succeeded in crossing the water, my horse swimming most of the way by the side of a canoe, along a crooked road cut through the jungle. We took breakfast in Mo village, beyond the lagoon, and traveled about three miles through the bush, like that in Liberia, to a beautiful prairie, adorned by several tall and graceful fan-leaf palms. After passing through several forests, farms and prairies, we entered a great wood, which continued with little interruption, for nearly thirty miles, to a more open country. The first stones, (iron conglomerate,) occurred about thirty miles from Badagry. The soil was generally good and the streams rather swampy. Near the centre of this great forest, though not immediately on the road, is a shabby little town which is distinguished as the birth-place of Adulè.

On Sunday, the 17th, we rested by a beautiful stream of clear water, about twenty miles from Abbeokuta. The woods were full of monkeys, parrots, horn bills and honey bees. Next morning we traveled about three miles through a fertile and heavily timbered body of land to the top of a hill, where we suddenly emerged into an open country, and my eyes were greeted with a more lovely scene than I had ever expected to behold in Africa—a vast expanse of undulating prairie, scattered over with palms and groves, and bounded in the distance by blue, mountainous looking hills. I felt that I had entered a new region; Guinea was left behind me. Passing through this lovely country, delighted by fresh beauties at every step, we arrived at the Ogun river, which flows by Abbeokuta, a little after sunset, and entered the city by twilight.

Abbeokuta is the capital of the very small independent kingdom of Egbá, which is numbered according to its position among the countries of Guinea, but in character is more nearly allied to Sudan. The whole population of this little state may be set down at 100,000, most of whom are in the capital city. On the east and southeast of Egbá, is the kingdom of Ijebu, (tortured by different writers into Jaboo, Yebu and Dshebu,) and east of this lies the larger country of Ibini or Benin. To the south and west of Egbá, are several unconnected towns, inhabited by a people, who are called Egbado (the lower Egbas) ; to the west of whom is the little kingdom of Iketu, which extends to Dahomy. Badagry and Lagos, (Eko,) on the coast, are independent towns, the latter of which is ruled by a king, who formerly professed allegiance to Benin. Midway between Badagry and Abbeokuta, is a very small tribe called Otta. The Ijebus, Egbás, Egbadoes, Ottas and Iketus, as also the people of Badagry and Lagos, speak the Yóruba language. All these people are similar in features, character and customs, but those near the coast are more barbarous than those of the interior. The Popoes and Dahomies are more degraded, at least morally, than any other people on this coast. They were probably the original owners of all the forest country between Badagry and Egbá, but have gradually retired before their Yóruba-speaking neighbors, till their language has almost disappeared from most parts of the coast east of Whydah The proper Yóruba kingdom, and the origi-

nal seat of all the Yóruba-speaking tribes, extends from
Benin on the east to Dahomy on the west, having the
Ijebus, Egbás, Egbadoes, and Iketus on its southern
border. The Yóruba country begins about twenty miles
north of Abbeokuta, or eighty miles by the road, from
the sea coast. No wonder if I entertained pleasing
hopes of soon being able to enter the country when
several of its mountains are in plain view of Abbeokuta.
Yet I was compelled to remain in Egbá and the other
low countries for eighteen months, before the chiefs
would give me permission to proceed. But this time
was not wholly lost, since I was employed in studying
the language, and in becoming acquainted with the
character of the people.

CHAPTER IX.

ABBEOKUTA AND THE EGBAS.

ABBEOKUTA — OGUN RIVER — ROCKS — SOIL — EGBA COUNTRY DESOLATED
BY WAR — ANCIENT GIANTS — WARS — DAHOMIES DEFEATED — MIS-
SIONARIES INVITED TO EGBA — SUCCESS — TRANSLATIONS — HAND OF
PROVIDENCE.

THE population of Abbeokuta is estimated by some
Europeans at sixty thousand, and by others at one hundred thousand souls. I approached the place with a confident expectation of reducing the estimate to twenty-
five or thirty thousand, for I could not believe that the
towns here were so great, when they were generally
small in other parts of Africa. Though it was nearly
dark when I arrived, I could still see enough to mitigate
my unbelief. It appeared to be truly an extensive town,
and my wonder was not diminished by traveling half a
mile to the Wesleyan station, which they said was almost
in the suburbs. Here I spent the night and rested for
two or three days. Proceeding then by daylight, I
found it about a mile to the first Episcopal station,
which was then in charge of Mr. Crowther, a native
missionary. Nearly a mile further, amid numberless
houses I was brought to Mr. Townsend's station, and it
was still two miles further to Mr. Smith's station near
the northern wall. The length of the town by the most
direct route was afterwards measured by a perambulator,

and found to be within a few rods of four miles. The width is from two to three miles. The walls, which include much open space, are probably fifteen miles in circuit, and the town itself is not less than ten miles in circuit. Observing that the houses are very large, and learning that the population of a house varies from twenty to one hundred souls, I felt entirely unable to guess how many thousands an accurate census would give to Abbeokuta. Here the matter is obliged to rest, but we all think it reasonable to estimate the population at sixty to one hundred thousand souls.*

Abbeokuta is situated on the eastern bank of the Ogun river, in latitude 7° 8' N., and, by estimation, about 3° 20' E. longitude. The river, which is here about one hundred yards wide, is navigable for canoes to the rapids near the southern wall of the town, and might be available for light steamers to a point about twelve miles lower down. The distance to Lagos by the river is about ninety miles, mostly through a rich but sparsely inhabited country.

The rocks about Abbeokuta are chiefly granite, many huge masses of which, in and around the town, arise to a height of two hundred feet or more. Much of the soil is not very fertile ; the water is pure, and the climate healthy. The surrounding country is generally open or sparsely timbered, being of the kind which is commonly called grass-field by the English, and prairie by ourselves. The absence of timber is attributable to long continued cultivation. Most of the Egbá kingdom, however, is very fertile, and covered with forests as other

---

* Such towns have gates at convenient points around the wall, and the farms extend in all directions from ten to twenty miles.

parts of Guinea. Fifty years ago this small territory
could boast of nearly three hundred towns, some of
which were considerably populous ; but now the village
of Oko-Obba, in the south-west of the kingdom, is the
only one remaining : all the others having been utterly
destroyed by war. Abbeokuta, which then had no
existence, is composed of refugees from about one hundred towns.

In ancient times, as their tradition relates, the Egbá
country was a province of the Yóruba kingdom. At
last a giant named Lishabbeh headed a rebellion against
an oppressive king, and the Egbás became independent
under a king of their own. Lishabbeh is still worshipped by the Egbás, and his farm, which it would be sacrilege to reclaim, is shown on the east side of the
Ogun, about twelve miles below Abbeokuta. Many
stories are told of this and other giants, who are represented as men of great stature. One of them, who belonged to the town of Igbehin, committed a sacrilege by
robbing the temple of Orishako, at Irawaw, in the west
of Yóruba, whence a law was passed, and is still enforced, that no Igbehin man shall enter Irawaw.

After a long time, the Egbás abolished royalty without substituting any efficient general government in its
stead; and this finally led to most disastrous results.
Jealousies between the chiefs and people of independent Egbà towns led to civil war, and the Yórubas and
Ijebus, by assisting first one town and then another, succeeded in depopulating the whole country. Some of the
last towns were destroyed about thirty years ago. It is
not improbable that these wars destroyed two hundred
thousand people. Multitudes were captured and sold to

the slavers, who shipped them to Cuba and Brazil, where great numbers of them are still living. Several thousands were re-captured on the high seas and carried to Sierra Leone. Many others fled to adjacent countries. Some of the captives are still in slavery to the Yórubas, as for instance at Ogbomoshaw, where the Egbás are said to number two thousand. Others again were sent to slave markets beyond the Niger, and found masters in Hausa and Burnu, or passed over the desert to Tripoli and Egypt. So great an overthrow of a whole tribe has seldom happened even in Africa.

Abbeokuta was founded about forty years ago by the refugees who were so happy as to escape the general destruction. At first a few persons took shelter on the top of a steep granite hill under the shelving sides of an immense rock. As this part of the country was not then inhabited, they found here a place of safety. Others joined them from time to time, and the new settlement received the appropriate name of Abbeh-okuta, "Understone." The remnants of each town, as they arrived, settled together around the original nucleus and called their locality by the name of their native town ; whence there are many districts in the city still distinguished by these names, as Akè, (the name of the old capital,) Igboro, Emmere, Igbehin, etc. The great rock which gave shelter to the first refugees, is worshipped by some under the name of *Olumoh*, "the builder." The old people still remember their former homes with affection, and sometimes express a desire to return, but the young men are opposed to resettling in the old towns, and insist on the policy of retaining command of the river and the trade to Lagos.

The enemies of the Egbás were not long in forming a resolution to destroy the new city. But their opportunity was already past. The united remnants of the nation had wisely placed themselves under the command of a single leader, a balogun (or general) named Shodekkeh, who proved himself equal to the task he had undertaken. The first assailants were the numerous and warlike Mahometans of Ilorrin, who returned defeated. Not long after, Shodekkeh repulsed the combined forces of Ijebu and Otta. An army sent from the strong city of Ibadan was equally unsuccessful. The fame of these victories reached the king of Dahomy, who made an alliance with Shodekkeh; and the Egbás began to be as much feared as they were hated.

All this time the people of Abbeokuta were cut off from direct communication with the coast, from which they desired to receive arms and merchandize in return for the slaves captured in their late successful wars. Lagos, which stands on an island, was too inaccessible, and too well defended by the armed canoes of its inhabitants, to be assaulted. Shodekkeh resolved to open communication with Badagry, by subduing his old enemies, the Ottas, and opening a passage through their country. The town of Otta was taken, but the people were permitted to remain on condition that they should not rebuild their walls. A strong party of Egbás then proceeded to Adú, on the Badagry road, which they besieged for several years, in the meantime cultivating farms on the eastern side of the town, while the besieged were doing the same on the west. In fact, the object of this siege was not to destroy Adú, but to give security to the Egbá caravans, which were now trading to Bad-

agry. About the year 1842, Shodekkeh died, and on
hearing this, the king of Dahomy treacherously marched
against the Egbás at Adú. It is probable that his only
design in this movement was to capture slaves ; but the
Egbás were victorious, and captured the king's royal
chair. Soon after this battle, they raised the siege and
returned home ; but the people of Adú thought best to
permit a continuance of the traffic between Abbeokuta
and Badagry. In 1852, the Egbás became masters of
the Ogun river, and opened an active trade with Lagos.

This story of Abbeokuta, considered apart from more
important subjects, would scarcely be worth relating.
But the most interesting portion of the narrative remains to be told. The Wesleyan missionaries, in
looking around for fields of labor, had fallen on Badagry, to all appearance one of the least hopeful points
on the whole coast. When the Egbás began their
traffic with Badagry, they met with the missionaries,
and carried home such curious accounts of their character and motives, that Shodekkeh and his people desired
to see them. About the same time (1838) several
Egbás, who had been re-captured from slave-ships and
civilized in Sierra Leone, returned to their countrymen
at Abbeokuta, telling wonderful things of Christianity
and Christian missionaries. The consequence was that
the Wesleyan missionaries were invited to Abbeokuta.
This was reported to Mr. Freeman, the superintendent,
who repaired to Abbeokuta, and was joyfully received
by Shodekkeh and the people.

In the meantime, some of the converted Egbás of the
Episcopal congregations in Sierra Leone desired to return home, and begged that missionaries might go with

them. Mr. Townsend was sent to Abbeokuta to make observations, and report on the prospects. In going up from Badagry, he met with Mr. Freeman on his way down. He also was well received by Shodekkeh, and on his return to Sierra Leone, the committee resolved on a mission to the Egbás.

In December, 1844, Mr. Townsend, Mr. Gollmer, and Mr. Crowther, a native missionary of the Yóruba tribe, who had been educated in Sierra Leone, arrived at Badagry to commence the new mission. By this time Shodekkeh was dead, and the whole country was so much distracted by wars that the Egbá chiefs were unwilling to let the missionaries proceed to Abbeokuta. They began to labor at Badagry, but finally, in July, 1846, Mr. Townsend and Mr. Crowther arrived at Abbeokuta, and were received with general demonstrations of joy. Many converted and unconverted Egbás in Sierra Leone now flocked to Abbeokuta, and the work has steadily proceeded in the country till the present time, notwithstanding two harassing persecutions against the native Christians. The Wesleyans also soon established themselves at Abbeokuta, and have continued to labor there with success. The different Wesleyan and Episcopal stations at present number about six hundred communicants. A great many people have abandoned idolatry. Mr. Crowther and Mr. King, both natives, have translated several books of the Old and New Testaments, which are handsomely printed and bound in separate books. Hundreds of people have learned to read their native tongue, and the whole tribe has advanced considerably towards civilization.

Let us look now at the steps by which God has conducted this work : the abolition of royalty by the Egbás ; their consequent civil wars ; the great rocks at Abbeo- kuta ; the refugees, who sought them for shelter ; the rise of Shodekkeh ; his victories ; the re-capture of slaves ; their conversion and return to their country ; the move- ments of missionaries ; and several other events in this history which remain to be related. Who would have predicted that the annihilation of the Egbá kingdom, forty years ago, would have led to such results as we now behold in this part of Africa ?

CHAPTER X.

BREAKING UP OF THE SLAVE TRADE.

EVILS OF THE SLAVE TRADE — OPPOSITION OF NATIVES TO SLAVE WARS —
THE DAHOMY ARMY — BATTLE AT ABBEOKUTA — BADAGRY BURNT —
LAGOS TAKEN BY THE ENGLISH.

WELL-MEANING people, who advocate a restoration of the slave trade, have considered but one side of the question. The old plea of our ancestors, that the negroes are national vagrants, who ought to be arrested by authority of law, and criminals, who deserve slavery as a punishment for their crimes, is correct in part only. Many of the interior tribes are far from being vagrants, or criminals. Besides this, it is utterly impossible to justify the wars by which the slave trade is supported. The annihilation of the Egbá nation, is a case in point. It is true, that these wars, except those of abominable Dahomy, were not generally commenced for the sake of capturing slaves; but once begun, for political reasons, they have commonly been nourished by the slave trade. At present there is peace on the Slave Coast, and it is the interest of the people to maintain it; but if the slave trade were restored, every petty war would be protracted as much as possible, for the sake of enriching the victorious party.

I have counted the sites of eighteen desolated towns within a distance of sixty miles between Badagry and

Abbeokuta—the legitimate result of the slave trade. The whole Yóruba country is full of depopulated towns, some of which were even larger than Abbeokuta is at present. Of all the places visited by the Landers, only Ishakki, Igboho, Ikishi, and a few villages remain. Ijenna (Janna) was destroyed a few weeks after my arrival in the country. Other and still larger towns in the same region, have lately fallen. At one of these called Oke-Oddan, the Dahomy army killed and captured about 20,000 people, on which occasion the king presented Domingo, the Brazilian slaver, with 600 slaves. The whole number of people destroyed in this section of country, within the last fifty years, can not be less than five hundred thousand.

The Egbás and Yórubas, who were the principal actors and sufferers in the merciless wars, were the most civilized and peaceable tribes in the country; remarkable for their love of agriculture and traffic, and among the last people in Africa whom we could suppose capable of such enormities as they persisted in committing for a space of forty years. Civil war was the cause of their madness. The brutish Dahomies, formerly the tributaries of Yóruba, entered into the strife from other motives, the love of rum and tobacco. At the time of my arrival in the country, many of the Egbás and Yórubas, looking round on their ruined country, felt sick of war and the slave trade, and sighed for a return of their former peace and prosperity. Hence Badagry, which was full of Egbás and Yórubas, had declared against the slavers, and opened her doors to lawful commerce and the Gospel. Hence, also, Shodekkeh had invited the missionaries to Abbeokuta. The country was now approaching a second crisis. The whole population was divided into two parties; one in favor of the slave trade, and of course opposed to missionaries and lawful commerce, and the other opposed to the slave trade as contrary to the best interests of the country. It was easy to foresee, even then, that this question must be decided in the battle field.

The main issue—the slave trade or no slave trade—was complicated with several others, and these, though confessedly of minor importance, were set forward as the prominent causes of the quarrel. Even the negroes of Guinea were ashamed to make war expressly in defence of the slave trade. They sought other pretexts. Some years before this date, Akitoye, the king of Lagos, had been dethroned by his nephew, Kosokkoh, who was now amassing great stores of wealth by an active traffic with Brazilian slavers. Akitoye, who was opposed to the slave trade, was an exile at Badagry, where he was protected by Abbeokuta. Hatred of Akitoye, and fears for the safety of the slave trade, prompted Kosokkoh to resolve on the destruction of Badagry. By way of preparation for this event, he opened communication with the slave trade party in the town, who now amounted to more than half of the population, and had a daring balogun (or general) for their leader. At some convenient time, a party of Lagos men were to attack Badagry, and the slave trade party in the town were then to fall upon Akitoye and his friends.

They had no doubts of being able to subdue Badagry, but they knew that scarcely ten days would elapse before their new possessions would be assaulted by the Egbás ; and the Egbás at this time were terrible enemies. Abbeokuta must fall or the slave trade must perish; and Lagos, with all her allies, could not venture to attack the Egbás in their strong hold. The king of Dahomy now remembered that the Egbás had worsted him in the fight before Adú, and he vowed to be revenged on the whole tribe, particularly for the loss of his royal chair. For twenty-five years the numerous regular army* of Dahomy, had been the scourge and terror of the whole surrounding country, always at war and generally victorious. King Gezo, who regarded his own Abomy as a large town, had no conception of such an immense city as Abbeokuta, and expected to overwhelm it with his troops as he had lately done Oke-Oddan. On my arrival at Badagry in 1850, I was informed that all these plans were matured. Kosokkoh and his allies were to subdue Badagry. Gezo was to make a desolation of Abbeokuta, the merchants and missionaries were to be expelled, and the slave trade was to be restored to the whole country. .

In the autumn of 1850, Consul Beecroft visited Abomy, and the king told him to remove the white people from Abbeokuta, for he had a quarrel with the Egbás about his royal chair, and was determined to destroy their town during the approaching dry season. Early in the following January, Mr. Beecroft came to Abbeokuta, and met the chiefs and people in a grand council. After relating all that he had seen and heard at Abomy, and reproving the Egbás for some of their misdeeds, an old man was put forward by the chiefs to answer the consul's speech. The appearance, language and manner

---

* Nearly half this army is composed of women, trained to war from their youth.

of the old man struck me with admiration. He replied, that as for the persecution of native Christians, it should never occur again at Abbeokuta. As for the slave trade, he affirmed that their ancestors were farmers ; they never sold slaves, neither did the Egbás desire to do so at present. As to the Dahomy's affair, he said, "When our father (Shodekkeh) was alive, the king of Dahomy professed to be our friend, and we exchanged presents. But when our father was dead, he turned against us. It is true that we fought his army and took away his chair, but we did not go into his country to attack him. He came to us."

On his return to Badagry, the consul was informed that Akitoye was a foe to the slave trade and a friend to the English ; that he was the rightful king of Lagos, whom Kosokkoh had expelled ; and that for these reasons, he was in daily jeopardy of being murdered, which would lead to civil war in Badagry. Under all these circumstances, the consul thought best to remove Akitoye to a place of safety in Fernando Po, and to report the whole case to the British government, as one which required the interference of the African squadron.

In the latter part of February, 1851, it was no longer a question whether the king of Dahomy would attack Abbeokuta. His army, the largest perhaps that he had ever commanded, was advancing through the Iketu kingdom, molesting no one, intent on the single object of the expedition. The Egbás were actively engaged in making preparations for the contest. Patrols were constantly on duty in every part of the town and surrounding country. Several times we had false alarms at night, when the women made the air ring with the shrill cry of "Elé! Elé!"—to arms! to arms! Christians prayed and heathens made sacrifices. For my own part I felt intensely interested in the result of the conflict. If the Egbás should be defeated, they had no place of refuge; for the Ijebus on the east and the Yórubas on the north were all unfriendly. Besides, the fall of Abbeokuta would totally blight the present -prospects of missions to Central Africa.

Early in the morning of the 3d of March, the scouts brought news that the army was approaching the city. I exhorted the people to stand firm, to reserve their fire, and take good aim. Ogunbonna, one of the baloguns, replied, "You will see that we shall fight." Toward noon, the Egbás, amounting perhaps to 15,000 men, all armed with guns, marched out at the Badagry gate, to meet the enemy. There was no noise and no gasconading, after the manner of the Golahs, but I could plainly see in their firm and solemn countenance, as thousands after thousands passed by, that they were prepared for the occasion. They were separated into three parties; the first proceeding half a mile to the ford on the Badagry road, the second, under Ogunbonna, crossing the river near the wall, and the third remaining not far from the gate. Soon after we saw the Dahomies advancing across the prairie in heavy squadrons, with flying colors. We heard afterwards that they numbered 10,000 men and 6,000 women. They divided into two parties, one coming forward to the ford, and the other, led by the king, proceeding over the plain to attack Ogunbonna. When sufficiently near, they made a furious charge, according to their manner, and the Egbás gave way. I saw Ogunbonna's division retreating rap-

idly towards the river, where they would be embarrass-
ed by the rocks and deep pools in the stream, and requested the division near the wall to run down and
cover them while crossing. They obeyed with alacrity,
but Ogunbonna rallied, and the battle began in earnest.
By this time the party at the ford were retreating upon
us with the utmost precipitation, closely pursued by
the Dahomies. Many of the Egbás who had remained
about the gate fled into the town and disappeared. I
attempted in vain to stop them. "Why don't you
stand and fight?" said I to one of the fugitives. "Hold
your tongue," he replied, and went his way. The party
from the ford were pouring in at the gates, and I feared
that they would not rally, but most of them took their
station promptly at the wall, and others defended the
gates with guns and swords so hotly, that some of the
enemy were cut down in the entrance. It was soon
evident that the town was safe. The guns were roaring along the wall for a mile or more, and Ogunbonna
still stood firm on the prairie. I hastened to Mr. Townsend's station to tell the news, and found the missionaries on a large rock, surveying the battle through a
telescope.

On my return to the wall after dinner,* I found Ogunbonna's men resting quietly on the battle field, and the
troops of the king, apparently ill at ease, were drawn up
at a safe distance. There was still occasional sharp skir-
mishing, sometimes at close quarters, about the Badagry
gate, but the greater portion of the enemy were sitting

---

* An article in a late number of Harper's Magazine contains two
mistakes : I did not drill the Egbás, and my acquaintance with the
Mexicans was several years anterior to the late Mexican war.

half way between the gate and the river. A resolute charge of the Egbás at this juncture, might have been very disastrous to the Dahomies, but it must have been really resolute, and withal well conducted, to be successful ; and for these reasons it was best' to let things take their course. Both parties slept on the field. During the night the king moved off, and was followed by the main body of his army about day break. They were closely pursued by the Egbás, with a continual roar of musketry, till the sound died away in the distance. At Ishagga, fifteen miles distant, the Dahomies faced about, and made an obstinate stand, but were again put to flight. While this was going on, Mr. Crowther and myself rode over the battle field, which presented a sad spectacle. According to the report of two men sent out by Mr. Townsend, 1209 of the enemy were left on the field. Their whole loss on the two days was probably 2,000 slain and several hundred prisoners. The Egbás' loss at the wall was not serious, considering the magnitude and length of the battle. This affair spoiled the terrible name of the Dahomies. Not long afterward the king made a treaty with the English for the abolition of the slave trade in his dominions, and his subsequent wars have been of little moment.

The signal defeat of Gezo was not sufficient to deter Kosokkoh and his party from their design of subduing Badagry. They succeeded in burning the town a few weeks after the battle of Abbeokuta, but the slave trade party, though considerably stronger than their opponents, were defeated with the loss of their leader.

In November, 1851, having at last obtained permission to visit Yóruba, I went down to Badagry to purchase supplies for the journey. I found the site of this once populous town now covered with fields of Indian corn, the property of about one thousand persons, who were living in rudely constructed huts. Two or three days after my arrival, Badagry was visited by Consul Beecroft, and several naval officers, who were bound for Lagos with a part of the British squadron "to make a treaty" with Kosokkoh for the abolition of the slave-trade. Kosokkoh, on his part, advise dand assisted by several Brazilian and Portuguese slavers, had prepared the articles of the treaty in the form of two or three dozen heavy cannons, with plenty of powder and ball. One of the armed steamers and all the gun boats were to sail up the river to Lagos to conduct the negotiation. The ex-king Akitoye was present to sign the ultimatum, and thenceforward to superintend the affairs of Lagos. There was to be no fighting, however, unless Kosokkoh should fire on the English "visitors;" for they alleged that an unprovoked attack on an African king might give umbrage to the French; but no one of course could censure the consul and officers for defending themselves, if fired on when they approached the town, as they intended to do with a white flag. Notwithstanding the diplomatic character of this expedition, I felt considerable desire to accompany it, but was prevented from asking permission to go by two considerations. In the first place, I was fearful that I might come to be recognized on this coast as an amateur; and then I was still more fearful that Lagos would not prove to be quite so manageable as the officers expected. They had evidently not reflected that six or eight thousand sturdy natives, backed by a dozen Europeans, and well provided with large and small arms, might happen to defend their houses and wives and children with something like vigor. After the ships were gone, I remarked to some of the English in Badagry, " Perhaps it will not be so, and I do not affirm that it will, but I should not be surprised if the English get whipped to-morrow." Of course this suggestion was hooted.

. Before nine o'clock next morning the negotiation commenced : bang-boom—we had been listening for it some time. "The English," said I, " are abolishing the slave-trade." Presently the conflict deepened. There must have been forty or fifty cannons. They were still thundering away at twelve o'clock, at one, at two ; and by this time I began to feel decidedly uneasy. If the negroes had fought so long they would fight to the end— the day was lost. And what next ? Why perhaps in due time an overwhelming swarm of furious savages would be in Badagry to take vengeance on the English merchants and missionaries. In such a case, my presence here could be of no advantage to any one else, and it might be very inconvenient to myself. I should think myself happy if I could get far enough the start of the assailants to hide in the swamp among the crocodiles, boa constrictors, leopards and hyenas. Or even if there should be no danger at Badagry, the people of Adú and Otta were known to be friends of Kosokkoh, and if I should attempt to pass through their country on the heel of his victory, they would shoot me for an Englishman. The people of Adú had already laid bullets in the road to indicate that no one could pass that way without danger of being shot. To remain at Badagry for a month or two after Kosokkoh's victory was intolerable, for I was now ready to proceed to Yóruba, and some of the people there would soon expect to see me. On the whole, I thought best to beat a precipitate retreat from Badagry, and pass through the Adú bush while the people were still frightened by the roar of the cannon, and ignorant as to the result of the battle. After a little delay I found some Egbá acquaintances who were willing to incur the dangers of the road, and we hastened away from Badagry. It was now so late in the day that we were obliged to sleep at Mo village, but the people there were friendly. Early next morning the cannonade was renewed at Lagos. Without thinking of the danger to the combatants, I was so selfish as to be glad of this, because it would frighten the people of Adú and Otta, and might deter them from shooting me. Still I had a suspicion that only one party was now firing and that Kosokkoh was rejoicing over his victory. We hurried on. Near to Adú we met a small party of men in the bush, but they passed us in silence. The bullets had been removed from the road. That same day we passed through the Otta country, and breathed freely on Egbá soil. Soon after my arrival at Abbeokuta, the news was brought and confirmed that the English had been defeated at Lagos. About thirty days after, however, they returned and, succeeded by hard fighting in driving Kosokkoh and his party from the town. They escaped to the Ijebu country, and continued hostile for about four years, when they made peace with the English and agreed to abandon the slave trade. Akitoye was re-installed at Lagos, and he reigned till September, 1853, when he died and left the king_dom to Dósomu, his son. English merchants and missionaries entered the town immediately after the expulsion of Kosokkoh, and an active trade soon sprung up with Abbeokuta. At present all the countries on the Slave Coast are in peace* and prosperity. Badagry hardly exists, but Lagos and Abbeokuta are increasing in population. The missions are in a very flourishing condition, and the Gospel is so much respected that king Dósomu, at the request of Consul Campbell and the missionaries, has promulgated a law forbidding all his subjects to labor, or to beat drums and fire guns on Sunday. This law is respected by the natives, and immediately after it was proclaimed all the merchants who had hitherto labored on Sunday, gave up the practice, except one, a black from Cape Coast Castle.

---

* On the 2nd inst. (Jan. 1857), I received letters from Africa, stating that the king of Dahomy has sent word to the Egbás to prepare for another attack this winter; and that Kosokkoh has given a similar warning to Mr. Campbell, the English consul at Lagos. An Egbá army is lying at Otta to overawe the disaffected people in that quarter.

CHAPTER XI.

AN ATTEMPT TO PASS THROUGH IKETU IN 1850.

DEPARTURE FROM ABBEOKUTA — IBARA — AIBO — AN ALBINO — PREACH-
ING — STRICTURES ON — SUPERSTITIOUS FEARS OF WHITE MEN — A
FINE COUNTRY — ROADSIDE MARKET — YERIWA RIVER — VILLAGES —
IJALE — RETURN TO ABBEOKUTA — ROBBERS.

Soon after my arrival at Abbeokuta, in August, 1850,
I applied to Sagbua, the head chief or president of the
Egbás, for permission to pass through to Bohoo. At
first he was evidently inclined to grant my request, but
he was reminded of a difficulty—the English missionaries had been refused permission to penetrate into the
interior, because the Egbás desired to retain them at
Abbeokuta ; and now if Sagbua should permit me as a
stranger, in whom he had no special interest, to pass
by the first comers into the country, they would have
been offended.* Sagbua soon changed his tone, and
declared that I must wait till the wars should cease, so
that I might travel in safety. The proposed journey
might have been perilous, and I accepted the old chief's
excuse without pretending to perceive the real cause of
his refusal. In the mean time, however, I teased him
every now and then with importuities to let me go,
and took occasion to make the impression, which was

---

* It is possible that Sagbua was also afraid of offending the Yórubas
by permitting a white man to enter the country.

really true, that I would choose to remain at Abbeokuta
ten years rather than be foiled in my attempts to
proceed.

As a compromise between my desires and those of his
advisers, or for some other reason, Sagbua readily
agreed that I might visit Iketu, the capital of the Iketu
kingdom, three days (65 miles) west of Abbeokuta, and
two east of Abomy. I gladly accepted this offer,
scarcely doubting that I could pass on from Iketu to
Igboho.

Having obtained a messenger from Sagbua to the
king of Iketu, I departed from Abbeokuta on the 9th of
September, about three weeks after my arrival, carrying
all my luggage, because I did not expect to return.
Our first day's travel was only nine miles to the populous
village of Ibara, which is surrounded, according to the
custom of the country, by a mud wall, and a ditch. My
guide, Agieh, conducted me into the market-place, where
I sat down under a large and shady wild fig-tree—(very
unlike our species) and was presently surrounded by a
suffocating crowd of men, women and children. This
thronging of curious gazers, who have the utmost disregard of heat and dust, is one of the annoyances to
which travelers must submit in every part of Africa.
But the people are always respectful, and seldom fail to
scamper away as soon as we approach them. They have
a particular aversion to looking a white man full in the
face, being afraid, I am told, of the "evil eye." I had
not been sitting long, before the chief sent to call me
into his house, where I found a low, narrow and dark
room provided for myself, and a spacious piazza for my
attendants. The crowd poured in upon us without

mercy, and continued bawling and laughing and sometimes pushing each other over, till the darkness drove
them away. Notwithstanding the uproar, I managed
to talk something about religion, employing my boy Sam
as interpreter.

Early next morning, we pursued our journey through
an unwooded, but well watered and tolerably productive
country. The few stones we saw, were clay stone, the
gneiss and granite having disappeared before we reached
Ibara. In the forenoon we passed by Ilewu and Ishagga.
We met a small drove of heavy-built black hogs, on the
way from Aibo to the Abbeokuta market. In a farm at
a distance from any town, I saw several bunches of
large snail shells,* suspended from the boughs of small
trees, to frighten away the monkeys and antelopes, by
their jingling when shaken by the wind. We arrived in
the afternoon at the small village of Ilugu, which was
destroyed by war some years ago, but is now rebuilding.
In front of a little órisha house, or temple, were two
wooden pillars, the middle section of which was carved
in the form of a woman, in a kneeling posture. In
strolling through the forest near the village, I lighted
on a flock of guinea hens, different from any I had seen
before, their heads being covered with a tuft of silky
black feathers. This species is incapable of domesti-
cation.

Leaving Ilugu, we passed over an elevated and nearly
level prairie, which stretched as far northward as the
eye could reach. This fine country might nourish thousands of cattle, where not one is to be seen. But why

---

* These snails, which are reckoned good eating, are frequently as
large as one's fist.

should the natives raise droves of cattle, when they do not know at what time their property and themselves may fall a prey to the ruthless marauder? When the Landers passed over this very plateau twenty years ago, the surrounding country was full of populous towns, scarcely one of which is now standing. The houses are in ruins, and the people are in Brazil and the grave. As we descended to the west, Sam exclaimed in the peculiar English of Sierra Leone, "See Aibo!" At first I could scarcely distinguish the brown grass thatched roofs from the prairie. Soon after I heard a roaring like that of waves dashing on the beach—"the voice of many waters, the voice of a multitude"—and Sam said, "They got market." Passing through the gate we walked three or four hundred yards through a forest along a broad road, lined with numerous little temples, some of which they said were dedicated to the devil. Then fording a stream where civilization would place a bridge, we ascended through a crowd of gaping natives, into the populous town of Aibo. As we proceeded along the street, to the house of the second chief, (or lieutenant governor) I saw an albino,* or white negro, running rapidly up a cross way to intercept us. I had scarcely entered the house and taken a seat, in the piazza, before he came and prostrated himself flat on the ground, according to their most respectful manner of salutation. Some time after dark, finding that he still lingered around us, I directed Sam to inform him that I would tell him something about the word of God. He appeared to be very glad, and replied, "That is what I have been waiting

---

* Albinoes are born of black parents, and their children are black. They are not a *race*, as some have supposed.

for all this time." He then proceeded to say, that he worshipped his órisha (idols) as his fathers had taught him, but he knew that Shangó, (their Jupiter,) could not hear him, and that Eshu (the devil), could not save him. If he lived at Abbeokuta, he would learn the word of God. One night he dreamed that a white man came to his town, (near Aibo,) to teach them, and that, said he, "is the reason I was so glad to see you." I preached to him for some time, giving him the prominent points in the history and doctrine of the Gospel, taking care to use very simple words which my interpreter could not fail to understand.* The crowd of people in the piazza and in the yard, listened with attention, but made no remarks. The albino said "My heart holds all you have told me," and went away, since which I have not seen him. The owner of the house, who was absent on my arrival, now sent for me. During our conversation, he remarked, "I was standing in the crowd and heard all that you said about the word of God. It is very good, but the Yórubas are so bad, that they will not do it."

---

* Preaching is too often lost to the heathen, through the complicated faults of missionaries. Instead of coming pointedly to the *facts* of the Gospel, some of them must needs deal out their trashy ethico-metaphysical disquisitions, which are odious at home and abominable folly in Africa. Then they preach *at* the people from year to year, through interpreters, rather than undergo the toil of learning the native tongue; and finally, they utter great swelling words which the ignorant interpreter never heard before in his life. Only think of a man perforating an interpreter who can barely read English, with such phrases as "immutable principles," or "the ineffable effulgence of the celestial world."

Since most of the towns through which the Landers passed, were soon after destroyed by war, the people of Western Yóruba became firmly persuaded that a like calamity would befal any town which a white man may enter. This absurd opinion was an article of sincere faith at Aibo. On hearing of my arrival, the chiefs and elders were concerned for the welfare of their town, and called Agieh before their assembly to show cause why he had brought me among them. An *alari* (observer, spy,) of the king of Iketu, who happened to be present, advocated our cause, and we succeeded in leaving Aibo in peace on the third day after our arrival.

The country west of Aibo, was beautiful and well cultivated. Seeing small parcels of fruit and other little articles lying beside the road, I asked Sam what it meant. "De put da for sell." "Well, where are the owners?" "Dunno, sa, in de farm some wha." "Don't travelers steal these things?" I inquired. "No sa, de cant steal um." In some places I saw a few cowries left by purchasers; and was so pleased with this novel kind of market, that I became a purchaser myself, leaving the cowries, which Sam, who knew the signs, declared to be the price.

At Ishala, we were met by a deputation from the chief, who said I must not enter the town. Passing through a fertile prairie country, watered by two branches of the Yériwa river, we saw Ijaka-oke and Ijakaodo, on our left, and arrived at Ijale, in the Iketu kingdom, about sunset. The watchmen, who were sewing cloth in the gate, received me courteously, but the chiefs and people were so fearful of the evils which might follow my entrance into their town, that I was obliged to sit in the gate till eight o'clock at night before they would decide to receive me. At first they treated me with great coolness, but after conversing with me for two or three days, and hearing all about my object in coming, they became very friendly. In the mean time they had informed the king of my arrival, and he sent messengers to see me. I explained the reasons why I had not sent to the king from Abbeokuta, told my Gospel message to them again and again, gave them little presents, and begged them to influence the king to let me proceed to Iketu. Two or three days after they returned and informed me that the king himself was anxious to see me, but the chiefs and people were utterly opposed to my coming, lest it might cause the destruction of their town ; and consequently, that the king desired me to leave his country and return to Abbeokuta. Nothing remained but to obey, and I bid farewell to Ijale. At this time there was war in every direction, and the country was full of robbers. As we approached the forest on the Yériwa, my people were so apprehensive of an attack, that I preceded them with my yager to encourage them. Two parties, one before us and one behind us, were attacked in one day, but no one molested us, and we arrived at Abbeokuta in safety.

Finding myself detained indefinitely at Abbeokuta, I now took up my abode in a native house, but the chiefs soon objected to this, and I was obliged to remove to Mr. Townsend's compound or mission enclosure, where I was furnished with rooms and boarded myself for about a year and a half, frequently making attempts to reach the interior.

CHAPTER XII.

INCIDENTS AT ABBEOKUTA IN 1851.

THE YORUBA LANGUAGE — A PULOH MAN — EGBA COUNTRY — HUMAN SAC-
RIFICES — OKO-OBBA — IMMODESTY — THE IDOL IFA — VISITS TO THE
FARMS — SLAVES — TOBACCO — ORO DAY — DEVIL BUSH

As THERE was no prospect at present of being able to
learn the Puloh language, I turned my attention to the
acquisition of the Yóruba. I endeavored in vain to employ a teacher among the Egbás, who had learned English in Sierra Leone, and was obliged to make the most
of my boy, Sam Jones. My method was to learn translations (sometimes incorrect ones) of short sentences,
such as I would need in conversation and preaching.
Every day I learned one lesson and reviewed another,
repeating the words aloud to habituate the tongue and
ear to the sounds of the language. Every principle I
discovered was noted down under its proper head, so as
to form a Yóruba grammar. After a while I united to
these exercises the continual reading of Mr. Crowther's
translations, which then consisted of Luke, Acts, Romans, and the Epistles of Peter and James. His grammar was too nearly a copy of Murray to be very useful
in a language like the Yóruba, where the idioms are so
very different. Although I attempted to speak as fast
as I could learn phrases, and faster, it was about
eighteen months before I could make myself tolerably

well understood. The great difficulty is found in the tones and accents, which must be uttered correctly to make the language intelligible. I used to be surprised, and sometimes vexed, when the people could not understand a sentence which I knew to be correct so far as regards words and idiom. It requires much practice to master the tones, and a man who has no ear for music will hardly do it at all.

Some time after locating at Abbeokuta, I was informed that the man from whom I purchased milk was a Puloh, who had been in slavery to the Egbás for about fifteen years. I employed him to teach me his language, but after giving me about two hundred and fifty phrases, he refused to proceed, alleging that attention to his master's cattle demanded all his time. This man, whose name was Jato, was mulatto-colored, tall, handsome, and intelligent. He was born at Sokoto, in Hausa, and his scars testified that he had been a warrior. I tried in vain to impress him with the truths of the Gospel, which may have been one reason why he refused to teach me his language. On my return to Africa in 1853, they informed me that Jato was dead.

Mr Hinderer, a German, who had been sent out by the church missionary society to study the Hausa language, finding it impossible to proceed to the interior, or to procure a teacher here, turned his attention to the Yóruba, and finally began a station at Oshielle, seven miles east of Abbeokuta. The chief gave him three or four little rooms in his large house, which he fitted up as well as he could for himself and native assistants. They soon had a little school and some converts. Mr. Hinderer used to tell me amusing anecdotes of the old chief, who, it seems, was something of a character. One day he showed Mr. Hinderer an old pair of breeches, saying that these were the first fine breeches he ever had, when he was a young man. Being in love at that time, a wily old priest, who wanted the breeches, proposed to him to exchange them for a charm, which would make him successful in his courtship. The young man perceived that the old priest only desired to cheat him, and he has kept the breeches by him ever since, as a memorial of the event.

Sometimes I paid Mr. Hinderer and the old chief a visit. On one of these occasions we rode several miles eastward into the Egbá country. It is certainly one of the most beautiful regions in Africa ; diversified by hills and valleys, woods and prairies, and scattered over with large gneiss rocks, some of which are nearly white. In one place we saw surprising quantities of gum in a forest of acacias. The land was unusually fertile. All this fine country is lying desolate.

One day at Oshielle, they brought in an Ijebu prisoner. Seeing the man exceedingly affrighted, I spoke kindly to him and offered him something to eat. This increased his fears into absolute terror, which almost bereft him of reason. For a considerable time he continued to reiterate. "*A o pa mi! A o pa mi! O tau! A o pa mi!*" "They will kill me ! They will kill me ! It is done ! They will kill me," etc. The people informed me that the Ijebus offer human sacrifices,* and that when a prisoner has been selected for a victim they always treat him

---

* This practice is uncommon in Yóruba, but not so in Dahomy, Ashantee, and some other countries.

kindly and give him food. The poor man, seeing Mr.
Townsend and myself in conversation with the chief,
supposed that we were about to purchase him, and when
I approached him with food and kind words, the awful
conclusion flashed upon his mind that the bargain had
been completed, and that we had bought him for the
purpose of being offered in sacrifice.

I have mentioned Oko-Obba as the only ancient Egbá
town remaining. On one occasion, I visited this place
in company with Mr. King, an amiable native preacher of
the Episcopal mission. The streams south east of Abbeokuta, though not boggy, are flat and grassy, and the
country appears to be sickly. Part of our way lay
through prairies, and part through forests and farms.
On the tall trees we saw and heard many horn bills, a
kind of bird as large as a goose. Sam told me that one
of their heads was worth half a dollar (1000 cowries)
to make a charm of. Three or four hours brought us to
the town which stands on a stream, embowered in the
forest. It is a double village, containing three thousand to four thousand inhabitants. We observed several
people whose noses had been obliterated by ulcers.
The place is undoubtedly sickly. The people are barbarous. Several young women, in full Guinea costume,
were dabbling in the creek wholly innocent of modesty.
Under a shed was a man consulting his Ifa, the órisha
which foretells future events. The ceremony was more
like a game of back-gammon than a religious exercise.
Although the responses are purely the result of chance
like the cast of dice, the natives believe in them as sincerely as an Irishman does in St. Patrick.

To acquaint myself with the language, intellect, feel

ings, and every-day life of the natives, I used to visit them on their farms, ten or fifteen miles from town, and remain two or three days. In the spring of 1851, I went with Sam and Shumoi, the cook, to the most distant farms up the Ogun river, whence it is not far to the Yóruba line. Most of the way the country was open, as usual, and covered with grass twice as high as a man's head. At last we came to one of the most lovely countries on earth, where prairie and forest are intermingled with endless variety of detail, as if designedly, to produce the most enchanting effect possible. Here we found one or two hundred men, women and children, in long open shanties, surrounded by goats and chickens. They lived in Abbeokuta, but were in the habit of coming and going as occasion required. The soil was rather good, and the country could not be sickly unless in defiance of cause and reason. The woods were full of antelopes, monkeys, red-tailed parrots, and Guinea hens; and the river, now very low, was encumbered with gneiss rocks, among which were numerous muscles, identical in appearance with oysters. Their taste was unsavory. At this season the stream was so clear that we saw a crocodile lying on the bottom, at the distance of thirty yards. Among the rocks we found a large white fish with its head bitten off. The scales of the fish were nearly as large as a dime.

Some months after this I visited the frontier farms north west of Abbeokuta. The prairies here were more than usually wooded. Ogunbonna and others were going out the same time to look after their farms. I was much interested in their sensible conversation, in which I took no part. After crossing the river, Ogun-

bonna began to point out the farms and forests to one
of the party, who it seems was a stranger to that place.
"That," said he, pointing to a forest, "belongs to
such a one :" "This farm is such a one's ;" and finally,
"This is mine." Here we stopped. The salutations
exchanged by Ogunbonna and his slaves, were patriarchal and cordial. I remained here for two or three days,
sleeping of nights in a shantie. Some of the antelopes
in the woods are as large as a pony, and others, though
full-grown, scarcely three times the size of a rabbit.
None of them are easily shot, owing to the height and
density of the grass. The slaves, at every cluster of
farm shanties, had their little uncut stone altar for sacrifice. One of the men at Ogunbonna's farm, was a Hausa
Mahometan, who held these rites in the utmost abhor-
rence, calling the people *ake* and *kaferi*, meaning to say
eke and *keferi*, liars and heathens. The overseer told me
privately that this man was wanting to run away and
go to Ilorrin. I was not surprised to hear it. A monotheist in bondage to a heathen less civilized than himself, instinctively feels the incongruity of his position.
But the heathen in bondage to the monotheist, generally
resigns himself contentedly to his fate.

In the borders of the towns of this region, tobacco
plants flourish spontaneously among the weeds. It is
sometimes planted by the natives, but never topped,
and the quality is very inferior. Wanting something
to do, and seeing that everybody used Brazilian tobacco,
for which they paid high prices, I undertook to make
myself useful by showing them how to produce the weed
for themselves. Several persons prepared hills, and
cultivated and cured tobacco in proper style, but the

quality was still poor. One reason might be that the land was too old, and too much exposed to the sun. There are now two or three natives in Abbeokuta, lately returned from Brazil or Cuba, who manufacture segars, having followed that business in America. The returning natives are introducing several other arts which may yet be useful.

One day the bellmen, or town criers, went over the city, beating their clattering unbrazed bells, and crying *atoto !* (equivalent to O yes!) to inform the people that on such a day Oro would make his appearance, and that all women and girls must remain closely shut up in the house, under penalty of death. *Oro,* which has its cognates in *orun,* the sun, and in *pharaoh, On, Aven,* etc., is a remote modification of sun worship. As the grand órisha of the Egbás, Oro is a personification of tne executive or vindictive power of the government; but all women are required to believe that he is a terrible spirit, who takes vengeance on violators of the law.* To give a man or woman to Oro, is only a figurative way of expressing legal punishment. On this occasion, a man was to be given to Oro for a murder, of which he had been convicted several days before. Early in the morning we heard the voice of Oro in the streets. This is made by whirling a flat stick, tied to a string, swiftly

---

* Another personification of executive power is called *Egugun,* literally *bones.* Egugun is represented by a tall fellow, fantastically clad from face to foot, who appears in the streets with a drawn sword in his hands, and speaks in a hoarse sepulchral voice. It is death by law, even to the king, to lay the hand on Egugun. If a woman should say that Egugun is a man, or should even hear it said, she would be put to death.

through the air. The voices soon became more numerous, some hoarse like the growling of a lion, others shrill as the scream of an eagle. All the doors in Abbeokuta were closed fast, and the houses are so constructed that the inmates are unable to see into the streets. When Oro cried near a house the women were silent, and the little children were frightened. Every man and every boy eight or ten years of age was in the streets. There was no market, no going out to the farms ; all business was suspended, even the mission premises were obliged to be shut.

Some time after breakfast I went to see the ceremonies. The absence of busy women from the streets and markets, gave the whole town a peculiar sort of aspect, as if something was wanting. Now and then some poor fellow, with a pot of water on his head, slipped through the streets, as if ashamed, and crept into the closed house, where his wife was to use the water in preparing his dinner. Several little boys, and some big ones, were seen with provisions, etc., to sell, but they had an awkward sheepish air about them, never attempted the usual cries of " hot yams!" " sweet sauce!" etc., and were clearly inadequate to the smiles and chat of the girls, whose places they were endeavoring to fill. I felt and predicted that the days of Oro were nearly numbered in Egbá; the absence of the women and girls was a chain too dreadful to be borne often. In the meantime, in passing by the houses, I had audible evidence that the women themselves, though resting, were ill at ease. Twenty or fifty women pent up for thirty-six hours in the interior court of the same house, and having nothing else to do, would talk of course, and feeling disagreeable by reason of their situation, would naturally say disagreeable things; and this occasionally led to a hubbub, which made the welkin ring again. The Oro day was probably the cause of one hundred fights, and ten thousand quarrels among the women of Abbeokuta.

In addition to the hanging, of which I was not a witness, there were some to be whipped ; one for a crime which the philosophical, canting, would-be reformer of France or New York would term a natural privilege. The Egbás are not so far humanized by the tendencies of the age as to advocate free-love, and their grave Sanhedrim had decided that the violator of the seventh commandment should be treated on Oro day to a good drubbing. Their method of inflicting the penalty may have been peculiar, but was not inefficient. The fellow was turned loose in the public square, whence, flying with the utmost precipitation to the nearest shelter, he was soundly flogged by nimble runners, headed off, and flogged back again, amid the shouts, jeers and laughter of everybody. I presume he will not readily forget that he was once given to Oro.

The " Oro bush," is a sacred grove* where the elders deliberate. The "devil bush" of the Guinea negroes is doubtless of the same nature. I slipped into one near Cape Coast Castle, and found nothing but a cleanly swept yard by the side of a large granite rock. In one of the Oro bushes, on the top of a hill, at Abbeokuta, was the skeleton of a man, with the cord still unrotted

---

* The Yórubas often worship in " high places," that is, on the tops of hills.

about his neck. This was probably the murderer above
mentioned. But there are other sacred groves and high
places besides those of Oro, and some of them contain
things offered in sacrifice, and pots of holy water, with
which they sprinkle the faces of children.*

---

* This affusion is not confined to the time of giving the child a name,
as among some of the ancient heathens, but may be performed and repeated at any time by the mother of the child.

CHAPTER XIII.

VISIT TO IKETU IN 1851.

DEPARTURE FOR IKETU — DAHOMY REFUGEES — A POOR COUNTRY — VIL-
LAGES — THE "KING'S FATHER" — SOIL — MANNERS AND CUSTOMS
— DIFFICULTIES — DEPOSING OF KINGS — PREACHING — MAHOMETANS
REBUKED — SLAVE MARKET — A FEMALE CAPTIVE — "SEND ME YOUR
HEAD!" — AMAZONS — DEPARTURE FROM IKETU.

SOME months after sending me back from Ijale, the
king of Iketu sent messengers to inform me that his
chiefs and people were now willing to receive me. Believing that they would desire me to remain at Iketu,
instead of going forward to Bohoo, I was rather unwilling to go ; but, on reflection, it seemed better to begin
a station at Iketu, than to remain at Abbeokuta, for
this would give us a route of our own to the interior.
I left Abbeokuta about a month after the great Dahomy
battle. On the Yériwa river we passed through the
extensive encampment where the invaders had rested
a day or two on their way to Abbeokuta. I was pleased
to find that they had done no injury to any of the villages where I had stopped on my way to Ijale last September ; for this afforded us a substantial argument
against the superstitious notion that every town which
a white man enters will soon after be destroyed by
war. The people of Aibo and Ijale received me with
great cordiality. When I asked the governor of the

latter place whether people thought the Dahomies were much worsted at Abbeokuta, he replied, "They were ruined." They informed me that some of the fugitives were still wandering about the country, unable to find their way home. Several had lately been caught by the farmers of different towns. Such as were found in the Iketu territories were sent home to their own country.

The soil beyond Ijale is generally poor, and badly watered. Twelve miles' journey brought us to Itobolo, where the villagers appeared to be less civilized than any I had seen since leaving the coast. Twelve miles further on is Ofia, which is only three miles from Iketu. While sitting under the huge fig trees which shade the market of Ofia, the chief of the village sent me a present of rotten eggs, and soon after came to salute me, having his head adorned, in true negro style, with red feathers.

As we approached the gate of Iketu, a young man came running to meet me, apparently with great joy, and saluted me in Portuguese. On hearing that I was not a Brazilian, he appeared to be mortified. He had been a slave in Brazil, and the ardent affection peculiar to his race could not forget his former country, although in that country he had been a captive and a slave. The high and massy clay walls, and the strong gate of Iketu surprised me. We passed along a rather broad street, to the house of Ashai, "the king's father,"* or

---

* This title was given to the prime minister of Egypt. We may mention, as a curious chain of coincidences, that in the Landoma language [on the river Nunez], the word for father is *agia*, and the same word, in variously modified forms, signifies father in different and

prime minister, with whom I was to abide during my stay at Iketu.

On inquiry, I was informed that Iketu is five days' journey, say one hundred miles, from Whydah, two days from Abomy, and seventeen from Ishakki, with which at this time there was no direct communication. Iketu is a small town of ten thousand to fifteen thousand inhabitants. There are no springs or streams within several miles of the place, and no wells had yet been dug sufficiently deep to reach water. All the water used in the town is collected from the eaves of the houses in cisterns or dry wells, dug to the depth of twenty or thirty feet in the tenacious clay. The soil in all this region is rather poor. In manners and feelings, the people of Iketu are more barbarous and Guinea-like than any of the other Yóruba-speaking tribes, except the Ijebus. But they excel all the tribes in this region, except the Effongs or Kakandas, in working lead, brass, and iron, and in carving images of wood. Some of their productions of these kinds are surprisingly well executed.

I soon discovered that the king had acted prematurely in calling me to Iketu. Only a few of the chiefs were willing to receive me; others had yielded a reluctant consent, and others had opposed my coming. African kings are not autocrats, as writers have frequently reported, without taking the trouble to examine into the facts. Several of the nobles in Iketu, declared that

---

widely separated districts of Africa. In Egbá, &c., the king has an officer called *agieh*, and *agah* is a title in Asia. The *agieh*, though now an inferior officer, may at one time have been a prime minister.

the king had transcended his authority by calling a
white man into the town contrary to their wishes.
Others, supported by the heathen priests and Mahometans, and by most of the people, carried their opposition
almost to actual rebellion. On the day of my arrival, I
had gone to the western part of the town, and stood by
an isolated house near the wall looking around at the
town and the country. That night the house was burnt
down. I suspected that this was done maliciously, in
order to convince the king and the people that misery
and destruction follow in the steps of white men. Next
morning I was called to a public audience of the king
and nobles. Only a few of the latter were present, and
my reception, though courteous, was not cordial. At
night, the king's house was set on fire and burnt down.
In the morning he ordered the chiefs to detail men to
assist in rebuilding his house. Several of them replied,
" Let the poor white man build it. But if you will send
him away, we will do any thing you require, even if
you should order us to go into the ground." The opposition was so strong, that the king was obliged to submit to these injuries and insults, but he sent word to
the chiefs that he would rebuild his house himself, and
that the white man should remain in Iketu. I desired
to leave, but this was not permitted, as it would amount
to an acknowledgement that the king was defeated by
his unruly nobles. Ashai thought that the opposition
would soon die away when the people discovered that
the king was inflexible. He declared, however, that I
must keep within doors for some time, not only because
my presence in the streets exasperated the chiefs, but
also for my own safety. I objected to close seclusion

as intolerable, and obtained permission to go out daily and sit under a tree near Ashai's house. The friendly portion of the people often came to see me, but the disaffected chiefs and their party kept at a distance.

After some days, Ashai informed me that they had learned (invented?) some particulars about the burning of the king's house. The conspirators had agreed to fire the king's house first, and while every body was gone to extinguish it, they would burn Ashai's house also, " and make the white man die in the fire." The king, fearing that some violence would be offered to me, had set guards around Ashai's house, but had neglected to guard his own, supposing that he was in no danger. The guard had remained at Ashai's during the fire, (which I knew to be true), and this, they said, had preserved my life. About the same time, the king sent me word that I must not eat of any thing which any one should send me, for he feared they would attempt to poison me. I was in the habit of receiving a bottle of milk from the king's own yard every morning. One morning, Sam came in with evident excitement, and said, " Please, sa, dat Filani man took a leaf out de milk slyly, before he po' it in de bottle." He had also refused to accept the usual pay. The bottle of milk was given to the dog, which in a short time was seized with a violent vomiting. But he was soon well, and I laughed at the coincidences which had excited my fears. Next morning I sent as usual for milk, and drank it. During the day, the dog had another fit of shivering and vomiting, which I fancied might be the effect of yesterday's poisoning, and thought that if I had given him half the milk instead of the whole, which caused him to vomit, he might have died. I drank no more milk in Iketu.

Ashai professed to fear that the king himself was in danger. All the food which any of the people sent to his majesty, was invariably thrown away. They said, moreover, that if all the chiefs should agree, they have a right by the law of the land to assemble, and say to the king, "You have reigned long enough," whereupon he must retire into his house, and take poison, to avoid a violent death. I had no fears of this extremity at present, for if the king should be deposed and killed, the "king's father," and several of the principal people must be slain also, under the pretence that he would need them in *orrun*, or hades—though the obvious design of this provision is to deter the chiefs from being too hasty in deposing the king.

By degrees I transgressed my prison bounds, and went further and further into the town to preach to the people. Ashai objected to this, but I asked him whether a king's messenger must not deliver his message. He said "Yes." "Then," said I, "you must not forbid me to deliver the message of the King of Kings, who has sent me to Iketu." Sometimes I met a party of the nobles, venerable old men, with long staffs in their hands, who never deigned to turn their heads and look at me. A few of the people tried to prevent others from hearing me, but their opposition only excited opposition in return. The people would hear and approve too. One woman cried out in the midst of the crowd, "whoever does not believe, he knows it ; I believe." The Mahometans, as usual in other towns, were bitter opponents. One day I met a party of them, and said, "Why do you

Mahometans go about telling lies on me ? You tell the people that Iketu will be destroyed because I have come into it. But you are the men who destroy towns with your two-edged swords. If you had the power, you would sell all these heathens for slaves. You know you would, for the Koran tells you to do so." This was said in the hearing of all the people, and the Mahometans felt it keenly.

Although Iketu has never been engaged in kidnapping, it has long been a great mart for slaves, where purchasers from the coast meet with sellers from the interior. One day, a very comely young woman, who appeared to be the victim of sorrow, came to see me. I inquired what she wanted. She replied that she was a native of Idoko, which lies to the east of Yóruba. She was a trader by profession, and while going to a neighboring market, she had been kidnapped and sold. After changing hands several times, she had at last reached the Iketu market, and expected soon to be carried to the coast for the slave ships. She had a husband and three children at home, whom she never expected to see again, but hearing of me, she had begged her master to come with her to see if I would not buy her that she might not be sent to Brazil.

At this time the Egbás were bringing many Dahomy prisoners to Iketu, to be redeemed by their countrymen. On the eve of the market day, it was reported that fourteen hundred armed Dahomies were coming to Iketu to take their countrymen by force. This news threw all Iketu into a ferment. The Dahomy traders were immediately ordered to leave the town, and messengers were dispatched to forbid the further advance of the troops, who deemed it prudent to retire. In the midst of the excitement, a man was heard to say, "The king has brought a white man into the town ; let the Dahomies come also." This was reported to the king, who imme diately dispatched some of his officers to punish the man for his treasonable speech. They waited on the poor fellow, and presented an empty bag, with the civil message, "The king says you must send him your head."

One of the Dahomy prisoners brought to the Iketu market, was a native of that place, who had been captured when a girl, and enrolled in the king's army of Amazons. Her parents found her out, and were delighted with the opportunity of purchasing her freedom, but she said, "No ; I will go back to my master." The Dahomy Amazons are said to have a perfect passion for the service, notwithstanding they are bound to perpetual celibacy and chastity, under the penalty of death. I know them to be furious in battle, but their chief utility, I am told, is to prevent rebellion among the male soldiers. They have a separate organization under generals and other officers of their own sex, and are deeply attached to the king.

After I had remained at Iketu about a month, Ashai informed me that I had better return to Abbeokuta, till such time as the king should send and inform me that the chiefs and people were willing to receive me. I readily agreed to this proposition, especially as it was not possible to pass on from Iketu to Yóruba. Ashai desired me to leave in the night, lest some malicious person should waylay and injure me, but I objected to running away like a thief, and remained in the town till about sunrise. The news of my departure seemed to spread through the town with great rapidity. As I retired through the farms, we heard the firing of guns and beating of drums, which I supposed was the rejoicing of my enemies.

During my stay at Iketu, my horse had declined so much, as to be worthless, and being unable to procure another, I was obliged to walk to Abbeokuta. The roads were full of water, and the streams which I must wade were swollen by the rains, but I arrived at Mr. Townsend's station in safety, and resumed my old quarters. About eight months after, the king and the once unfriendly chiefs sent me a joint invitation to return, but I was now in the act of departing for Yóruba, and could not accept the invitation.

CHAPTER XIV.

VISIT TO BI-OLORRUN-PELLU, IN FEBRUARY, 1852.

MESSENGERS SENT TO ISEHIN — INVITED INTO YORUBA — OPPOSITION—
ABERREKODO — ERUWA — SCENERY — BI-OLORRON-PELLU — WHITES IN
AFRICA — A CHIEF'S BIBLE — EFFECTS OF PREACHING — HEATHENS WITH-
OUT IDOLS — IRAWAW — TRAFFIC — CANDID MAHOMETANS — INVITED
TO AWYAW — FARMS — ANIMALS — HUNTING — THE UNICORN.

In October, 1851, about twenty months after my arrival in Africa, I received the first letters from home. Of
late I had almost ceased to write, and began to fear that
none of my communications had been received, or why
should they not be answered ? Possibly my friends had
heard a false report, that I was dead, and I had long
since been laid aside among the forgotten. I now learned
that my letters had frequently been received and answered, but although I had been careful to employ the
proper agents on the coast, they had either failed to receive or neglected to forward anything which had been
sent to me from America. The joy of receiving letters
was speedily followed by an increase of funds, and to
crown all, I now at last heard of an open road to Isehin,
in the heart of Yóruba.

As it was not proper to visit Isehin without the permission of the king, I went to Sagbua for a messenger
in his name to go with one of my own, and ascertain
whether the king was willing to receive me. Sagbua

referred me to Shumoye, the chief general of the Egbás.
Though I had no previous acquaintance with Shumoye,
I went to see him. "What white man is this?" he inquired. They told him. "Well," said he, "I have never
eaten any of his money," intimating that he was under
no obligation to assist me, because I had never given
him a present. After some explanation, he agreed to
send me to Isehin within a few days, with the messengers of Asehin,* who were then at Abbeokuta. Before
the appointed time the messengers were gone, and I
found that I had been deceived.

It is vain to trust in princes. I next went to a private man, who had some sort of jurisdiction over the
Isehin road. "O yes," said the courteous old gentleman,
"you shall have a messenger, but the man is very drunk
to-day, and you must come again to-morrow." Next day
I found him sober, and soon had my messengers on the
road to Isehin. They returned in about two weeks, and
made a full report of their journey, even to the little
presents which they had received from different chiefs
on the road. They had slept the first night at Aberrekodo, where the governor said that I should not enter
his town, but I might pass round it. Next day they
reached Bi-olorrun-pellu, on the top of a mountain.
Bíoku, the chief, received them kindly, and gave them a
goat, but said to them, "You may as well go back, for
Asehin is a child, and will be afraid to see the white
man." They replied that they could not return without
delivering their message, and Bíoku then sent a man

* Each king here has his peculiar title, as Asehin, king of Isehin.
Alake, king of Egbá, Alaketu, king of Iketu, &c.

with them, to introduce them to the king. On the third
day they reached Awaye, and Lashimeji, the govern-
or, expressed great joy that a white man was coming
to Yóruba. On the fourth day they passed through
several villages, some of which stood on high mountains, and arrived at Isehin. They found the king an
old man and a cripple. He received them kindly, and
promised to call a council to consider my proposition,
but refused to accept the little Yóruba book which I had
sent him as a present. There were many Mahometans
in Isehin, " about three hundred" of whom attended the
council. It is scarcely necessary to add, that under
such influence, the king declined to receive me.

On their return to Bi-olorrun-pellu, Bíoku said " I told
you that Asehin is a child. Go tell the white man that
if no one else will receive him I will. My town is small,
but I have plenty of hogs, and cows, and sheep, and am at
peace with all my neighbors. He may stay here as long
as he chooses. When I was born my parents called me
Bíoku, (i. e., If he don't die, implying that he would be
great if he lived). Twenty years ago, when the country was ruined by war, I came to this mountain to build
a town. Everybody said we could not succeed. I replied, Bi-olorrun-pellu, (if God be with us,) and we gave
that name to the town. The city of Ijaye sent an army
to destroy us, but we killed their balogun (general) and
cut off his head. When all the roads were closed by
kidnappers, I took my own cowries and paid Ibadan
to open this road, and let us have trade. The road is
now open. If the white man will let me know when he
is coming, I will send messengers to meet him at Aberrekodo." This message was good news to me, and I

resolved to go. Just then, however, another invasion
was threatened by Dahomy. Commander Forbes, of the
British Navy, was at Abbeokuta, making active preparations for the expected war, but Ogunbonna and some
others desired that I should be present also, and I
thought proper to remain. After all, the king of Dahomy
was too wise to pay Abbeokuta another visit, and I lost
two months by waiting for nothing. On looking back
upon my efforts to reach the interior, I may say with
an old wanderer on the shores of Africa, " Per varios
casus, per tot discrimina rerum," &c.

At last, a little more than two years after landing in
Africa, I found myself ready to proceed with a fair
prospect of success. Then all of a sudden came a new
and unexpected difficulty—my carriers backed square
out and refused to go. I engaged others, and they also
violated their contract. I persisted in my determination to go, and my servants deserted me. It was useless to rely further on native converts. I picked up two
fellows, not fit for servants, and applied to Ogunbonna
for carriers. Somewhat to my surprise, he declared I
should have as many as I needed. With a light heart I
passed through the gate and took the road to Yóruba.
After traveling twenty-two miles, over a fine prairie
country, we arrived at Aberrekodo. True to his word,
the governor refused to let me enter the town, but I
passed round to the northern gate, where we met Bíoku's
messengers. Many people flocked out to see me, to
whom I talked, as well as I could, without an interpreter. A fine looking woman, leaning on the arm of a
man somewhat younger than herself, was pointed out to
me as a sister of Attiba, the king of Yóruba. Her mien

was at once graceful and rather imposing, and I found her quite intelligent in conversation.

Next morning, I was anxious to proceed, but was informed that the governor had given orders to detain me, till he could send forward and ascertain whether Bioku was really willing to receive me. I replied, "You have made me sleep without the gates, like a wild beast, and I will not sleep here again. Go and tell the governor that I shall proceed at once or return to Abbeokuta." Several messages were exchanged, and it was two o'clock in the afternoon before I obtained permission to proceed. We traveled about six miles over an undulating prairie, rather thickly covered with low scrubby trees, to the Ofiki river, which is thirty feet wide, and obstructed in places by rocks of gneiss. Four miles further is the village of Eruwa, which stands on a steep and naked mountain of granite, several hundred feet in height. The ascent was so difficult, that my horse fell repeatedly, and in one place was injured by sliding several yards down the smooth rock. The governor gave us a handsome reception. In the morning I strolled over the village, which might contain one thousand inhabitants. The houses were crowded in among numerous large bolders of granite, which were frequently surmounted by little corn cribs, built of mortar and thatched with straw. The views from Eruwa are very beautiful, On the south and west, there is a wide expanse of undulating prairie, traversed by meandering tree-bordered streams, and dotted here and there with wooded hills and huge masses of naked granite. Immediately on the north, is a rugged mass of mountains, whose peaks and gorges present many picturesque landscapes. At this season, the beauty of the scenery was heightened by the intermixture of gay flowers, and bright green leaves, with the dark foliage of evergreens.

Our road from Eruwa lay through a gorge directly over the mountains. . In some places the strangeness, wildness, and beauty of the scenery, made an indescribable impression on my feelings. Beyond the mountains, is a fertile valley, which was mostly occupied by farmers of Bi-olorrun-pellu. As we approached the village, which stands like Eruwa, on a rock mountain, we met two women, who looking suddenly up, and seeing such a figure as myself, bolted into the bushes, exclaiming *èmaw!* i. e., monster! A sick traveler overheard two negro women who were nursing him, conversing in this style: "He looks like folks"—"Yes, but he ain't." No philosophical ethnologist ever doubted the proper humanity of Africans more sincerely than some of the Africans doubt ours.

The eastern entrance to Bi-olorrun-pellu, is a narrow pass between two great bolders, at the top of a precipitous ascent. Having performed the difficult task of leading my horse to this point, I mounted, and rode several hundred yards through intricate and narrow streets, to the house of Bíoku, the chief. Although the sun was not warm, my people insisted on my raising my umbrella, so soon as I had entered the town, merely to gratify their own vanity; for an umbrella in Yóruba is quite as honorable distinction as a coach and six and servants in livery, among "certain parties"—mediæval fogies—in some civilized countries. The sensible old governor received me without any of the useless

preliminaries common on such occasions, and after a
few salutations and inquiries, directed his people to
conduct me to the rooms which had been prepared for
my reception.

My first employment was to see the village, which
contained about two thousand inhabitants, and to give
every body an opportunity of seeing me. So far as I
ascertained, there was only one man in the town who
had ever seen a white man before. He professed to
have seen many, not only a few like me on the sea
coast, but a whole city of white people of a different
kind, some where in the east. His story was briefly
this: that he had been for many years a dresser of morocco leather; that he had traveled in this occupation
one month's journey to a large town called Sokoto, and
thence two months further to a town called Waiangarana, which was inhabited almost wholly by whites.
Here he resided for several years, and learned to speak
their language, some specimens of which he readily
gave me. To my questions, he replied, that some of
the people there were fairer than myself; that they
dressed differently; that they were neither idolaters nor
Mahometans, though he could not tell what they worshipped; that the weather was always warm there,
and that there was another small town of white people
near to the large one, in which he resided. I could only
set the whole story down among several other doubtful
and inexplicable things which one hears in Africa.

One day Bíoku sent for me and showed me his Bible,
a cheap duodecimo copy, published by the British and
Foreign Bible Society, and probably sold or given to
him by some Yóruba man, who had resided in Sierra

Leone, as a re-captured slave. He knew it to be the word of God, and treated it with great and perhaps superstitious respect. How eagerly he would have read it, if he had only been able! But the heavenly message was sealed up and shut out from his soul. He next invited me to the house of his *ennikeji*, associate, or lieutenant, and showed me all his idols, and the other symbols of his religion. They were neatly arranged in a broad niche or little room, and concealed by a curtain. When I told the old man of the Saviour revealed in the Bible, he listened with great attention, but could not agree that his own mediators, of which the images were only symbols, had no power with God. In Africa, as every where else, the doctrine that Christ is all in all, the one and only Saviour, is a stumbling stone to the natural man.

For several days the people were too much engaged in looking and wondering at the white man, to pay much attention to the Gospel. It was not long, however, before a number of persons were deeply interested. I was told that one or two of Bíoku's sons had laid aside their idols. For several days a middle aged woman, named Oyindala, came almost every morning to hear me preach. When I first observed her, she was evidently under deep concern, but I thought best to let her pass without any special instruction. She had not yet spoken to me. At last she came to see me, with a countenance beaming with joy, and began to tell me how she had been distressed, since hearing the word of God, and how she now believed in Jesus the Saviour. Next day she brought her idols to be destroyed. Although it is my uniform manner to give prominence ,to the historical facts of the Gospel, including baptism, I was rather surprised when she said, "I want you to baptize me." Knowing that I must soon go forward, and might never see her again, so as to instruct her in all things which follow baptism, (Matt. xxviii. 20,) I felt constrained to refuse her request. Some judicious brethren in America have regarded this refusal as a violation of the commission. My own opinion is, that I ought not to have left the village. If I had baptized Oyindala and some others, who were ready, and had sent home an ardent appeal for help, the mission might at once have been established on a firm basis. But I then thought that I should explore the country and prepare for establishing ourselves in some of the large towns. In fact, I was too curious to see the country.

Another of my hearers named Alaiju, used to visit me almost every evening, to converse and ask questions. I have never seen a person who appeared to be more burdened by the power of the Word, but for several days, neither he nor I made any allusion to his feelings. My old-fashioned Baptist brethren have a proverb, that "the fruit will fall when it is ripe," and this is precisely my own opinion. Nevertheless, while I abstained from saying anything special *to* such people as Alaiju, I frequently made special remarks *for* them. In due time Alaiju introduced his own case by this remarkable declaration: "I have no idols; I am not a Mahometan; I have nothing of this kind to lay down, but I am a sinner and I want to be saved." Now was my time to show him how God could be just and the justifier of him that believes in Jesus.

We have frequently thought that all heathens are

idolaters, but this is not the case in Yóruba. I have met with several of both sexes, who declared that they had never worshipped an idol. This is a natural result of the pure theism of their natural religion. Everybody in that country believes in one true and living God, of whose character they often entertain surprisingly correct notions. Most of the people worship certain imaginary creatures whom they regard as mediators between God and men ; but there are some who reject such mediation, and attempt to hold direct communication with God himself. So far as my observation extends, this class of people are usually sensible and moral, and easily impressed by the doctrine of atonement and mediation as propounded in the Gospel.

In regard to humanity and civilization, the people of Sudan are far in advance of the Guinea negroes, and the two classes have little community of feeling. The former are even afraid to go down to the coast except at a few points, and the traffic between Guinea and Sudan is mostly carried on at certain border towns, as Iketu and Aberrokodo, which lie four or five days' journey in the interior from the sea board. The line of traffic through the latter place had been suspended for years, till very lately, but there was already an active caravan trade between Aberrokodo and the interior. As the caravans passed through Bi-olorrun-pellu, many traders and travelers came to see me, which gave me an opportunity of hearing from various parts of the interior, and of sending the Gospel message to the people of distant towns. From time to time, I have met with men from the interior who had never seen a missionary ; and yet they had obtained some correct knowledge of the

Gospel from travelers. One of the strangers who visited me at Bi-olorrun-pellu was a son of the chief of Irawaw, a town in the west of Yóruba. He paid great attention to the Gospel, and urged me to visit his town. Irawaw is the head-quarters of the idol called *Orishako*, which on account of its being expensive, is chiefly worshipped by the aristocracy and the wealthy. The symbol of this *órisha* (idol) is not an image, but a large iron bar manufactured and consecrated in Irawaw. The people have told me a curious story of which the following is an outline : In ancient times there was one of the *six-fingered* giants* of those days living at the Egbà town of Igbehin. Being summoned to Irawaw to take an oath by Orishako, he became enraged with the priests, killed them and every body else he could lay hands on, and carried off ten of the sacred iron bars. It was then decreed that no Igbehin man should ever again enter Irawaw, and the law remains in force to this day.

Among my other visitors were several Mahometans, who generally listened respectfully to the word. One party in particular appeared to be much impressed. When they first came their spokesman introduced them by saying, "We have long heard that there are people in the world who are better acquainted with God than we are. After a while we heard that some of them (the English missionaries) had come to Badagry ; then

---

* I must express a slight suspicion that the people never heard of six-fingered giants till some of their countrymen returned from Sierra Leone. Still I have heard no facts on which the suspicion is founded.

they came to Abbeokuta, and now you have come into Yóruba. The people told us that you are a good-natured man, who receives everybody, and we have come to hear you talk." I told them about the history of Christ, and the Gospel plan of salvation, and they raised several objections from the Koran. In speaking about making war on the heathen, as the Koran enjoins, I said, in the figurative style which always pleases the Africans, "I am a soldier; I have come here to fight with the heathen and with you Mahometans; here is my sword (taking up the Bible)—the true sword of God. I use it with my tongue. When this sword enters a man's ear and pierces into his heart, he is killed, not his body, but his soul is killed to the love of sin, of idols, of Mahomet, and he rises a new man, to live a new and holy life for God." This made an impression, and I followed it up warmly for a few minutes with doctrine and exhortation. When they arose to depart, at the end of a long conversation, their spokesman said, "You have smitten us with the sword, but we are not offended." These men continued to come for several days, and even permitted their caravan to leave them behind, that they might hear more of the Gospel. At last they departed, and, like many others to whom I have preached with considerable hope, I have seen them no more from that day to this.

Aggaw-Ojjah, the capital of Yóruba, often called Awyaw, lies four days' journey to the north east of Bi-olorrun-pellu. The king soon heard that a white man had entered his dominions, and instructed his messengers, who were going to Abberrekodo, to see me and inquire what I wanted. I took particular pains to tell them again and again, what the Gospel is and requires, and charged them to rehearse the whole matter to the king. About two weeks after this, the messengers returned, saying that the king was much pleased with the word of God, and desired me to come and see him. As this step might have involved Bíoku in trouble with the chiefs of Ijaye and Ibadan, who were too strong for the king, I was obliged to defer a visit to Awyaw till some future period.

Most of my mornings at "Bíoku's place," as the village is often called, were spent in the piazza of my house, sitting on a mat, and preaching to the people who sat around me. In the afternoon I often took solitary rambles through the surrounding farms, and occasionally spent several hours in clambering up the steep and rugged mountains. The country was full of game, as monkeys, rockdoves, coneys, partridges, squirrels and a sort of hedge-hog, among the mountains and rocks; and guinea-hens, another kind of partridge, crested cranes, antelopes, etc., in the farms and prairies; and I generally carried my gun, not only for amusement, but to defend myself, in case of necessity, against leopards and other beasts of prey. I seldom made an excursion without meeting with some little adventure. One day, on the mountains, I caught a young monkey, alive and sound, and carried him home, to the great amusement of the people. At first he was much affrighted, but soon became quiet. After I had tied him in the piazza, he sat very demurely for some time, as if in deep meditation. When I offered him a piece of banana, he extended his hand slowly and took it; but after nibbling a little, laid it down, apparently too much afflicted to eat. It was only a few hours, however, before he appeared to be quite reconciled to his lot, and he was soon performing as many antics as if he had wholly forgotten his misfortune.

On another occasion I shot a very large hawk of a peculiar kind, which I was anxious to examine. Seeing some women passing along a mountain path, and knowing that they would be glad to eat the hawk, I called to them to go and get it. As we approached the place where it had fallen, something leaped away through the rocks and bushes, and I prepared to shoot an antelope, but we soon found that a leopard or tiger-cat had borne off our prize.

I was in the habit of making diligent search every where, high and low, for inscriptions on the rocks ; not because I really expected to find any, but still I thought it might be possible. To the west of Bioku's rock is another still higher, called Imeggeh, which is two or three miles in circuit, and so precipitous that the people assured me that the summit was inaccessible. I had a fancy, and at last a strong desire to ascend this rock and look for inscriptions. The northern side was a perpendicular precipice several hundred feet in height. By repeated examinations and trials I found a place of ascent on the south. After climbing a somewhat steep hill for a distance of three or four hundred yards, I came to a flat of rich level land planted in Indian corn. By the side of this little farm, I discovered an old man in a snug lodge under a shelving rock, with no other companions than his hens and chickens. No hermit could desire a more quiet or romantic spot to act the fool in. Further on was a great mass of granite, penetrated by a horizontal fissure into which I walked till the darkness compelled me to return.   Climbing the rock with some difficulty and danger, I at last reached the summit, which I found covered with bolders and brushwood, except a few acres of naked granite at the eastern end. In this almost inaccessible spot there had once been a village, as I knew by the basins which the women had worn in the rock in pounding corn, and by the stone trough, now broken, in which the blacksmith had tempered his tools.   These were the inscriptions left by the poor villagers to commemorate their existence.   I read them with melancholy interest.   Nothing but the terrors of war had planted a village in such a place as this. Here perhaps the unhappy people had suffered the horrors of siege and famine, or had been driven over the edge of the precipice by fierce assailants.

Once or twice during the dry season, the chiefs and principal men, followed by a multitude of people with dogs, have a grand ring-fire hunt, in which they take abundance of game, including buffaloes, leopards, antelopes, hedge-hogs, rabbits, rats, terrapins, &c. Bioku's hunt came off during my stay at his village. In the evening all the game taken was brought in and laid at the feet of the chief and elders, who distributed to the head of each party to be divided among his followers. My own share was a small antelope and a tortoise.

Several of the villagers told me of an animal, called *agbangrere*, which has the form of a horse, the feet of a cow, and single horn in the forehead, like that of a large antelope. This creature is sometimes slain in Yóruba, but the unfortunate slayer is sure to die within a year. Only one had been killed in these parts for a long time, and the skull of that was buried in the stack of bones before the hunter's temple, at Bi-olorrun-pellu, but I could not be permitted to pull down the stack and remove it. The horn of one was produced, and proved to be nearly as long as my arm, black in color, coarsely rugose below and smooth toward the point. They stoutly denied that it was an antelope's horn, and said that the person who owned it, held it sacred as a sort of órisha, or idol. Bíoku himself confirmed all these statements. They declared further that king Suta had a living unicorn at Ilorrin. Three years afterward, when I went to Ilorrin, I asked the king's people whether they had ever seen a unicorn? They replied, Yes, that one had been brought into the town as a present to the king ; that it was shaped like a horse, but was not so large— that it had cloven feet like those of the large antelope, (*ira,*) that its color was sorrel—that it had a large black horn on its forehead, that it refused to eat, and that the king had it taken out of the town and killed.

The king's slaves had eaten its flesh, but no one knew what became of the horn or the skull. If such an animal exists in the country, some of us will probably be able to procure a skull before long.

CHAPTER XV.

VISIT TO AWAYE, KE-EFO, AND IJAYE, IN 1852.

DEPARTURE FOR IŠHAKKI — AWAYE — OKE-EFO — RETURN TO AWAYE —
A PRINCE BANISHED — VISIT TO IJAYE — LAND GIVEN FOR A MIS-
SION — RETURN TO THE COAST — EMBARK FOR LONDON.

Soon after my arrival at Bi-olorrun-pellu, I sent messengers to Ishakki, five days' journey northward, asking
permission to visit that city. On their return, the men
reported that they had been favorably received at every
place, and that Okkerre, the chief of Ishakki, was much
pleased to hear of my coming. I now fancied that all
my difficulties were ended. But I delayed for the sake
of preaching in Bioku's town, till the news of my coming had spread far over the country, and Kumi, the
chief of Ijaye, had sent orders to the towns on my road
to prevent my going further into the interior. The king
also was determined to persuade me to turn aside to his
town, though he durst not command me, for fear of giving offence to Okkerre and Kumi, both of whom desired
to see me.

Just as I had completed my arrangements to proceed,
the king's messengers came to me the third time, and
urged me to visit Awyaw. I declared that I could not
do so, and alleged the well known opposition of Asehin
as an excuse. The chief messenger replied, " If you
were willing to go, we could take you through the air,

rather than leave you behind." I told him that my promise was out, and I must start to Ishakki to-morrow.
He was evidently not pleased, and I feared that he
would go before me and raise some hindrance at Awaye.
To prevent this, I arose at two o'clock in the morning,
and set out as quietly as possible, but the king's messengers had already departed. They probably left Bi-
olorrun-pellu the evening before, soon after dark. As
there was no moon, we had a difficult time in descending the mountain, and clambering over the rocks, which
obstructed our road a mile or two further on. Several
kinds of birds which slept on the trees in the prairies
began to chatter and scream an hour before day. At
sunrise we found ourselves in a wide prairie, partially
wooded and well watered by clear rocky streams.
Every now and then we passed over a great flat rock,
and occasionally by the foot of a granite hill, several
hundred feet in height. Mt. Adó was in plain view
before us, with a cloud resting on its bosom, at some
distance below its summit. It was four o'clock in the
afternoon before we arrived, weary and hungry, at
Awaye. To my surprise and mortification, the gate
keepers shut the gate in my face, and told me that I
must not enter the town, till Lashimeji, the governor,
should return from Ijaye. As my carriers were now to
leave me and return to Bi-olorrun-pellu, I bivouacked
under a tree, where I was soon surrounded by a crowd
of men, women, and children, anxious to look at the
white man. At first, I laid my misfortune on the king's
messengers, but the people soon informed me that
Kumi wanted me to visit Ijaye, and had given orders
that no one should assist me in proceeding to Ishakki.

What should I do now? Ijaye is not more than sixty miles from Abbeokuta, and not at all in the direction which I wished to proceed. Why should I turn aside for two weeks or a month, and then retrace my steps to Ishakki and the Niger? I made offers for carriers to convey my luggage to Oke-Efo, but the people declared that the governor had forbidden them to assist me. Next morning, I renewed my efforts with no better success. "Very well," said I, "you shall see what I can do." So I packed two loads on my horse, and gave three to my servants and a stranger, who agreed to help us, and set out on foot with a cheerful heart, carrying my gun and blankets.

Nearly all the Yórụba prairies are partially wooded with low bushy trees, but beyond Awaye we entered an open woodland country, such as we see in America. A country of this character in Africa was so unexpected, that I was delighted beyond measure. It seemed that I should never grow weary of looking once more on an open grassy forest. The whole country appeared to be full of antelopes, some of which (the ira) made tracks almost as large as the buffaloes which roam through the same woods, only more sharp-pointed, like the track of a deer. Eight or ten miles beyond the town, we cross-ed a creek, and passed over a flat piece of ground, where the rocks are trappose—the first of the kind I had seen since leaving Monrovia. The mountains a mile or two beyond the creek are granite, and so steep as to be difficult of ascent. My horse was unable to carry his loads up some of the acclivities, and we were obliged to take them ourselves. Night overtook us in the midst of the mountains, and we lay down beneath the spreading branches of a large *osson* tree, which was loaded with yellow fruit as large as peaches. The wind whistled among the mountains all night, and next morning the ground was covered with the golden fruit, which had the flavor of large red haws, only it was more pleasant and juicy. Three or four miles over an elevated plateau, covered with beautiful farms, brought us to Oke-Efo—the Mountain Glen, which is girdled about by towering hills, with a fine open view to the west. Finding the gate open, I rode in, and was about to ascend into the town, when I was met by a deputation from the chief, who declared that I must return, and encamp behind the wall, as they could not presume to receive me, contrary to the orders of Kumi. They conducted me to a pleasant camping place, by a clear brook, and the chief sent me provisions.

The stranger who had assisted us from Awaye, could not accompany us further, and my horse had been too much injured by the fall on Eruwa rock, to bear the fatigue of carrying a heavy burden up and down the mountains. My only expedient was to send two of my servants to Ishakki for carriers, while myself and the third should remain and take care of the luggage. But the rainy season had already commenced, and as it would require eight or ten days to get carriers from Ishakki, it was necessary first of all to make a tent or booth of grass, to protect us against the weather. On learning my determination, the good-natured people took hold of the work with alacrity, and soon completed our shelter. It was finished just in time to shield us from one of the most violent rains I have ever seen. The mountains were shaken by continuous peals of thunder, and the rivulets were converted into mighty torrents, which bore away earth and stones in their raging currents.

One night after I had lain down, some men hailed from the hill above, and announced themselves as messengers from Akiólla, Kumi's eldest son, who, as heir apparent, bore the title of *Daudu*. They said, "that Lashimeji had returned from Ijaye, and Daudu with him ; that Kumi, whom they called Areh (i. e., generalissimo or military prince) wanted to see me ; that he was the owner of all this country, almost to Ishakki, and was not willing to let me pass through it to another chief ; that if I had come to preach, I had gone far enough to begin, but if I would build a house in Ijaye, and if some of the white men would live there, Areh would give me permission and messengers to go wherever I might choose at some future time. I saw at once that there was no hope of further exploration at present, without incurring the risk of giving such offence to Kumi, that he might entirely forbid missionary operations in this part of the country. It was useless to reason with the messengers, who had no discretionary powers, and as I had not yet sent forward to Ishakki for carriers, I agreed to return to Ijaye.

On the following morning, the people took up my luggage, and ran cheerily forward to Awaye. The gate stood wide to receive me, and I was greeted by many a hearty salutation as I rode through the streets to the residence of the governor. My own feelings, however, were far from cheerful. My ardent and too precious hopes were blighted, and the disappointment preyed so much on my feelings, in spite of my better reason, that

I fell into a dysentery, which came near endangering my life.

Akiólla requested me to rest a few days at Awaye, till he should visit several neighboring towns. One evening, he returned and informed me that the people had loaded him with presents in the towns which he had visited, and that I must wait till he should make a tour to several other places. Soon after, it was reported through Awaye, that Daudu was extorting tribute contrary to law, that he was a bad man, and had spoiled his name, etc. Fearing that these extortions were sanctioned by Kumi, I had thoughts of refusing to visit him. One night, Akiólla came into town in great haste, and leaving his women and other attendants with Lashimeji, posted off without resting, to Ijaye. The mystery was easily explained. Kumi had heard of his high-handed measures, and was so much enraged, that he had sent two executioners to behead him His precipitate flight was designed to escape the executioners, and throw himself on his father's mercy. I learned afterward, that when he arrived at Ijaye, he took refuge in the house of the balogun, or general, who could scarcely prevail on Kumi to change the sentence of death into that of degradation and banishment. At last it was agreed that Akiólla should be expelled from the country, that his wives and all his property, except his horse, should be confiscated, and that Kumi's second son should receive the title of Daudu. Akiólla fled to Attiba, the king, who at first received him with favor, but afterward sent him away for fear of Kumi's resentment. He then retired to the eastern borders of Yóruba, and entered the army of some prince in that region,

where he still remains. On his father's death, he will
probably make war on Ijaye, to recover his rights as
hereditary prince of that city and its dependent territories. Like his father, and unlike his younger brother,
he is a man of unconquerable will and powerful intellect, and I have little doubt that he may yet be the
ruler of Ijaye.

These untoward events involved me in new embar-
rassments. I was not free to proceed to Ishakki, neither
would Lashimeji permit me to visit Ijaye, without
again hearing from Kumi. At last the desired permission was obtained, and I departed in company with
some of the governor's people. To avoid going through
Isehin, where they were not willing to see me, we took
the prairie road to the river Ogun, and traveled the
greater part of the distance without seeing a farm or a
human being. The country is well stocked with elephants and buffaloes. Here is a fine country from
twenty to thirty miles in width, and from one hundred
and fifty to two hundred in length, almost without inhabitants. It reaches nearly to Abbeokuta on one side,
and to the Niger on the other, and indeed we may say
that the desolated Egbá country belongs to the same
great wilderness. It is capable of giving ample susten-
ance to three hundred thousand colonists; and can
boast of unusual advantages in regard to soil, climate,
and facilities for traffic.

We found the village at the river Ogun overflowing
full of travelers, which is no unusual occurrence in this
land of caravans. Of course I preached and talked
to as many as possible. After lying down, I heard some
of the travelers conversing solemnly and sensibly about

the Gospel. Such an incident, here on the wild banks of an unknown river, in the interior of Africa, more than repaid me for all the toils and troubles I had seen in the country.

As the governor of the village refused to let me proceed till he should consult Kumi, I was obliged to remain till messengers should go nearly twenty miles to Ijaye and return. I attempted to amuse myself shooting birds, but soon grew weary of the sport. Seeing a fine school of large fish in the shallow water of the river, near the village, I made inquiries, and was informed that the people worship them as a sort of órisha or idol. They were white scaly fish, with large mouths, something between a mullet and a trout. They were very gentle, and would almost run out of the water to meet the women who fed them. To kill one of these fish, would of course be sacrilege.

The river at this point is about sixty yards wide, and considerably deeper than a man's head. As usual in Yóruba, the people have no canoes. Things are carried over on large gourds, which contain sufficient air to float three or four hundred pounds. The gourd is directed by the ferryman, who swims behind it and pushes it forward with his hands. When a person is to be conveyed, he and the ferryman sit down up to the neck in the water, with the gourd between them, and embrace it, taking hold of each other's arms with their hands, so that the ferryman may swim and push his gourd and his passenger across together. For this comfortable ferriage, the traveler pays two hundred cowries, which is ten cents.

The messengers were not long in returning from Ijaye,

with orders for the white man to proceed. I laid my
clothing on the gourd to keep them dry, and swam the
river in my own way. The land for several miles was
level and tolerably fertile, but unoccupied, after which
it was broken, rich, and covered with luxuriant crops of
Indian corn. We approached Ijaye from the north. I
observed that the women whom we met were not afraid
of me as in other places, and my attendants told me
that some took me for a Puloh, while others contended
that I must be a white man. An immense crowd followed me through the streets to Areh's house, where many
were already assembled. The old chief gave me a
hearty reception, and sent nearly half a bushel of eggs
after me to my lodgings. All the natives suppose that
eggs are the favorite diet of white men.

The good people of Ijaye were mad with curiosity
to see me. In the house they thronged me to suffoca-
tion ; they blockaded the streets wherever I went, and
if I rode into the farms, they swarmed after me like
an army. To preach was to waste words in the air ;
they could do nothing but stare and wonder.

Kumi never once alluded to the manner in which I
had been brought to Ijaye, but he sent for me to his
house and his garden, again and again, in order to hear
the Gospel, and ask questions about its requirements.
At last he told me to ride over the town, and select
whatever place I chose to build on. There was only
one good place vacant within the walls, and of course I
selected that. The people who had followed me objected strenuously to this selection, declaring that the place
was haunted by a malignant spirit called Akalasho,
who had uniformly destroyed every man that attempted

to settle there. Areh himself confirmed this report, and refused to give me the land. I was obliged to select an inferior place, and this he said should be reserved for me till I could go to America for more missionaries and return. My travels had now come to their natural termination. Having no money to build with, in Ijaye, I resolved to return at once to America and report progress. Leaving most of my luggage with Kumi, to wit, a couple of nearly empty boxes, I took the remainder, and set out for the coast, to seek a passage to some civilized country. It was now June, which is the wettest part of the year, but I was too impatient to wait for better weather. The road from Ijaye, to Abbeokuta, is little more than two days' journey, but it had now been closed for a long time in consequence of enmity between the two cities. It was said to be so much infested by robbers, that I durst not travel it, but as I could not conceive how a road, which no one had traveled for years, could be much infested by robbers, I resolved to risk the danger, rather than go twice as far by a frequented route. They finally yielded to my determination, and I hired two men to accompany us to the borders of the Ijaye farms, and put us in the right way. This being Friday, we pushed on in hopes of reaching our destination to-morrow night, or at least in time to attend church on Sunday. Night overtook us in the midst of the prairies, and we kindled our camp fire on a flat rock. By four o'clock next morning, we were up and moving. After pushing through the tall wet grass, for two or three miles, we entered a forest, as dark as Egypt, where nothing but the density of the bushes could keep us in the narrow path. We groped on, hoping soon to emerge

into the prairie, and presently found ourselves on the
banks of a river eighty yards wide, which was evidently
too deep to be forded. Ever and anon, some sportive
fish leaped up and fell back with a plash, into the water.
"What river is this?" I inquired. None of the party
had been here before, but they thought it must be the
Ossa, a tributary of the Ogun. When it was day, we
discovered a dim path which wound through the forest
for some distance, and brought us to the stream at a
place where it was less than twenty yards in width.
We passed over and pushed on through the forest, for
the prairie on the south of the Ossa, but were soon
brought to a stand by seeing the broad river once more
before us. The width and appearance of the stream indicated that it might be fordable, but the fear of the
water, and of the crocodiles which might be in it, deterred my natives from attempting to wade over. Crocodiles are not apt to infest a stream where it is broad,
rapid and shallow. Laying off my clothes, and taking
a long staff in my hand, I felt my way across the river,
and found the deepest places scarcely four feet. Our
course now lay southwest through a fine uninhabited
country, full of wild beasts and honey bees. Toward
night we arrived at Bi-olorrun-pellu, thoroughly drenched
by successive showers. We were still two days' journey
from Abbeokuta, at which place we arrived on Tuesday
evening, five days after leaving Ijaye.

The expulsion of Kosokkoh from Lagos, had opened
the Ogun to the Egbás, but there was little navigation
as yet, because the hostile Ijebus, on the right bank,
were in the habit of shooting the people in the canoes.
Dangerous as the roads might be, I was obliged to go,

and after some delay, I succeeded in finding two men
who agreed to carry me in a little canoe. Hoisting the
stars and stripes on a bamboo staff, and laying six loaded guns at my feet, we pushed off into the rapid current, and were soon gliding through the hostile district.
From time to time, the canoe-men pointed out places
on the bank from which the Ijebus had recently fired
into canoes. The river was one hundred to one hundred
and fifty yards wide, and deep enough for a large steam-
boat. The whole country is covered with a heavy
forest and almost without inhabitants. If any of our
fashionable philanthropists are silly enough to sigh
for " a lodge in some vast wilderness," I would recommend the banks of some river in Guinea. His position
would have at least one advantage—to keep him out of
mischief. We slept the first night among some fisher-
men on the left bank of the river. Next day we arrived at Lagos, where I found several English merchants and missionaries. The effects of the recent
bombardment were every where visible. After waiting
about a month for a passage, I embarked on a Hamburg
brig, and made a most disagreeable voyage of one hundred and three days to London. Thence I went to America, and sailed again for Africa, with two other missionaries, on the 6th of July, 1853.

CHAPTER XVI.

BEGINNING OF THE YORUBA MISSION.

RETURN TO AFRICA — SICKNESS — WAR — DEATH OF MISSIONARIES — STATION AT IJAYE — ERECTING HOUSES — BAPTISMS — ARRIVAL OF MR. CLARK — PREACHING — EXPLORING TOUR — REMOVAL TO OGBOMOSHAW.

On the 28th of August, 1853, J. S. Dennard, J. H. Lacy, and myself, with our wives, landed at Lagos for the purpose of proceeding to Ijaye in Yoruba. Mr. and Mrs. Dennard were both attacked with fever on the same day that we landed, and were confined to their beds for about a week. After their recovery we were still unable to proceed on our journey; for Kosokkoh had assembled his forces to retake Lagos from the English, and the lake and river were infested by his canoes, while the land routes were in possession of his adherents. Finally, the officers of the British squadron resolved on a gunboat expedition to drive the enemy from the lake. They were not able to capture any of the armed canoes, but they drove them into the eastern Ossa river, and burnt two or three villages of the disaffected natives. This we thought was our best time to risk a voyage to Abbeokuta. Should we delay a few days, the armed canoes might return, and the terrified natives in the villages would take courage to murder us, which they would hardly venture to do at present. We engaged three or four canoes to convey ourselves and property, and left Lagos about seven o'clock in the morning, not without apprehension of meeting with rough treatment on the lake or at some of the villages on the river. Mr. Dennard and myself thought it lawful to charge our double-barrelled guns with heavy shot. On arriving at the mouth of Agboyi creek, which we were to enter, we were pleased to see a white flag suspended from the branches of a tree. Not far from the village was a strong stockade-fence across the creek, with an opening large enough for canoes, but too small for a gun-boat. The villagers were surly and taciturn, and we were glad to find ourselves safely beyond their borders. By the evening of the second day we had passed the northern boundary of the dreaded Ijebu country, and entered the territory of our friends, the Egbás. Soon after reaching Abbeokuta, the remainder of our party were laid up with African fever. Mr. Lacy's eyes were so much affected that he returned home to avoid total blindness. Mr. Dennard returned to Lagos to begin a station there for the purpose of forwarding supplies to the interior. His wife died of fever early in January, and he then removed to Abbeokuta, where he died in June, 1854. He had obtained land for a station at Abbeokuta, but had not yet commenced building. The station is to be resumed.

About two months after landing at Lagos, myself and wife proceeded alone and sorrowful to Ijaye, to begin the Yóruba mission. Mr. Mann, of the Church Missionary Society, had preceded us by several months. Kumi welcomed me back to Ijaye, and told me that my land and the boxes I had left in his charge, were all safe. I rented two rooms in a native house, to live in till I could build. They were about seven feet wide, and scarcely six feet high to the ceiling, with very low doors, and no windows. The heat was intolerable, especially to my wife, who was in bad health, and not accustomed to African weather. But there was no remedy, except in building a better house; and to this work I devoted myself with so much zeal, that I had little time, and, I confess, but little inclination to preach, for several months. The first labor was to clear the land of bushes and wild sugar-cane, a gigantic and useless sorghum twenty feet high. Some of the chiefs volunteered their people to assist me; but I found this plan so uncertain and expensive, that I resolved to hire laborers by the day for the future. In clearing the land, we discovered and killed two or three civet-cats.

The next step was to make mortar for the walls of the house. My laborers were now divided into several parties : 1, men and boys were employed to "dig dirt" to make the mortar; 2, women and girls to "bring water" in large calabashes or earthen pots; 3, others to "tread mortar;" 4, others to "make balls" half as large as one's head of the tempered clay; 5, others to "carry balls" to the building; 6, "builders," who made walls of the soft balls by throwing them with force upon the wall already built, and patting the new wall into a proper form; 7, girls or boys to "hand balls" from the ground or scaffold to the builders; 8, a "wall trimmer," who plumbed the walls, and trimmed them, while yet soft, with a wooden shovel; 9, "stick cutters," who brought rafters, etc., from the woods; 10, "grass getters," who brought in grass for thatching; and, finally, "thatchers," who covered the house when fin-

ished. The wall is built in layers, a foot and a half or
two feet high, and each layer must dry a day or two in
the sun before receiving another, otherwise the house
will fall.

When properly built and well dried, such a wall is
very strong, and if neatly plastered, is equal in appearance and comfort to any other wall.

It is scarcely necessary to say that it kept me busy
to superintend all parts of the work. But worse than
all, there were some things, as plumbing, and occasionally trimming, which I was obliged to do with my own
hands. In about ten weeks the walls were finished.
Then we put on the joists, and a lathing of palm leaves,
and made a fire-proof ceiling of earth or mortar. Preparing the joists and thatching, required two weeks
more; so that we removed in our house about the first
of February, 1854. The floor was made of beaten clay,
and neither it nor the clay walls were fully dry, which
endangered our lives.

In June, 1854, I erected a little chapel, twenty by
thirty feet, which was large enough for our congregation. In July, I baptized a man, and not long after,
a woman. In September our hearts were made glad by
the arrival of Wm. H. Clark, as a missionary of our
board. Not long after this he baptized a man and a
woman, and I baptized another man. We both remained
together at Ijaye till the autumn of 1855, when I removed to Ogbomoshaw, fifty miles further in the interior,
and began another station. A few months previously
to this removal, J. M. Harden, a colored man from
Liberia, began a station at Lagos; so that we now had
three missionaries and three stations.

Our labors during the year 1855, consisted of building,
preaching, and traveling. Mr. Harden erected a commodious mission house at Lagos. Mr. Clark and myself
completed a large one at Ijaye, designed in part for the
accommodation of new missionaries till they shall pass
through the acclimation fever.

Our preaching labors were incessant and ardent, so
that every corner of Ijaye heard the Gospel. A volume
might be filled with interesting incidents connected
with these labors. Many times the people heard with
such rapt attention, that a stranger would have thought
that the whole town was on the point of turning to
God. Others opposed, at times, with equal ardor. In
one district of the town, the opposition was so violent
that I could not make my appearance but they would
begin to cry out, *ekpa órisha*—" wonderful órisha." One
evening, after meeting with two or three such recep-
tions, I was moving homeward rather sadly, when a
company of men who were sitting under a tree requested
me to preach to them. A little further on, the request
was repeated by others. People often came to our house
on purpose to hear; others came merely to look at us,
and their visits were often annoying, but our duty to
Christ and to souls required us to exercise as much
patience as possible. Some missionaries refuse to receive promiscuous visitors into their piazzas, but I dare
not say that they are guiltless. It is not enough to say
that the people may hear the Gospel in the chapel. We
are commanded to be "instant in season and out of
season," in preaching the word. Conversation is more
useful than technical declamation. The friendship
gained by social intercourse has a powerful influence

over the heart of the heathen, and the exclusiveness and crabbedness of missionaries excites the ill will of the natives.

Most of the missionaries in Africa preach in English. In Sierra Leone and Liberia, and at some other places, the native must understand English or live and die without hearing the Gospel, though it is administered regularly in his town. Very few of those who pretend to understand English, can comprehend what is said in the fine classical style of the missionary. Sometimes the preacher is a German, whose accent would puzzle an Englishman, much more an African interpreter. Vast amounts of preaching are thrown away by missionaries. At Cape Coast Castle and other places, a native man interprets from the lips of the English speaking preacher. What the interpreter calls "high English," or "deep English," is often an unknown tongue to him, and of course he can not tell the people what the preacher has said, though he is sure to tell them something. Under the best circumstances, the Gospel is much impaired by passing through the mind and lips of an ignorant interpreter. Even some of the missionaries who speak the native tongue, do it most imperfectly, for they have never intended to undergo the patient and protracted labor which would make them masters of the language. The one great fault of some missionaries is a desire to discharge their duties with the least possible trouble. They can not endure the annoyance of intercourse with the natives; they can not submit to the toil of mastering a barbarous tongue; they can not preach and talk everywhere in addition to the chapel services.

In February, 1855, Mr. Clark visited Ogbomoshaw, a large town fifty miles northeast of Ijaye. He was so cordially received by chiefs and people, that he resolved to make this his field of labor. The propriety of this location depended somewhat on the willingness of Ilorrin to allow us an open road to the interior. We still felt that Central Africa was our destination, and if we could not be allowed to protract our line of stations through Ilorrin, it would be proper to neglect Ogbomoshaw for the present, and locate ourselves in Ishakki. To ascertain the feelings of Ilorrin toward the missionaries, I made a visit to that town in April, 1855. The king promised to give us land for a station, and we hoped rather than believed that he would keep his promise. In July of the same year, Mr. Clark departed on a long tour to Ishakki, Igboho and Ilorrin, to ascertain the prospect of extension and usefulness in that direction. His reception was very encouraging, and he returned, believing that the whole country occupied by the heathen, was now open to missionaries.

Not long after Mr. Clark's return from this tour, I left Ijaye with my wife and household affairs, to settle in Ogbomoshaw, or if possible, in Ilorrin. None of my journeys in Africa had heretofore been so full of vexations as this. The hammock-bearers who carried my wife, were so badly trained, and withal so careless, that she was in constant jeopardy of a dangerous fall. The luggage bearers, of whom there were about thirty, were more quarrelsome and untractable than any I had met with since I left the Golah bush in 1850. And to crown all, it was the rainy season, and both of us were in bad health.

Our first day's journey was scarcely a dozen miles. Next day we trudged on through muddy forests and prairies to the river Obba, which was now swollen by the rains, and eight or ten feet in depth. I persuaded the superintendent of the ferrymen to give us an early passage across the stream next morning, but when the time arrived, he refused to carry Mrs. Bowen and the luggage over unless I would pay exorbitant ferriage. I soon discovered that all these troubles were fomented by several Guinea men, whom he had unfortunately employed as carriers, but it was not possible to dismiss them here in the bush and to engage others.

It was nearly ten o'clock before we were ready to commence crossing the river, and the crossing itself was a far more serious matter than all the obstinacy of the natives. My wife was obliged to float across by means of a large calabash, as described in a previous chapter.* She waded into the water to the depth of three or four feet, and embraced the huge buoyant gourd in her arms. The ferryman, standing on the opposite side of the gourd, embraced it also, taking hold of her arms above the elbow, and in this manner she was propelled across the stream up to the neck in water. To encourage her, and to render assistance if needed, I swam close behind the ferryman, and was truly glad to see that her countenance indicated no apprehension of danger. Her servant was floated across by another ferryman, and she was soon redressed and ready to pursue the journey.

Our luggage had been brought over in good condition

---

* Page 174.

on the calabashes, but the carriers were still on the other side. They now informed me that they would go no further, unless I would increase their wages. I told them that I had paid them enough already, that no one had ever treated me so meanly before in Yoruba, and that I would not give a single cowry more to such mean fellows. "Then we shall return home," they replied. "Go and welcome," I answered, "and I shall leave your loads here on the bank of the river." So saying, I set my wife on the horse, and departed, walking before her, regardless of mud and water. Two or three hours after, when Mrs. Bowen and myself were both much fatigued, the rogues came up with us bringing all the loads and the hammock as cheerfully as if nothing had been amiss. If they had not come, we should have been obliged to sit by a fire all night, and I found that the journey, still two days to Ogbomoshaw, would have been more than Mrs. Bowen could well accomplish. I have left my carriers before, when alone, but will never attempt it again when traveling with my wife. I had no thought, in fact, that riding on horse-back would have given her so much fatigue. After all our difficulties, we arrived safely at our destination, on the fourth day after leaving Ijaye. Every body condemned the bad conduct of the carriers, who now appeared to be heartily ashamed.

After renting a house and making all possible arrangements for the comfort of Mrs. Bowen, I visited Ilorrin, to make a second and decisive effort to settle in that Mahometan town as a missionary.

CHAPTER XVII.

VISITS TO ILORRIN IN 1855.

DEPARTURE FOR ILORRIN — OPPOSITION — THE COUNTRY — A VILLAGE
PRIEST — RECEPTION AT ILORRIN — CONFERENCES — ARABS — LARGE
TOWNS — DASABA THE CRUEL — PAST EVENTS AT ILORRIN — THE PU-
LOHS — MEN WITH TAILS — A SECOND VISIT TO ILORRIN — NEW MIS-
SIONARIES — DISTANCES FROM LAGOS.

ILORRIN, (written Alori in Arabic,) is the town which
Lander mentions, under the name of Alorie. Its inhabitants, consisting of Pulohs, Hausas, Kanikès and Yórubas, are mostly bigoted Mahometans. The Pulohs
are the ruling people, the king himself being of that
tribe, and the Yórubas are the most numerous. For
several years past, the missionaries have frequently
met with Ilorrin traders at Abbeokuta, Ijaye and other
places, and the stories which they told of the extent
and civilization of their town, excited our desires to
visit them. When I proposed to go there in 1852, they
affirmed that no Christian could be permitted to enter
the town. If I should attempt to go, the king would
send messengers to meet me and compel me to return.
This story and others like it, and even worse, were repeated by the Ilorrin people who came to Ijaye in 1853
and '54. The road moreover, was infested with robbers,
and was often dangerous. Some of the people, however encouraged me to go, and affirmed that a large

minority of the citizens of Ilorrin were heathens, who
would be glad to hear the Gospel.

When I resolved to visit Ilorrin in 1855, I asked
Kumi to send an official messenger with me that I might
have the protection of Ijaye, but he considered it a deli-
cate matter, and dissuaded me from going. According
to custom, I ought to have sent to the king for permission to visit him, which would have placed me under
his protection; but I felt certain that he would not
suffer me to come, and I entertained some little hope
that if I should approach him boldly and unreservedly
as the messenger of Christ, he might agree to let me
live in Ilorrin and preach the Gospel. For the sake of
making the least imposing appearance possible, I selected two little boys as my only attendants. I believe
that almost every body in Ijaye disapproved of my going. The Mahometans were vexed, and the heathens
freely expressed their fears, that the bad people of Ilorrin would murder me.

At that time, the caravans were guarded from one
town to another, by soldiers who were sent by the
chiefs to protect the traders from robbers. A great
company were going from Ijaye to Ogbomoshaw, and I
fell in among them without ceremony, as if I had been a
native. After traveling several miles through farms,
we reached a forest country which extended twenty
miles or more to the Obba river. We encamped at
Oddeh, a farm village, the Mahometans apart from the
heathens, and myself on the outskirts of the latter. It
is not often that the natives are rude or insulting in
their behavior, but the Ilorrin Mahometans on this oc-

casion, appeared to cast off all restraint. Some declared that the king would order me back before I reached Ilorrin ; others, that no one would give or sell me any thing to eat ; others, that my boys should be taken and sold for slaves, and others, that I should be killed. The heathens took my part, but urged me to return home. Next night we slept at the Obba river, where there are three high mountains rising abruptly from the plain. The Mahometans renewed their opposition. On the following day we passed through a beautiful prairie country, and arrived at Ogbomoshaw. The Mahometans renewed their threats and insults, and the heathens begged me to go no further.

During the two or three days which we remained at Ogbomoshaw, I traveled over the town, and preached to the people. Some approved and others contradicted. When the caravan assembled at the gates they appeared to be three thousand strong. I was surprised to find my old persecutors so mild and courteous. As I turned away from a party with whom I had been conversing, one of them observed, " That man knows very well what he is doing." An old market woman, who sat near the gate, said to me, " Don't be afraid of these Ilorrin people. They came here once to fight with us, and if it had not been for God our Lord, they would have destroyed us; but we drove them away. Go on, and don't be afraid." We encamped that night on the Obba, five or six miles from town. The country next day was prairie, rather thickly covered with low crooked trees. About twenty miles from Ogbomoshaw, we crossed the first stream which flows to the Niger. Several plants which are common nearer the coast, were no longer seen, and I now began to meet with plants and birds which I had not seen before in Africa.

About sunset I stopped at one of the numerous villages which lie around Ilorrin. The venerable old Mahometan priest, or religious teacher of the village, came to see me, with a present of eggs. After he retired, some of the villagers told me that he was accustomed to say, "It is not the Mahometan or the heathen who will be saved, but the man who serves God in his heart." I was not prepared to hear such a doctrine in a suburban village of Ilorrin. The people listened to the Gospel attentively, and raised no objections.

On arriving at Ilorrin next morning, I rode through the first and second gates without ceremony, and alighted under a tree. "Why did he come in?" exclaimed one of the gate keepers. "Stop there; put his loads down outside." The carriers put down my loads as directed, and I waited a short time to see what would follow. After a little, I walked good-naturedly into the gate house, and asked for water, which was brought by a timid girl. "Why didn't you send a messenger, to let the king know you were coming?" inquired the old captain of the gate. "Because I am a messenger myself," I replied. A little conversation put him in a better humor, and he sent men to inform the king of my arrival.

In about two hours orders came from the king to let me enter the town. A noisy crowd of people ran before and followed after us. I was first conducted to the house of Dangarri, the prime minister, and then, after some consultation, I was delivered to Nasamu, the exe-

cutioner, who carried me to his house, and informed me
that I must not go out into the street. For several days
I could not walk across the yard, but he or one of his
men would be at my heels. All this was very annoying,
but I resolved to keep quiet and cheerful, as if I were
not aware of the fact that I was virtually a prisoner.
Nasamu, though always armed with a mace, or heavy
iron club, with which he had executed more than two
hundred men, was rather a pleasant man, and decidedly
polite and easy in his manners.

Many people came to look at me, and I often improved
such opportunities by preaching. Nasamu and his wife,
and one of his men, named Mama, paid so much attention that they were evidently impressed. I fancied that
Nasamu was rather uneasy as to the result of my visit,
and I overheard some of the king's wives saying,
"May God give the king patience that he may let the
white man out." One day, when no one was in the
piazza, except Nasuma's wife and myself, she informed
me that the king and nobles, and chief alufás (doctors
and scribes,) were holding councils every night, with
their Korans spread out before them, to determine what
they should do with the white man. I made no inquiries
as to what any of them had proposed, but it required
several sleepless hours at night to bring myself into a
state of mind which could agree to submit quietly to
indignity or violence.

One forenoon Nasamu announced that the king was
riding by, and wanted to see me in the street. He was
attended by several armed men, some of whom were on
horseback. Nasamu and those with him, prostrated
themselves before the king, and directed me to do the

same. I raised my hat and bowed three times, and they let it pass.

A day or two after this, the king sent for me, to attend a public audience. He was seated behind a screen or curtain, with two or three hundred nobles, alufás and principal men in front, on his left hand. They were sitting on the bare pavement, with their shoes off, but their heads were covered with caps and turbans. I was directed to sit directly in front of the king at a distance of about thirty feet. Several interpreters and attendants took their seats between me and the king, a little to his right. He began the conference with many and oft-repeated salutations in the Yóruba language, and then proceeded to interrogate me in the Hausa language, which the interpreters translated. The object of this may have been to give all, both Hausas and Yórubas, an opportunity of hearing all that was said. He asked my name and age, the name of my mother, whether I were an Englishman, the name of our king, whether I were a Mussulman, (Mahometan) and what was my object in coming to Ilorrin. I answered each question as it was propounded, and they gave me ample time to express myself fully. When I replied, "God is our king," I felt as no man can feel who acknowledges an earthly monarch. King Suta appeared to be impressed by the declaration, for he answered, "God is enough." When I said that I was not a Mahometan, they inquired whether I knew Mahomet? I told them yes, I had two Korans. "Do you serve Moses?" they continued. "No; Moses wrote the truth, but he was my fellow-servant, not my master. We deny allegiance to all creatures, even to

angels." Glances and smiles of approbation told that
this speech had produced the intended effect. At last,
when they demanded my object in coming to Ilorrin, I
was just in a frame of mind to speak freely of salvation
through Christ. They listened attentively, and offered
no objections. When I had finished, the king told me
to return with Nasamu, and we left them to discuss my
proposition to come and live in Ilorrin.

I was informed that the king and most of the nobles
were much pleased with our interview. On the following
day I went out to the river Assa, which flows not far
from the southern wall, and found it to be about forty
yards in width. It is not navigable to the Niger, owing
to a ledge of gneiss rocks, some distance below Ilorrin.

A few days after my first audience, the king sent for
me to have a private interview, and requested me to
bring the *dinjila*, or New Testament. This time he raised
the curtain, and had me to sit near to him. Only one
man was present. The king examined the Bible which
I had brought, and requested me to read to him. I read
and translated Luke's account of the conception. We
then had the following conversation :

"Why do you wish to live in Ilorrin ?"

"To preach the Gospel."

"What do you say when you preach ?"

I gave him a brief, distinct outline of the Christian
religion.

"We are Mahometans here."

"I know you are Mahometans, and that is the reason
I want to live among you, and teach you the whole word
of God."

"I am very much afraid that your religion will spoil ours."

"God commands all men, high and low, to repent and believe the Gospel."

"If any man should believe here in Ilorrin, what would he do?"

"If any one should believe, I would baptize him in the river Assa, and thenceforth, if he were really a believer, he would lead a new and holy life."

Hereupon he fixed his eyes on the ground for some time, as if in deep meditation, and muttered to himself in Hausa (which he supposed I would not understand), "There are Mussulmen, there are heathens, there are Christians." (Nasara.) But he evaded an answer to the question, whether I should be permitted to live in Ilorrin. To me it seemed morally impossible that a strenuous and bigoted Mahometan people would permit me to live among them avowedly to convert them to Christianity.

Nasamu now informed me that the king was greatly pleased with me—that he called me a very wise man—that he would give me a horse now, and a house in Fada when I should return. Fada is the aristocratic quarter round about the king.

My reply to him was, "Nasamu, you know I told the king that I did not want money, or horses, or slaves, or ivory—only to preach the Gospel. When I come, I shall want to live in some retired place, that I may preach to the poor as well as to the rich. I can not live in Fada. You must let me be a poor man in Ilorrin." I said this with great earnestness; because I felt it, and because I was determined, at all hazards, not to involve myself in any political relation or favoritism. There is nothing which I regard with more supreme contempt than the desire of the Catholics and some others, to court the favor of princes. This method of conducting missions has never converted a nation to Christ, and never will.

There were several Moors and Arabs at Ilorrin, and some of the latter were as fair skinned as myself ; in fact I suspected one as being, as his countenance indicated, neither more nor less than an American, but I afterwards supposed myself to be mistaken. One of the Moors, who professed to have been at Kasandria and Stamboul (Alexandria and Constantinople), treated me with great friendship, and appeared to be much interested in my case. On one occasion, he said to all present, pointing to me, "These people are the masters of the world." He told me that he had seen the ships of my country in the Mediterranean. While I was shut up in Nasamu's house, he came to see me almost daily, and sometimes sent his wife and little daughters. One of the girls, who appeared to be about twelve years of age, was a bright-eyed brunette, of surpassing beauty, and modest to excess. My friend had great doubts whether the people of Ilorrin would receive me, but, said he, "If they reject you here, you can go to Iseh, six days' journey to the east, which is nearly as large a town as this, and more civilized. They will receive you." When called before the king, this Moor and the Yankee Arab were both present. The latter appeared to be in great favor, as he was sitting on the king's right hand, behind the curtain. He was said to be a sherif, or lineal descendant of the prophet.

I took occasion to ask Nasamu and others whether they knew anything of a town called Iseh, and they informed me that it was a very large town on the river Kanpe, six days eastward from Ilorrin. Somewhere in that region the people dig copper from the ground. Six days' journey beyond the Kanpe, is the largest town in Africa, which bears the name of Aw-waw. Ilorrin, Ilesha, Ibadan and Abbeokuta are towns of the second class compared with Aw-waw; and Ijaye, Ogbomoshaw, Offa, Sokoto and Kano of the third class.

Lander mentions the civil wars in Nufe, which he calls Nyffe. It appears that the rupture has never been healed. Three or four years ago one of the rival kings, called Dasaba the Cruel, attempted to form a confederation for the destruction of Ilorrin. In the meantime he was growing more and more obnoxious to his own subjects, and, at last, in the year 1852, the citizens of his capital, Ilade, on the Niger, revolted, and drove him from the throne. Ilade was burned in the conflict, but he was not able to suppress the insurrection. The emperor at Sokoto, finding that Dasaba's power was fairly broken, ordered him to repair to Ilorrin, and reside there as a private citizen. One morning, king Suta sent me word that Dasaba had arrived, and that I must come and see him do homage. We found an immense crowd assembled in and around the court, and a strong body of horsemen drawn up in the public square. The king motioned for me to approach, and caused me to sit about six feet in front of him, on his left hand. Presently Dasaba and his retinue made their appearance. I have never seen a handsomer man, or one so superbly majestic in his bearing. He advanced with a slow and firm step, and prostrated himself at Suta's feet, with an air that said more plainly than words could express, "I am not conquered." It required no prophet to foretell that he will stir up another war, if possible.

Ilorrin once belonged to the Yóruba kingdom. About fifty years ago, the Imalle or Yóruba Mahometans conspired with the Hausas and Pulohs to subdue the heathen and erect a Mahometan nation. For some years they were uniformly successful, owing to the Puloh and Hausa cavalry. Aw-yaw,* the capital of Yóruba, and many other cities were destroyed ; and the Pulohs boasted that they would not cease till they had subdued all the country to the sea. While this was going on, so many refugees, outlaws and desperadoes, assembled at Ibadan, on the borders of the forest country, that it grew from a small town to a large city, which felt itself able to oppose the progress of the Pulohs. A bloody battle between the armies of Ibadan and Ilorrin resulted in the signal defeat of the latter, and put an end to their conquests. Since that time they have been content to maintain their independence. A Puloh man, named Absalom,† who was a relative of Bello of Sokoto, and of Dendo of Raba, became their king, and was succeeded by the present king Suta, whom the Yórubas call Sheeta.

The people of Ilorrin are a mixture of Yórubas, Pulohs or Fellatahs, Hausas or Gambareés, Kanikès or Bornuese, and Nufes or Tapas. Most of the people of all tribes speak the Yóruba language. Nasamu, him-

---

* This town was known to us as Eyeo, or Katanga. The Hio country of old authors, is Yóruba.

† Such names as David, Mary, &c., are common in Sudan.

self a Kanikè, informed me that Burnu, (which means
Noah's ark or ship)* is not the name of a country, but
of a single town in the Kanikè kingdom. He affirms
that the Kanikès are descended from the people of Barba, (Lander's Borgoo,) on the west of the Niger. The
Hausas or Gambareé tribe, are probably the mixed descendants of the Kambri or Cumbrie people, who live
along the Niger above Busa. The Nufes are allied by
their language to the Yórubas, but they are more civilized, and have superior skill in the arts. They are said
to be the only people in Sudan who still retain the art
of manufacturing glass. At present this art is confined
to three towns, one of which is west of the Niger, about
two days' journey from Ilorrin. From anecdotes which
I heard of king Moses, and of Mallam Shaiki, "the
Lion King," I infer that the people of Yakobu or Jacobu,
east of Nufe, are far from being barbarians.

But the Pulohs, (called also Fulahs, Fellahs, Fellatahs and Fullanies,) who are the rulers at Ilorrin, are
by far the most interesting people in Central Africa.
According to their own account, their ancestors were
white, and they still call themselves white men. I have
already expressed a conjecture that they may be the
Psylli or Psulloi of ancient history. Jato, my Puloh
teacher at Abbeokuta, informed me that the original
country of his people was Pelli, which lay in some unknown region of the coast. Some of the tribe relate a
tradition that their people once lived about Massina
near Timbuctu, whence they dispersed by four emigra-

---

* This town is said to have been built on the spot where the Burnu,
or ship of Noah, landed after the flood.

tions to the Senegal, to the Susa country, which they
subdued and called Futa,* to Barba and other countries
west of the Niger, and to Hausa, where they have
founded a great empire which extends to Ilorrin. Their
language is not African; it is not Shemitic. In Africa
they are called red people. Some of them are black,
others mulatto colored, and others almost white. The
women plait the hair on each side and tie it under the
chin. They have the same cast of countenance as white
women, and some of them are decidedly handsome, like
the mulatto creoles in New Orleans. I noticed one who
would have passed for a sharp-nosed woman in any
country. Some of the old men have projecting noses
and chins, and reminded me of old Scotsmen. Somewhere in the east, but how far I could not ascertain,
there is a tribe of red men called Alabawaw or hide
wearers, who are said to speak the Puloh language,
though they do not appear to be politically connected
with the Pulohs of Sokoto or Kano. They live in villages, and like other Pulohs have many cattle. Their
religion is Mahometanism. There are other tribes of
red men who are heathens, but their language is not
Puloh. The Azbens, who live on the southern borders
of the desert, were declared to be entirely white like
myself. This was the only white tribe known to the
people of Hausa and Kanikè.

None of my negro and Puloh friends had been very
great travelers, excepting now and then a man or a
woman who had been a slave in Fezzawn, as they called

---

* This name has long ago been referred to Phut, the grandson of
Noah, from whom it is thought by some that the Fulahs are descended.

it, or Kasandria. Nasamu and others with whom I conversed the most had no personal knowledge of any country beyond Yakobu, Mandara, Kanikè, and the Desert. But the Moors and Arabs, who had been every where, had told them wonderful stories of still other countries and tribes far off in the east. Somewhere on the other side of Yakobu is a tribe of people called Alakere, none of whom are more than three feet in height. The chiefs are a little taller than the common people. The Alakere are very ingenious people, especially in working iron, and they are so industrious that their towns are surrounded by iron walls. Beyond these are a tribe called Alabiru, who have inflexible tails about six inches in length. As the stiffness of their tails prevents the Alabiru from sitting flat on the ground, every man carries a sharp pointed stick, with which he drills a hole in the earth to receive his tail while sitting. They are industrious manufacturers of iron bars, which they sell to surrounding tribes. All the fine swords in Sudan are made of this iron. The next tribe in order are the Alabiwo, who have a small goat-like horn projecting from the middle of their forehead. For all that, they are a nice kind of black people and quite intelligent. A woman of this tribe is now in slavery at Offa, near Ilorrin. She always wears a handkerchief around her head because she is ashamed of her horn. There are other people in this "Doko" region who have four eyes, and others who live entirely in subterranean galleries. These wonders were affirmed by natives and Arabs. If the "German surgeon in the French service in Africa," had heard all this, he would doubtless have reported that he had found men at Ilorrin with *two* extra vertebræ instead of one. But the most singular *lusus naturæ* of which I have yet heard was the "French savan," who fell among the Arabs and heard such vivid descriptions of tailed men, that he went home and reported that he had actually seen one. No savan as yet, I believe, has published a scientific description of the roc's egg. After all, if there are white men in France with long ears like asses, why should there not be negroes in Africa with short tails like baboons?

On the day that I left Ilorrin, the king sent for me to visit him at his private house. Dangarri now informed me that I should have land to build on, "your own house, your servant's house, *and the house of God.*" With this assurance, I was dismissed to go home and make preparation for removing to Ilorrin after the close of the rains, or in about six months. Nasamu and several others accompanied me to the gate, and I bade farewell to Ilorrin surprised and pleased, yet doubting as to the final result.

On leaving Ijaye in the fall of 1855, as previously stated, I left my wife at Ogbomoshaw and went to Ilorrin on a second visit. I soon discovered that something was wrong. Nasamu had various complaints to make against other white men who had been there since my visit; that they had come with a large retinue of servants; that they were stern and unsocial, etc., and I received intimations that the balogun, who was absent at the time of my visit, was hardly willing for white men to live in Ilorrin. Some of my old friends were not quite so cordial as before, but others, including one respectable Puloh man, declared themselves the friends of the Gospel. When called before the king, they requested me to repeat the doctrine of the Gospel, to which they listened in silence. The king then informed me that I might live in Ilorrin, provided I would not preach, to which I replied it was impossible. "But," said I, "let me come and preach to the heathen." "What if some of the Mussulmen should believe?" he inquired. I replied that no man can govern the heart of another. "It won't do," said he; and here the conference ended. Every body appeared solemn, not to say affected.

A few days after, when about to leave, the king sent for me again. After salutation and a little conversation, he asked me to preach. As I began to speak I heard a noise of footsteps, and the court, before empty, was soon filled by two or three hundred people who entered, I do not know where or how. When they were seated I proceeded to preach with all my power. On my telling the king that my desire to live there was for his salvation and the salvation of his people, some young men in the outskirts of the congregation began to laugh, but hearing no response they were soon silent. The whole assembly was deeply serious. As the discourse proceeded one man leaned further and further forward till his head almost touched the ground. No one spoke till I had finished. The king then said, "We do not reject God, but we are Mussulmen." He told me further, to go and build a house in Ogbomoshaw and come occasionally to see him. We parted in friendship and evidently with mutual sorrow. I was not much disappointed, for I had always feared that the Mahometans would not receive us as missionaries. If such a course had been possible, I would have entered the town quietly, and have tried to preach without attracting public attention. But my color and the customs of the country compelled me to appear before the king, and he as a Mahometan prince could not do otherwise than reject my proposition to convert his people. Perhaps if we had gone as traders we might have got a foothold in the city.

On my return to Ogbomoshaw, the chief gave me a beautiful building site near the northern wall, about two hundred yards from the gate to the Ilorrin road. By the end of three months I had completed a comfortable cottage of three rooms, a servants' house, kitchen, etc. and surrounded the whole with a wall five feet high, inclosing a space about forty yards square.

At Ogbomoshaw, as elsewhere, the Gospel immediately began to make a good impression. Many listened with attention and interest; a few professed to have abandoned idolatry, though their sincerity may be doubtful; and one man, not a resident of the place, openly renounced Mahomet. When about to leave and return home, he came to ask me how he should pray, now, since his change of opinion.

In February, 1855, our mission was reinforced by the arrival of Mr. and Mrs. Phillips from Georgia, and Mr. Beaumont from Alabama. Mr. Phillips remained at Ijaye, where his wife soon fell a victim to the fever of the country. Mr. Beaumont came up to Ogbomoshaw. The mission has since been strengthened by the addition of Messrs. Trimble, Priest and Cason, and their wives. Our whole force now consists of eight men, five of whom are married. The first station is at Lagos, on the sea coast, in charge of Mr. Harden, a colored man from Liberia ; and the most interior station is at Ogbomoshaw, which stands at a point where the fauna and flora of Guinea begin to give place to those of Sudan. The distance from Lagos to Abbeokuta by the river Ogun is about ninety miles ; thence by the road to Ijaye, sixty miles ; thence to Ogbomoshaw fifty miles ; thence to Ilorrin twenty-eight miles ; and thence to Ilade on the Niger about fifty miles : so that in going from Lagos to Ijaye we travel one hundred and fifty miles, to Ogbomoshaw two hundred miles, to Ilorrin two hundred and thirty miles, and to the Niger two hundred and eighty miles. By a direct road the whole distance would be less than two hundred and fifty miles.

CHAPTER XVIII.

A JOURNEY FROM YORUBA TO SIERRA LEONE, IN 1856.

DEPARTURE FROM OGBOMOSHAW — HEATHEN NOTIONS OF PROVIDENCE — A
CANOE VOYAGE — IMPROVEMENTS AT LAGOS — MONROVIA — SIERRA LE-
ONE — BAPTIST CHURCHES THERE — MISSIONARIES NEEDED — A SCHOOL
OF NATIVE BOYS — SUCCESSFUL MISSIONS.

IN the spring of 1856, various circumstances required
my return to America. When we left Ogbomoshaw, a
crowd of people followed us some distance on the road,
expressing many wishes for our safety during the journey. Our carriers on this occasion were everything that
we could desire. One evening, in the wide, uninhabited
country between Ijaye and Abbeokuta, we were over-
taken by a tornado, or thunder-cloud with wind, which
gave me an opportunity of ascertaining the feelings of
the heathen natives in regard to the providence of God.
While the black clouds were advancing from the horizon,
the hammock-bearers frequently exclaimed, "May God
not let it rain!" One said, "God is king." Finally,
in a part of the prairie which was rather more than
usually wooded, it began to rain, and the carriers then
prayed, "May God not let it be much!" A few minutes
after, a gust of wind and rain came full in our faces,
and the people, looking up at the bending trees, exclaimed, "May God spare our lives!" and one of them
added *Olorrun aku*, "Salutation to God," a phrase which

is incapable of translation into English, but which implied profound respect and submission on the part of the speaker. On such occasions as this, when there appears to be danger, the people forget their *órisha* (idols,) and call on *Olorrun* (God). The rain was soon over. On reaching the water we kindled large fires and passed a comfortable night.

The following night was spent in a village about twelve miles north of Abbeokuta. A bachelor resigned his house to myself and wife, and the carriers slept in the piazza and yard. After we had lain down, some one raised the alarm of *ejo! ejo!* "a snake ! a snake !" The serpent was killed, and the people resumed their pallets. Soon after I heard a man, lying in the piazza, apparently talking to himself and saying, "It is God delivers men ! That snake came into the yard and bit nobody !" Then after a pause of a minute or two, he resumed, "All mankind are in pit ; it is God delivers them." Poor man ! how ardently and affectionately I then wished that he could know more of that God, of whose power and goodness he appeared to have so clear a conception.

We descended from Abbeokuta to Lagos in a canoe. The river was so low that we were often aground on sandbars, and it took us four days to make the journey, but the novelty of the scenery compensated in some measure for the tediousness of the voyage. We arrived at the lake just after dark, and the wind was so high that we were obliged to lie in the mouth of the creek amid swarms of musketoes. One of our canoe men, a new hand, was alarmed at the roaring of the wind and waves, and declared that he could not proceed to Lagos,

or if he did he would never go out into the roads to
look at the large ships. "If Ossa is doing this," he exclaimed, "what is the ocean itself doing?"

The mangrove swamp around the mouth of the creek
was now covered with tide-water. As a troop of monkeys were leaping from tree to tree, probably on their
way to a convenient sleeping place, one of them leaped
upon a dead branch, which came down with a plash into
the water. Hereupon the whole troop of monkeys set
up a vociferous screeching and grunting, as if fully
aware of the uncomfortable condition of their companion. He doubtless regained his position, for after
some time the cries of the monkeys subsided as if they
were satisfied.

Toward midnight the wind subsided, and the lake
was soon so calm that we pursued our journey, and
arrived at Lagos before day-break. This was about the
first of May. I had not been here before since October, 1853, to see the improvements which had taken
place in the town. The merchants, missionaries and
wealthier natives had erected about a hundred houses
(as I was told) in European style, a number of which
were good buildings which cost several thousand dollars. About a dozen vessels were lying in the roads,
and I was informed that if steam lighters were sent
out to ship the palm oil, they could receive one dollar
per hogshead for two hundred hogsheads a day. Still,
the traffic of this place is only in its infancy. If roads
were opened to Ibadan, Ijaye and other places, the
quantity of oil might be greatly increased from these
quarters.

For the last four years, Western Africa has enjoyed

the advantages of a monthly mail steamer from England. During this period there has been a great increase of traffic and of passengers. The steamer in which we took passage from Lagos to Sierra Leone was uncomfortably crowded. I was pleased to see that several American houses have been established on this part of the coast since 1850, when not one existed.

During the few hours which the steamer stopped at Monrovia, I went ashore and looked over the town. The place is evidently growing in prosperity. But nothing pleased me so much as the renewed and special efforts which our missionaries are making for the conversion of the natives. Such efforts are not only the sacred duty of those who must give an account for souls, but one of their highest interests, as citizens of a nation which is destined to derive much of its population and strength from the civilization of African tribes.

When we arrived at Freetown several boatmen boarded the ship to convey passengers to the shore, one of whom approached us and said, "Plenty America man live ashore."

"How do you know we are Americans?" we inquired.

"By de tongue," he replied.

We stopped at a hotel kept by an emigrant from Virginia, who appeared to me as white as any woman, though she claimed to be a free negro. She has been in Freetown many years, and besides making a good living, has uniformly maintained a high reputation for every kind of probity.

I have already mentioned the fact, that some of our American negroes were colonized in Sierra Leone about sixty years ago. A few of these colonists were Baptists. They formed themselves into a church, and although neglected by their brethren, while Pedo-Baptists were spending large sums in missions to the colony, they have still maintained their existence. In 1853, brethren Dennard, Lacy, and myself ordained two ministers, Brown and Thompson, at the request of these brethren. They were then divided into two churches in consequence of a schism. Sometime after this, Mr. Thompson removed to Waterloo, and received an appointment as a missionary of the Southern Baptist Board. Mr. Brown remained at Freetown, and the Board granted one hundred dollars toward his support. One part of my design in stopping for a while in Sierra Leone, was to form a better acquaintance with these Baptists, and if possible to extend their influence to the Yóruba residents. I found that the schism had been healed, and that the religious prospects of the church were improving. Still there was great need of more efficient aid. Mr. Brown is a very worthy man, who ought to be more adequately supported, as he has suffered a physical injury which disqualifies him from laboring at his trade as a blacksmith. Few of the natives, except the so-called Eboe tribe, attend the Baptist meetings. Of this tribe there are several members, some of whom might be useful, if missionaries were sent to their country on the lower Niger.

So soon as the Yóruba and Egbá people discovered that I had come from their country, they gathered around me like bees. Every one had something to say and something to ask, if it were only for the sake of hearing me speak in their native tongue. I felt a great desire to remain and preach to them for several reasons.

1. Because comparatively few among them can understand English sufficiently to learn the Gospel well from English teachers ; 2. Because many of them are still heathens ; 3. Because many of the professed Christians are unconverted—some of the worst and basest men at Lagos have been in the church at Freetown ; 4. Because my having been in Yóruba, would 'give me peculiar influence over the Yóruba people in Sierra Leone ; 5. Because we need converted and educated natives in our Yóruba missions ; and 6. Because there are many natives of other tribes in Sierra Leone, who never go into the chapels to hear the Gospel. Freetown itself is a great and important missionary field, especially to those who preach the Gospel as preached by the Baptists, and in that manner which we believe to be proper. I am not aware of the light in which this remark may be regarded by some readers; nevertheless, Sierra Leone does need the doctrine and the practical common-sense preaching and management which Baptists can give them, and which none are better qualified to give than the Baptists of our own country.

Freetown is a great resort of Fulahs, (Pulohs,) and Mandingoes, two fine intelligent races, who adhere to the Koran, and seldom hear a word of the Gospel. They ought to receive the special attention of a special missionary—not of a gentleman in gown and slippers, but of a discreet, open-faced, open-hearted man, who will go into their resorts, and introduce and reiterate religious conversation, in such a manner that they can neither get angry, nor fail to learn the truth. To suppose that they will learn English and attend the chapels, is to expect more than they have done, or can do. Even those

of them who speak English, are deterred by many religious and social motives from attending the chapels.
And yet on almost every part of the coast, they must
learn English, and go to chapel, or die in their sins.
Will any one at Bathurst, or in Sierra Leone, or in Liberia, deny the general truth of this statement?

In one of my rambles beyond the borders of Freetown,
I entered a native school, where about two hundred boys,
lately rescued from slavery in the interior, were learning to read and speak English. They were of all ages,
from about five to ten or twelve, and in every sort of
imaginable garb. Some were smartly clad in shirts and
trowsers; others had nothing but shirts; others nothing
but trowsers, and others nothing at all. A merrier set
of noisy little fellows was never seen. After a few
years, they will be put to trades and service of various
kinds, so that every one of them will have an opportunity of becoming a useful and prosperous citizen of a
civilized colony. In this way, Sierra Leone has added
greatly to her strength, thus setting an example which
Liberia should be zealous to follow.

I regard Sierra Leone as one of the greatest triumphs
of modern benevolence. The missions there were commenced in 1804. For a long time they were unfruitful;
for the negroes of Guinea, in their present state, and
surrounded by present social and idolatrous influences,
are not very susceptible of Christian instruction. After
a while, the British cruisers began to send in cargoes
of re-captured slaves, who were different from any
natives heretofore seen in Sierra Leone. They were
the citizens of Yóruba, Nufe, Hausa, Kanikè, and other
nations of Sudan, who had been captured in war, and

sent down to the coast to be exchanged with the slavers for tobacco, guns and powder, and other articles of civilized commerce. The nude and half-nude captives were taken in charge by the missionaries, and placed under instruction, according to their age and condition. The children improved rapidly in school, and the adults soon gave promise of becoming useful colonists. From time to time, their number was increased by the arrival of fresh cargoes. Large numbers of them joined the churches of the Episcopal and Wesleyan missionaries. Some became acceptable preachers, and valuable schoolmasters. Some became creditable scholars in the various branches of education. Others prospered in business, and became comparatively wealthy merchants, the owners of ships and extensive warehouses. The richest native in Freetown, a Jalof, is said to be worth about £100,000, or $500,000. Several of the Nufes, Yórubas, and Eboes, became wealthy. The natives of Sierra Leone, at present, are a respectable, civilized, and Christian community. There are twenty-three chapels in Freetown alone, several of which are handsome and commodious stone buildings, with basements for lecture rooms, school rooms, etc. The people now pay for the instruction of their children in the day-schools. The religious contributions of the Episcopal congregations for last year, amounted to $3,262. The contributions of the Wesleyans were probably not inferior. This, we must admit, is astonishing liberality for a few thousand converted Africans.

The Sierra Leone missionaries with whom I became acquainted, appeared to be men of excellent character. Judging from the work which they have done, their predecessors must have been men of the same stamp. None but discreet and laborious men could have produced the results* which are witnessed in Sierra Leone. But the present missionary work of the colony labors under one great defect—a scarcity of men. The duties of the missionaries are too onerous. Some of them, as

---

* The last Report of the Sierra Leone Missions were as follows:

EPISCOPALIANS—(*English.*)

1 Bishop.
12 Ordained European Missionaries.
3 Native Missionaries, (others ordained since.)
1 European Industrial Agent.
3 European Female Teachers.
8 Native Christian Visitors.
56 Native Teachers.
7 Native School Mistresses.
3 Seminaries.
59 Schools.
5181 Scholars.
15 Stations.
3354 Communicants.

WESLEYANS.

4 Circuits.
31 Chapels.
3 Other Preaching Places.
7 Missionaries.
5 Catechists.
133 Local Preachers.
63 School Teachers.
24 Schools.
2897 Scholars.
6461 Communicants.
361 On Probation.

I know, and I suppose all of them, labor beyond their
strength ; and yet their charge is so large and unwieldy,
that the people can not receive that enlarged degree and
kind of instruction which their advanced condition demands. The chief duty now in Sierra Leone, is not to
evangelize the congregations, but to train evangelists
for the extension of the Gospel—to give a higher Christian tone to converts—to extend their influence to the
surrounding heathens, and to send well-instructed Christian Yórubas, Nufes, etc., as missionaries to their native
countries. This can not be done effectually without
more laborers, and some change of plan. In a word,
the time has come in Sierra Leone to separate the pas-
toral from the strictly missionary work.

The people of Sierra Leone consist of re-captured
slaves from almost every part of Africa ; and if missionaries were going to any point of the west, east, south,
or interior of the continent, there would be an à priori
probability that they could obtain interpreters, if not
Christian schoolmasters and other assistants, at Freetown. But this opportunity will not continue long. Of
late there are few arrivals of re-captured slaves, and
the children who are brought up in the colony will not
be so well qualified for interpreters in every part of
the continent, as are their fathers. Now is the time to
invade Africa with swarms of missionaries.

It is vain to regret now that a few wrong headed
young preachers blighted the English Baptist Mission,
once planted in Sierra Leone. If the men first selected
as missionaries, had been prudent and persevering, the
Baptists also might look to Sierra Leone for native assistants to every part of Africa ; but now there are

scarcely any native Christians in the Baptist Church, except a few Eboes. As the opportunity has not yet passed away, and will not entirely cease for the next twenty years, we ought yet to improve it. A well-conducted Baptist mission in Sierra Leone, would add a new element of vigor and spirituality to the missions already existing, and might provide our missionaries to other parts of the continent with valuable native assistants. Liberia is an important field, but can not promise the same secondary advantages which may be realized in Sierra Leone.

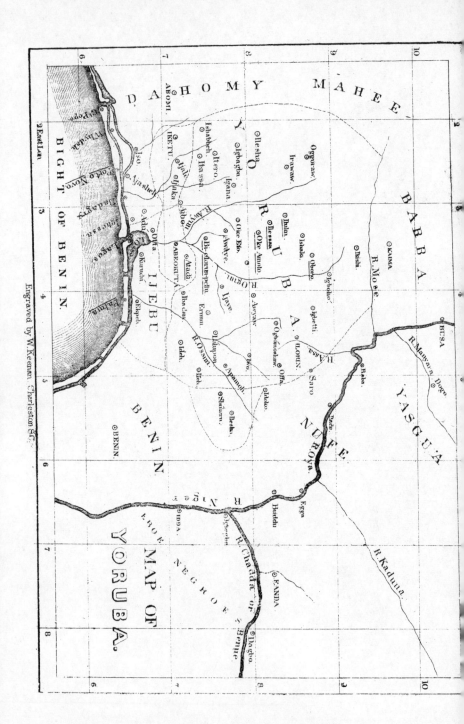

MAP OF YORUBA.

Engraved by W. Keenan, Charleston S.C.

CHAPTER XIX.

GEOGRAPHY OF YORUBA.

BOUNDARIES — POPULATION — TOWNS — SURFACE — MOUNTAINS — PRAI-
RIES — SOIL — STREAMS — SWAMPS — SPRINGS — WATER.

THE boundaries of Yóruba are not accurately known.
The southern limit lies between Ijaye and Abbeokuta,
about eighty miles by the road from the sea. On the
north it is bounded by Nufe (called also Nupe, Nyffe
and Tapa) which extends to a distance of thirty or forty
miles this side of the Niger. On the east of Yóruba
we hear of Effong (Kakanda) Igbona, Ijesha. and Ifeh.
On the east are Barba (Borgu) Mahee and Dahomy.
The country between Yóruba and the sea is occupied
by the tribes of Iketu, Egbá, Egbado, Otta and Ijebu.
All of these tribes, as also the people of Ifeh, Ijesha,
Igbona and Effong are branches of the Yóruba family,
and speak varieties of the same language.

An English writer supposes that the people who speak
Yóruba amount to three millions. This estimate is not
too high, if we include the surrounding tribes of the
same family. We have been informed that the Yóruba
language is much spoken in Nufe, along the Niger, and
in Barba, north of Mahee. Scarcely any other tongue is
spoken at Badagry and Lagos and other places on the
coast between Whydah and the Delta. Re-captured
Yórubas are numerous in Sierra Leone, and are found

at Fernando Po, on the Gambia, and in other places along the coast. Many native Yórubas are in slavery in Brazil and Cuba. I have seen a Yóruba woman, the wife of a Bedouin, who affirmed that she had been to Stamboul or Constantinople. According to her and others, there are Yóruba slaves in Tripoli, and Fezzan, and all over Central Africa.

The eastern parts of Yóruba, and the countries of Ifeh, Ijesha, Igbona and Effong, have not been visited by the missionaries. We are assured however that there are many large towns in that region.

The population of the large towns with which we are best acquainted may be stated in thousands as follows; Lagos, (Eko,) 20,000 ; Ajasheh, 15,000 ; Abbeokuta, 60,-000; Iketu, 15,000 ; Ishabbeh, 20,000 ; Iganna, 20,000 ; Ishakki, 25,000 ; Igboho, 20,000 ; Ikishi, 25,000 ; Ilorrin, 70,000 ;* Offa, 30,000 ; Ejigbo, 20,000 ; Iwo, 20,000 ; Ideh, 20,000 ; Ibadan, 70,000 ; Ijaye, 35,000; Awyaw, the capital of Yóruba, 25,000 ; Ogbomoshaw, 25,000 ; Isehin, 20,000.

Besides these, there are numerous smaller towns, containing from 1,000 to 10,000 people. The average population of the whole country is probably not less than ten persons to the square mile. I should not be surprised if it is twenty. Fifty years ago it must have been much greater, and it is now again on the increase.

The surface of the country is generally undulating, in long and gradual swells. From the flat sea coast, where there are neither hills nor stones, the country rises grad-

---

* This town may contain 100,000 people; we have never said 500,-000, but in comparing it to New York, we alluded simply [as we said] to its extent.

ually, yet rapidly, to the watershed between the Gulf of Guinea and the Niger. As well as I could ascertain by the barometer, Abbeokuta is 567 feet above the sea, Ijaye 997 feet, and Ogbomoshaw 1305 feet. Fifteen miles beyond the last place the streams flow to the Niger. The most elevated land in Yóruba is about the head of the Ogun river. The mountains there probably rise to a height of three thousand feet above the level of the sea, which is at least one thousand feet more than the highest hills about Ogbomoshaw.

There is no continuous chain of mountains in Yóruba. In passing from the sea to the Niger, we may pursue routes which will frequently bring us in contact with rugged masses of hills, but other routes are so level that a railroad might be constructed without a single deep cut. If a traveler should pass through the country along one of these level routes, he would see nothing more than some occasional solitary mountain or little cluster of mountains rising abruptly from the level plains. But if he should climb to the top of one of these, he would see scores of others rising at various distances all around him. Hence those who have passed along roads which lead them over the hills have concluded that Yóruba is a mountainous country, which is the reverse of what is true.

The first mountainous hills we meet as we go from the coast to Awyaw are the huge piles of granite in and around Abbeokuta. Going westward sixty miles to Iketu, I saw no hills and no granite except near to Abbeokuta. Thirty miles north-east from Abbeokuta brings us to the rocky mountains at Eruwa and Bi-olorrun-pellu. This mass of hills, which is some twenty or thirty miles in circuit, is surrounded by level land. These mountains, which rise several hundred feet above the plain, are partly wooded and partly composed of naked granite, the immense masses of which are piled together in all sorts of fantastic forms. The scenery here is indescribably beautiful. About twenty miles to the north of this are a dozen or two hills of naked granite, the largest of which, Mt. Adó, is about three miles in length and several hundred feet higher than the plain. The southern end is a perpendicular cliff. It is inhabited by rockdoves, celebrated for the beauty of their eyes, but though I could distinctly hear their hoarse cooing, they were too high up the rock to be visible. Twelve miles further I encountered the rude and rocky hills of Oke-Efo, which it took me two hours to ascend. Not far from the road is a little village perched like an eagle's nest among the highest cliffs.

One of the highest mountains in the country, is at Igbetti, between Igboho and Ilorrin. Mr. Clark has visited this place, and found the town of Igbetti on the mountain. The people of Ogbomoshaw have told me that the harmattan wind, which they call *awyeh*, is a huge man, who resides in Igbetti hill. During the dry season he flies out over the country and makes cold weather. The harmattan is a cold north wind which comes from the direction of Fezzan, the highest part of the Great Desert. In Hausa it produces frost and even ice,* but in Yóruba I have not seen it sink the mercury lower than 60.°

The road from Abbeokuta to Ilorrin is level, but we

---

* So say the natives, and Clapperton affirms the same.

pass by the foot of several mountains. Those on the Obba river beyond Ijaye rise to the height of one thousand feet or more above the plain. A few miles beyond this a long ridge is divided to the base by a perfect valley, a mile in width, so that no obstruction is offered to the road. In fact there would be no difficulty in opening roads through every part of Yóruba.

Liberia, and other large districts in Western Africa, are covered with heavy forests with an exceedingly dense undergrowth of shrubs and climbing plants, which is called *the bush*, both by Europeans and the natives. But these forests are an exception to the general character of the African continent. Southern, Eastern, and Central Africa are open grassy countries with a scarcity of timber. When I was at Sama, four days' journey from Monrovia, the natives told me it was five days more to the Boonda country, where the ground is covered with grass instead of bushes. I suppose that the open country is not more than one hundred miles on a direct line from any part of Liberia. From Badagry and Lagos the forest-country extends to the interior about forty miles and is interspersed by numerous little prairies. All the country about Badagry is prairie. Badagry mount, as it is called, is only a clump of trees on the open plain. Almost the whole of Yóruba is a prairie, scattered over with small spreading trees. There are some forests, however, especially on the rivers, some of which are several miles in extent. One of the largest lies between Ijaye and the Obba.

Careful observation has fully convinced me that the African prairies are simply the result of long continued cultivation, followed by annual burnings of the tall

grass. Our own western prairies are probably the
farms of the hypothetical mound-builders. If England
were now abandoned to a sparse population of hunters,
it might remain a true prairie country for indefinite
ages. Some prairies, however, like deserts, have resulted from the drying up of seas. But there are none
such in Yóruba. Here, as in America, if there should
be no more burning of the grass, the prairies gradually
return to the state of primeval forests. Some qualities
of soil however in both countries would regain their
timber much sooner than others.

The soil of Yóruba is various; sometimes decidedly
fertile, especially in the ancient forests; often quite
poor, perhaps from exhaustion; but generally of medium quality. In most places it has a good proportion of quartose rocks and sand. It is mostly of a gray
color, in which it differs from that of Golah, etc., which
stains the water of the St. Paul's river yellow; and
from that of Eastern Africa, which imparts a red color to
the full Nile.

The streams of Yóruba are generally clear, except
when swollen, but in some places receive a milky white
color from the potter's clay which abounds in all parts
of the country. Small streams flowing over rocky or
sandy beds are numerous, but there are no large rivers.
The Ogun above Abbeokuta is about one hundred yards
wide, but too rocky for navigation even by canoes. Below the town it is rather wider, and is navigable for
canoes except in the latter part of the dry season. The
Ossun, according to the natives, is about as large as
the Ogun, and less encumbered with rocks. The river
Ossa flows parallel to the coast from the westward to

Lagos, where it spreads out into a wide lagoon thirty
or forty miles in circuit. This lake as also the lagoon
or river which comes into Lagos from the east, is called
Ossa. The Assa at Ilorrin is forty yards in width, but
navigation is prevented by rocks. In short, there is no
inland navigation in Yóruba. No part of the kingdom
however, is much more than a hundred miles from the
sea on one side, or the Niger on the other. By reference to the map it will be seen that Yóruba is a sort of
peninsula, or in the oriental style of the interior, *an
island*. Its position in regard to the sea and the Niger,
its healthiness, and the facility with which roads may
be constructed, all conspire to make it one of the most
important portions of the African continent. If colonized by civilized blacks from America and properly conducted, it would soon command the trade of all Central
Africa, to which it is the natural key.

The proper Yóruba kingdom is perfectly free from
swamps. Even in the low country along the coast,
there is little swamp except in a few places near the
sea. Universally in the interior the soil is dry and
rocky, and the streams are not subject to great freshets
as in America. The reason is that the rains are more
uniform and gradual.

The only lake is the Ossa, already mentioned. There
is scarcely a pond of an acre in extent in Yóruba. I
have never heard of lakes in the interior except the
Tsad or Tsaddi (Chad) and other smaller ones near it.
Congo people have told me of a large sea in the interior of their country. On further inquiry I became convinced that they were speaking of the Indian ocean,
where white men come in ships to sell cloth and buy

ivory. The eastern Africans also speak of a great inland sea navigated by large ships, and they have affirmed that the people who lived there built castles of stone. Their sea is the Atlantic and the castles are the Portuguese settlements. To convince me that there is a sea and civilized people in the centre of Africa, would require better evidence than the vague reports of ten thousand ignorant and often mendacious natives. The temptation to lie in all such cases is your own love of the marvelous, which the people are not slow to perceive. If however there is a sea in the interior of Africa, we may feel confident that Prestyr John* is king of all the surrounding country. Lake Ngami, I may observe, is only about thirty miles long by six or eight wide.

Most of the streams in Yóruba cease to flow during the dry season. Even the Ogun has been known to stand in pools. I have seldom found a good perennial spring. In most parts of the country there is a stratum of tenacious potter's clay a few feet below the surface of the ground, which arrests the rain water and causes it to ooze in the valleys without forming springs. The wells are usually shallow. Sometimes they are mere pits into which the people descend and dip water. When a well is private property, which is often the case, the owner draws and sells to the women at the rate of two or three cowries for a large pot full ; about one cent for fifty gallons. When they draw at public wells, every woman brings her own bucket, which is simply half of a large

---

* Prestyr John was a Tartar prince who was reported to have embraced Christianity. A hundred years or two after his death—if ne ever lived—the Portuguese were thrown into "intense excitement" by their expectation of finding his glorious kingdom in Central Africa.

calabash or gourd tied to a string. In the centre of Ogbomoshaw there is a fine spring issuing from a mass of gneiss. The owner of the spring has cut a circular basin in the rock, from which a woman dips and sells to thousands of customers. In the evening, which is "the time that damsels go out to draw," this spring is worthy of a visit.

The water in Africa is generally good, but always warm. When the thermometer stood at 85° in the shade, it sank to 75° in a cold spring at the foot of mountains 1500 feet high. By exposing our drinking water to the wind in porous earthen jars, it becomes a little cooler.

10*

CHAPTER XX.

SEASONS AND CLIMATE.

RAINY SEASON — DRY SEASON — SPRING — TEMPERATURE — WINDS — THE
HARMATTAN — CLOUDS — MORNINGS AND EVENINGS — THE BEST TIME
TO TRAVEL — DISEASES OF THE NATIVES — DISEASES OF WHITE VISITORS
— FEVER — DYSENTERY — DEBILITY — CAUSES OF DISEASE — HEAT —
DAMPNESS — MALARIA — HOW TO PRESERVE HEALTH — TAKING COLD —
CLOTHING — HOUSES — BATHING — DAMP BEDS — LAWS OF MALARIA —
DIET — MEDICINES.

THERE are two seasons, the *dry*, corresponding with
our winter, and the *wet*, extending through the greater
part of our spring, summer and autumn. The first rains
begin gently in March. June, or occasionally May, is
the wettest month in the year. From the middle of
July to the latter part of September, we have a fine cool
season, with a few showers. The latter rains are in
October and November. The heaviest showers do not
occur when the sun is vertical, but after he has passed
over and is retiring either to the north or south. When
he is approaching us from the northern tropic, there is
little rain, and there is none, or nearly none, as he
ascends from the tropic of Capricorn.

The quantity of rain that falls in Yóruba is comparatively small. Four inches at a time is considered a
remarkable shower, and more than twenty inches in the
wettest month is bad weather. The torrents of which
we read in other tropical countries are not poured from

the skïes of Yóruba. The thunder is about as severe
as in the Southern United States, but from some cause,
I have never seen a tree that had been struck by lightning. Houses are set on fire every year, but this may
be chiefly the work of the "thunder worshippers," to
whom such houses are lawful plunder. In one case,
however, the lightning killed a woman in the streets.

The *dry season* begins in the latter part of November.
By the middle of January, many trees, especially in the
up country, cast their leaves, as if in sympathy with
their brethren of the chilly north ; by which means they
enjoy that season of repose which is said to be necessary
to the perfection of timber. This season is the hottest
time of the year, except when the harmattan blows from
the north, which sinks the mercury to about 65°, and
occasionally lower. The heat would be still greater,
were it not for "the smokes," caused by the burning of
the prairies, which obscure the sun. There is also a perpetual breeze from the south-west, as at other seasons.
The arrival of the harmattan usually produces a little
rain, so that we have three or four light showers every
dry season.

The approaching *rainy season* is preceded in February
by a degree of moisture in the atmosphere, the effects
of which are soon visible on vegetation. The tender
grass springs up from the dry earth, and many trees are
loaded with gay flowers, which are soon followed by
new green leaves. The season of spring is distinctly
marked, and very beautiful even here in the torrid zone.
It is seen to the best advantage among the mountains.
The dark green foliage of the evergreens, mingled with
the bright young leaves of spring, and interspersed

every where with large and small trees covered with
various colored flowers, the whole disposed in endless
variety over valleys, and gentle slopes, and steep hill
sides, with masses and spires and piles of rock rising
among the trees, present a picture of inexpressible
beauty. But even here the undefinable somberness of
Africa hangs over the scene. There is something wanting, something saddening. I suspect, however, that
half the shadows which seem to rest on African scenery are cast over by our own feelings. We are far
away from the land and the people we love, cut off
from civilization and sympathy, exiles in a remote barbarous country, where we must die and be buried, and
these circumstances impart a hue to our feelings, which
can scarcely fail to be reflected on everything around us.
If the mountain scenery, and the wide green undulating
prairies of Yóruba, were our own native land, inhabited
by our own people, they would seem as bright as the
brightest scenes of earth.

The heat of this country is not excessive. The average in the dry season is about 80° at Ijaye, and 82° at
Ogbomoshaw, and a few degrees lower during the
rains. I have never known the mercury to rise higher
than 93° in the shade, at Ijaye. The highest reading at
Ogbomoshaw, was 97.5°. Still the weather appears
very hot, especially in the sun. The very beasts and
birds, and insects are lazy. Frequently, I have wan-
dered over the farms of an afternoon, for exercise and
recreation, taking my gun to shoot birds, but they
were all asleep in the shady groves, and I have returned without so much as a dove, after walking several
miles. I once watched a pair of hawks building a nest

in their usual season, which is the hot month of December. They might generally be seen perched contentedly on the boughs of their tree, and it was only at intervals that they brought a branch or a twig to deposit on their nest. It took them a month to finish the work of a few days. At another time I observed a wasp building his nest on the ceiling of my room. Most of his time was spent in idleness, and the nest was no larger than the end of my thumb at the end of five weeks. Even the ants, industrious as they are, work only in the cool of the day. Though a million may sometimes be found at six o'clock in the morning, they are all gone to their cool underground galleries long before noon. The people are equally cautious of heat, generally spending their noons under the shade of trees, or dozing in their cool piazzas. Europeans should take plenty of exercise in the cool of the day, but the un-African energy with which they do everything, is not favorable to their health in this land of stagnation.

The winds in Yóruba, besides the little whirlwinds, which occasionally move leisurely over the plains, are of three kinds:

1. Night and day, at all seasons, a damp and cool south-west wind comes in from the Atlantic. It appears to be fully as strong at Ilorrin as in the low country, though not so damp.* There are no gales or hurricanes in this country.

2. The African tornado is merely an ordinary thunder-gust, which seldom has power to blow down a tree, or

---

* Since writing this, I have found the winds in the interior quite variable in the dry season.

unroof a thatched house. This wind usually comes from
the north-east, and the cloud, in which it occurs, moves
directly to meet the south-west breeze. When the two
contrary winds meet, there is a short calm, which is followed by wind and rain from the thunder cloud.

The harmattan, called *awyeh* by the natives, is a cold
and very dry north or north-east wind, which blows for
a few hours at a time, at intervals of three or four
weeks in the dry season. It feels decidedly cool in
Yóruba, and on one occasion caused the mercury to sink
to 60°. Once on the mountains, I saw both men and
dogs shivering under its effects, but I had left my thermometer behind. Its dryness causes excessive evapor-
ation. The average of the hygrometer in the dry season
is about 6° at Ijaye, and 10° at Ogbomoshaw; but I
have seen the harmattan separate the mercury in the
two tubes to 25° in a few hours. Everything is affected
by this unusual dryness. Our skins feel husky, and the
books gape, as if for thirst. Once my table made such
a loud outcry against this loss of moisture, that I drew
off the cloth, expecting to find it split. We accuse the
harmattan of doing us no good. It only chills and dries
us for a few hours, and then resigns us with wrinkled
skins and worsted feelings to the heat and moisture of
the climate.

The upper regions of the air appear to be little dis-
turbed by winds. The scirrus, which at home is generally seen hurrying away to the south-east, lies here in
Africa as motionless as the moon. The lower clouds
are frequently no more than a few hundred feet in height,
and move before the south-west breeze. We seldom
have two cloudy days in succession.

The mornings in Yóruba are damp and chilly, owing to excessive dews. Fogs are not common. By ten o'clock the heat is oppressive, and continues . so till about four. The dew begins to fall before sunset, and soon after dark the damp air is often disagreeably cool. In fair weather the nights are very beautiful, the moon and stars shining with surprising splendor. Sometimes a meteor glides across the sky, but they are not so common here as in higher latitudes. Once, when sleeping by the wall of Abberrekodo, because they refused to receive a white man into the town, I was aroused a little after midnight by thunder and wind. A great cloud lay in the east glowing like fire, with the bright lightnings playing on its edges. There was a loud roaring in the cloud, which could not be attributed to the wind, but there was no rain. Sometimes after sunset, bright streams of light ascend from the west, like the tails of comets, and the surrounding clouds and skies are tinged with the brightest colors. I have seen nothing like mirage in Africa, though it is common enough in Western Texas.

We are never prevented from traveling by rain. Some of my longest journeys have been performed in the wettest months of the year. The best time, however, is in August and September, when the air is cool, and there is little rain. The dry season is too hot, and we are frequently troubled to find good water. In some places, water is sold by women, who sit by the road side for this purpose. It is immaterial at what time the missionaries arrive at Lagos. They can come to the interior without danger at any time. Even in June there is seldom rain during the whole day, and after a few days'

rain, there are commonly a few days of fine weather.
These are the times to travel in the rainy season.
Every traveler should have a tent, and boots, trousers,
and poncho of India rubber.

The climate of Western Africa, especially at a distance from the coast, has no bad effect on the natives.
Neither men noi women come to maturity in any respect
earlier than Europeans. They are robust and healthy,
subject to few diseases, and frequently live to a good
old age. I state these facts explicitly, because many
mistakes on these points have got abroad, and have
even found their way into the works of standard authors.

The diseases of the natives are not malignant. The
country is visited by no choleras, plagues, or other epi-
demics. Agues are not common. Fevers continue from
one to three weeks, and, in the latter case, are liable
to prove fatal by wearing the patient out. I have
known but one case of dysentery to terminate in death.
The remedies for fever are medicated baths and pounded mixtures, which they drink in *ekkaw*, a sort of sour
gruel or mush, which is a common article of food for
the sick and the well. For dysentery they take roots
and herbs, and abstain both from meat, and from all
hot articles of food. I have seen several cases of asth-
ma, for which the natives esteem gunpowder an excellent remedy, though I believe it never cures them.
Some are afflicted with chronic liver complaints, which
they seem unable to cure. This is the disease which
Europeans have called consumption. Sore eyes, frequently ending in blindness, is a very common ailment.
Numbers have applied to me for remedies for this and
other lingering diseases, but in no case have they per-

severed in the use of means for more than a few days. In treating cases of gonorrhea, chiefly with indigenous remedies, I have been more successful. I have met with a few cases of epilepsy, and two or three of insanity. Measles and whooping cough are surprisingly rare. Small pox is common, and, strange to say, is very little regarded, because it seldom proves fatal. The patient strips himself bare, and lies on a mat till the disease runs its course. Though the whole body is equally exposed to the light, only the face is pitted. Whatever may be the proper treatment of small pox in other countries, the best plan in Yóruba is to let it alone. In Abyssinia, where they try to cure it, many die. Boils, ulcers and various cutaneous diseases are common in the sicklier parts of the low country, but not in the interior. The African leprosy appears to be nothing more than a scrofulous disease. It is not contagious. I have seen several cases of elephantiasis. Colds and rheumatic affections are common, especially in the rainy season, for the people are exceedingly imprudent. I have seen a good many cases which appeared to be nothing more nor less than dyspepsia. Bad teeth are fully as common as among the most civilized of mankind. Crooked spines and deformed limbs are more common here than among whites. According to the natives, the Guinea worm is found only where the people drink bad water. Many of their ailments are laid to worms in the stomach and intestines. If a man feels any unusual sensation in these parts, he pronounces it a worm, and wants medicine to kill it. The above are the chief diseases I have seen in the country. On the whole the people are more healthy, and far less liable to die from acute and violent diseases, than we are in America.

To Europeans the climate of the low country especially is very dangerous. Some years ago it was said that the average life of Europeans on this coast was only about two years, and I suppose that there has been no improvement. An old resident declares that of about one hundred white children born on the coast, only one or two have lived to the age of ten years, even of those who were soon taken to England. Mulattoes on the coast, born of debilitated brandy-drinking Englishmen and Dutchmen, are generally feeble. I think we may fairly conclude that no race could ever be fairly acclimated in Guinea, unless they were endowed with the nerves and the skin of the negro. Individuals, however, may be half acclimated, and live here in tolerable health for many years ; but to do this, they must spend every fourth or fifth year in a better climate. This is the opinion and the practice which observation has forced upon European residents.

The principal diseases to which white people are mostly subject in this country are fever and dysentery. Fever presents itself in several forms :

1. The true *acclimation fever* generally occurs within a month or two after landing ; sometimes within a few days. The sooner the better, for if it be much delayed it assumes a new type, and is more dangerous. Proper acclimation fever appears to be little else than an excited state of the nerves and arterial system, with few, if any, bilious symptoms. In itself it is scarcely more dangerous than an ordinary cold, but the debility which follows may result in serious consequences. In my

own case the fever was so light that I was not laid up
till the fourth day, and was not aware in fact that my
indisposition was the dreaded African fever. For the
next four days, till the fever left me, I was on foot most
of the time. The fever came on at its regular period
without the least symptom of chill or yawning, and re-
mitted perfectly in a few hours. The excitement of the
nervous system was rather pleasant than painful.

2. The *bilious fever* is dangerous. This is the fever of
natives, of acclimated persons,* and of those who escape
the acclimation fever at the proper time. In some cases
the skin is decidedly yellow, but if vomiting should
occur, it differs in nothing from that of ordinary fevers.
The acclimation fever scarcely requires treatment, and
patients are liable to be injured by being drugged, but
the bilious fever may, and often does, baffle the utmost
skill of the most experienced practitioners who have been
on the coast. In no disease perhaps is a little bad treatment liable to produce a greater amount of injury. It
should always be remembered that the patient is debilitated, and has no strength to spare.

This fever presents several irregularities. In one
case there was severe vomiting and purging of blood,
with a badly intermitting pulse, and great prostration.
After various remedies had failed, a mixture of sugar of
lead, laudanum, ipecacuanha wine, epsom salts and pot-
ash, arrested the vomiting in three hours, and tonics
completed the cure. Depleting measures would have
killed the patient.

---

* Some deny that the two fevers are different, except in the degree
of violence.

In other cases the fever is clearly *congestive*—a be-numbing, paralyzing chill, with little or no reaction. One of my colleagues, Mr. Dennard, died of this dreadful disease in the second paroxysm. I have little doubt, humanly speaking, that he might have been saved, but the kind people, among whom he was, were ignorant of this disease. A gentleman died at Lagos in the first paroxysm. In the published account of his death his disease was called "fever and apoplexy."

3. Regular old fashioned *agues* are not uncommon, after a man has been some time in the country. I believe the paroxysm usually occurs every other day, and the disease will terminate on the eighth day, especially if opposed a little by quinine. Sometimes a little fatigue or exposure will throw a person into a chill followed by a smart fever, and the matter ends there. It is not the beginning of a spell of fever, but an accident, and the person passes on as if nothing had happened.

4. A kind of *typhoid fever* is liable to follow relapses. No disease in the country is so dangerous as this. Sometimes the very best remedies are wholly powerless. The stamina of the patient is gone, and he sinks from day to day without hope of recovery. For this reason a convalescent patient should be exceedingly careful to restrain his voracious appetite, imprudence in diet being the chief cause of relapses.

Dysentery also is a dangerous disease, though not so common as fever. It arises from two causes, cold and imprudence in diet. Sometimes it approaches very gradually, or gives warning several days beforehand. Then is the time to apply remedies. I have never known mercury and chalk to fail of curing it.

The bane of African residents is *debility*. This is not merely relaxation, arising from the constant heat of the climate, but a state of actual disease, consisting in general derangement of the system. The liver acts badly, the digestion is impaired, there is frequently costiveness, weakness, languor, chilliness, wandering pains, a quick pulse, enlargement of the spleen, nervous irritability, etc. In this state a man is but poorly qualified for the discharge of his duties, and if he should be attacked with fever or dysentery, his constitution may not be able to withstand it. In most cases, death is not so much the result of the violence of the disease, as of the debilitated state in which it finds the patient. This is the chief reason why people should go home and reinvigorate their constitutions every four or five years.

It must not be supposed, however, that a resident in Yóruba, at least, is always half dead with debility. I have repeatedly walked three or four days' journey at a time, keeping up with the natives, wading streams, climbing mountains, sleeping under trees without a tent, and living on the usual food of the people. Such exposures would be unfavorable to health in any climate, and I can not think that a climate where white men can do all this is sufficiently bad to excuse them from missionary duty.

The *causes* which render the African climate unhealthy are confessedly obscure. So far as known they appear threefold—heat, moisture, and malaria.

1. The *heat* of this climate, as already stated, is not excessive ; but it is constant, there being no cool, bracing season, to invigorate the system. It is said that a tropical climate is unfriendly to the constitution

of people from cold countries, in various ways: 1. It relaxes the muscles, and impairs the vigor of the stomach and other organs, which can not be deranged without injuring the health; 2. It produces debility, both by relaxation and excessive perspiration; 3. It excites and deranges the liver; 4. The air which we receive into the lungs, though equal in volume to that which we have been accustomed, is less in absolute quantity, because it is rarefied by heat, and hence contains less oxygen.

2. The *dampness* of this climate arises from the rains, the heavy dews, the moist south-west wind, and the dense vegetation which prevents the sun from drying the earth. The moist night air produces a chilly sensation, and causes disease by deranging the functions of the skin. This degree of chill is perfectly harmless to a strong man in his own country, but it proves too much for a debilitated European, in the sickly climate of Africa. It is a fact worthy of serious attention, that our diseases here generally result from catching cold, which is very easily done. Dampness also appears to increase the activity of malaria. Hence there are two strong reasons why we should avoid the night air, and keep our rooms as dry as possible.

3. Many of the causes which are thought to produce *malaria*, are found in Western Africa. 1. There are swamps on most parts of the coast, though it is true they are neither numerous nor extensive; 2. The ground is often flooded by the rains, and then dried by a hot sun; 3. The forests are always damp, and the prairies, covered with a very dense coat of tall grass, are seldom quite dry. In both these cases, heat, and moisture, and decaying vegetation, conspire to taint the air. 4. In

most places, the water is arrested within a few feet of
the surface, by the stratum of clay; and here we have,
for four months in the year, the concealed water and hot
dry surface which is said to produce the most deadly
miasmata. We may say, then, that the hot days, the
damp chilly nights, and the causes of malaria everywhere visible, are sufficient to account for the unhealthiness of Africa to Europeans. The negro is healthy,
because he is perfectly accustomed to the malaria, and
has a skin adapted to heat and moisture, and a peculiarity of nerves, to wit, a diminution of sensibility,
which fortifies him against all these causes of disease.
Heat, dampness, and malaria, are found in other countries, and these I believe are always sickly. Some are
even more so than Guinea. Bishop Heber tells of a
district in Asia, which is so unhealthy for a part of the
year as to be forsaken by monkeys, tigers, and birds.
During the sickly season, on certain parts of the Nile,
cattle must be removed from the bottoms to the highlands, in order to save their lives. There are no such
districts in Western Africa. The peculiarity here, is
the vast extent of country which is uniformly unhealthy
to Europeans. In Central Africa, where the prairies are
more scantily covered with grass, there may be a good
climate. The unhealthiness of Guinea appears to be
unalterably fixed in cosmical causes, the shape and position of the surrounding oceans and continents producing a perpetual vapory breeze from the south west,
and the geological strata which favor the production of
malaria.

The *means of preserving health*, so far as possible in this
climate, should be carefully studied and constantly

remembered. They consist in general terms, in avoiding the causes of disease.

1. Several rules must be observed to counteract the effects of *heat*. 1. Exposure to the hot sun is injurious, and unless we are in active exercise so as to produce free perspiration, it is liable to bring on a dangerous attack of sickness. Our times of going out should be the morning and evening. During the heat of the day, we should remain in the shade,. and always when the sun is warm, we should carry an umbrella. Traveling stretched on one's back in a hammock, must be very injurious in sunny weather. We had far better endure the fatigue of riding on horse-back, or even of walking, than to be wrapped up all day in a sultry hammock cloth.

2. As to other heatings apart from that of the sun's rays, we should always bear in mind that it is not the state of being hot, but the manner of getting cool again, that does the injury. Every sudden depression of temperature is dangerous, whether we are overheated or not. A man may catch cold and take a fever or dysentery by sitting in a draft of air, between doors or the like, while sitting in the open air would do him no harm whatever. When walking, riding or laboring, we should lay off our coat, and put it on again the moment we stop. It would be better to wrap up in a cloak when we stop, than to keep our coats off and suffer too sudden a decrease of temperature. So much caution may seem needless, but if we do not learn it from some other source, our own bitter experience will teach us. Two gentlemen were traveling in Africa on foot. When they stopped to rest, one would throw himself down in

the shade without his coat to enjoy the cool breeze. The other would button his coat to the chin and saunter about till he was cool. The first was soon in the grave, the latter was not greatly affected by the climate. However agreeable it may be to cool off in a refreshing breeze, we should remember that in this case a man may feel most pleasant when he is catching his death. Capt. Clapperton lost his life in Africa by lying on the ground to rest and cool.

3. Our *clothing* should be light to prevent our suffering with heat, but of some material which will not permit us to be too suddenly cooled when heated, or at any time by the fresh breeze. For myself, thin flannel underclothing is better than silk, especially in the rainy season. When the son of Mungo Park arrived at Akra on his way to search for his father in Central Africa, he adopted the native costume, which leaves the body mostly naked, but he soon fell a victim to the climate. It is a good plan to change the coat in the heat of the day, or lay it off. Of rainy days, and especially at night, we should not go out without a thick coat or a cloak. A man should never sleep in his flannels. The skin is sufficiently taxed without the labor of re-absorbing impure perspiration.

4. Nothing is more conducive to health in Africa, than frequent *bathing*. It cools the body, and what is still more important, it keeps the skin in a clean and healthy condition. To enjoy health with the skin habitually loaded with filth, may be set down as an impossibility. On the other hand, if the skin were always kept clean, and its pores open, by a proper temperature, it would not be easy to get sick. The natives in most

places are among the most cleanly people in the world, washing their bodies daily and their clothes often, which, I suppose, is one reason of their good health. Sometimes, when I have neglected bathing for a few days, I have felt the evil all over my system, and on such occasions have come out of the bath, commonly an open stream, with feelings wonderfully renewed. I made a free use of soap, brushes, and coarse towels.

It is not every one that knows how to bathe. Before entering the bath, we should walk briskly for a few minutes to produce a little perspiration. Then douse yourself in *cold water*—warm is injurious to well people —scrub briskly for four or five minutes, wipe dry, and walk for a quarter of an hour. The design of getting into a perspiration before bathing, and of walking afterward, is to produce a good reaction, without which the bath may do more harm than good. Many people have a mistaken notion that we must not go into the water in a perspiration. The injury which has resulted in such cases arises wholly from staying in too long, and from not taking exercise after coming out.

Every possible precaution should be taken to guard against the bad effects of *dampness*. I have never been injured by a good wetting, as for instance in a shower of rain. Partial wettings have seldom left me wholly uninjured. In wet weather our rooms, and especially the bedroom, should be dried by clear charcoal fires. The coal may always be bought, if you know where to find it, commonly from the blacksmiths, or iron smelters. I would recommend charcoal fires in the room in the fore part of the day, with the windows open. They should be closed by four o'clock p. m., after the room has cooled, and before the damp air of evening has entered it. In a close room, charcoal fires would produce death.

Nothing is more injurious than *damp beds.* The mattresses, &c., must be regularly sunned or dried, if we expect to be healthy. Even in America, when people sleep away from home, they frequently catch cold, and lay the blame on a strange bed. The truth is, that many good ladies ignorantly thrust their visitors into beds, which have neither been sunned nor occupied for a month. To be sure, the sheets are very clean, but the bed is full of filthy poison for all that, being stale for want of sun and air. Thousands of deaths are caused by the washerwomen, who are too careless to dry the clothes well before bringing them in. What would produce a cold in America, may cause death in Africa. For the same reasons that we avoid other dampness, we should be careful of wet feet and clothing, and the night air.

Fortunately, several laws of *malaria* are so well known, that we may measurably guard against it by availing ourselves of this knowledge. All we have to do, is to build the right kind of houses, in the right places, and to keep closely within them at the right times.

1. To protect the clay walls against rain, our houses in Africa are always surrounded by a piazza. This should be weather-boarded above and below, and there should be shutters to close the open portion of nights and rainy days, so as to exclude the damp and chilly air. Ventilation should enter the rooms above the doors and windows, which should be closely shut about sunset. This alone would be almost sufficient to protect us

against three causes of disease—chilliness, damp and malaria. But still further, we should build our houses two stories high, and live on the upper floor, because malaria is most abundant nearest to the ground. It has been observed in sickly localities in the West Indies, that two thirds of the cases occur on the ground floors.

2. Since malaria moves with the wind, our houses should never be built to the leeward of a place where it is known to be abundantly produced. When I arrived at Ijaye in 1852, I selected a beautiful site for building, but they declared the place was bewitched, and all who had attempted to live there had died. The chief confirmed this story, and absolutely refused to let me have the ground.

In 1854, I chanced to enter the forest behind the wall, where I discovered one of the few swamps I have seen in the interior—a filthy, reedy marsh, containing three or four acres, and lying directly to the windward of the enchanted field. Then I understood the nature of *Akil-asho*, the malignant spirit, who is said to wander of nights about the place I had selected for a station.

3. In general our houses should be built in the centre of the town, and not in the suburbs, because malaria is far less active in the midst of a crowded population. Charleston, S. C., is comparatively healthy, but I have been told that a stranger can not spend a single night in the adjacent country during the sickly season, without danger of fever. To escape fires we should cover our houses with tiles. At Lagos, where thatched and tiled houses stood side by side, the former were burnt, and the latter left uninjured. Tiles are better for health than grass. The leeward side of a town, other things

being equal, is healthier than the windward, because the effluvium of the city is less deleterious than the malaria of the forest, which it arrests.

4. The house should stand in an airy situation. It has been found that the malaria is carried away from such places by the wind, so that they are healthy though the poison is generated on the spot.

5. The sides and tops of hills should be avoided, for two reasons :—1. The winds carry malaria to the highlands, where it is retained, perhaps by the attraction of the ground ; and 2, it travels with fogs, which are naturally drawn towards the hills. There is a hill in the centre of Ogbomoshaw, a beautiful place, which they pronounce sickly, and leave unoccupied. Several houses once stood on the hill, as the ruins show. In such cases it is good to be advised by the natives, even though, as at Ijaye, they mix their information with superstition.

6. The healthiest places near a sickly river are immediately on its banks, and the leeward bank is best. The reason appears to be that malaria near the water is attracted by it, and absorbed. Ships anchored a mile from the African shore are perfectly free from danger of malaria. The immediate banks of our southern rivers are healthier than higher places at a considerable distance.

7. The leaves of trees, like water, appear to absorb malaria; at least, trees are known to be a protection, and should be planted near the house, where none are already standing. They should not be so numerous as to prevent the drying of the earth by their shade.

8. It is well known that malaria is much more abundant or active by night than by day. Sailors may come

ashore in Africa daily, without danger, but dare not sleep there a single night. It may be that the vapors of night are the chief means by which malaria breaks away from the attraction of the earth, and rises into the air; or, on the other hand, the chilliness of night may condense and concentrate it near the ground. However this may be, we must *avoid the night air*, if we desire to escape the effects of malaria. When "the pestilence walketh in darkness," we must be closely shut up in our rooms, with the piazzas also closed. If we must go out, it is said that breathing through a silk handkerchief thrown over the face is a protection.

No mortal can live long on the Pontine marshes in Italy; even riding along the road through them by night has cost men their lives. Yet a story is told of a man who built a house there, and lived in it in perfect health. His sleeping-room was as nearly air-tight as possible, and he never exposed himself to the open air after the dews began to fall, nor till they had dried off in the morning. By building proper houses, and observing all the rules of health, I have little doubt that Europeans would almost escape the effects of the African climate.

Attention to *diet* is even more important in Africa than in other countries, for here we are all a sort of invalids.

1. We should eat *temperately*, because our digestive organs are not able to bear excess. For the same reason, we should eat nothing but the most wholesome food. That fruits are the proper diet in tropical countries is a mere theory, and a false one. They are decidedly injurious to health in Africa. In colder latitudes, berries, etc. are needed, and there they are found. They are

not here. A negro would think you a blockhead, if you
should talk of his living on pine apples, bananas, and
other trash, fit only for monkeys. His food is yams,
beans, Indian corn, vegetables, meat and palm oil. This
is the proper diet for Europeans, except the beans and
the palm oil. Boiled, or even fried plantains are wholesome. A friend of mine, to whom I preached this doctrine, said, "Look at Mr. ——, he is always eating
oranges." I replied, "Yes, and he is always sick."
Not long after he was dead. Good sherry wine and ale
are sometimes useful as medicines, except where there is
inflammation of the liver, &c. Gin and brandy are not
so. It is true that most people use them, and it is
equally true that most people die.

2. We should eat *sufficiently*, because we have no
strength to waste on medical asceticism. Some that I
have heard of starved themselves on coming to Africa,
and probably lost their lives in consequence of the erroneous notion, that a depleted body is better able to withstand the assaults of disease than a strong one. Acclimation fever is not an acute disease, and death commonly happens in consequence of the debility by which
it is followed. I have mentioned that relapses are very
dangerous. The reason is because they find us weak ;
but a man may weaken himself so much by starving,
that the first attack is equal to a relapse.

Plenty of moderate *exercise* in the cool parts of the day,
or in the shade, is not only advisable, but indispensable
to health. Nothing is equal to this in curing or miti-
gating debility. It gives tone to all the organs of the
body. Judson thought that the average life of missionaries in his part of the east, was about five years, and

that inactivity killed them. Few better reforms could
be introduced into missionary life, than for each member
of the corps to labor three hours every day at some useful mechanical art, which would give relaxation to his
mind, and vigor to his body. For myself, if I live, I
propose to put me up a little shop, and try to learn
the art of making chairs, tables, and spinning wheels.
Even fatigue is not hurtful, unless carried to excess. I
have walked on my journeys, till my bones ached, and
yet I soon felt all the better for it. In Liberia, when
some of the emigrants who came out about the same
time that I did, were moping about with swollen ankles,
an old settler pointed them to me, and said, "Look at
that man; he is always going, and see how much better off he is than you are."

For the sake of the people, we ought to preach in the
streets at least once a day, but loud talking and mental
excitement are not the right kind of exercise for health.
We must have recreation. Hard study is well nigh as
baneful as malaria. Ease without indolence, activity
with moderation, should be the motto in Africa.

As to the means of *curing disease*, I have but little to
say. I will mention three rules, however, which in the
absence of medical knowledge, I have found very useful, and would recommend to others.

1. Endeavor to have a clear knowledge and view of
the *symptoms* of the disease you are obliged to prescribe
for, noticing everything, great and small, and contem-
plating the aggregate of all the symptoms, as consti-
tuting one corporate body, (so to speak) or one disease.
I should think it best to consult none but the best
authors, leaving quacks and reformers to those who

have less at stake than you or your patient have in a case of African fever or dysentery.

2. In applying remedies, strike at the symptoms, which are matters of fact, and not at the *name* of the disease, which may be a mere shadow. If your patient is hot, try to cool him; if cold, try to warm him; if he vomits, try to allay the irritation of his stomach, &c. It is easy enough to find, or think you find, the name of a disease, and the name of the drug which they say is good to cure it; but if you deal in names, you will probably kill as many missionaries as you cure. Never mind the name, and try to relieve the pains and troubles of the sufferer.

3. Never administer a medicine, unless you have first ascertained that it will not aggravate any of the symptoms. For the uses and contra-indications of medicines consult *Pereira's Materia Medica*, a work which I would scarcely exchange for half a library. To prescribe at random, without consulting the symptoms in this way, is often worse than to give no medicine at all. Beyond all doubt, many a man who has died would have got well of himself, if he had not been drugged. And yet drugs are very useful, when rightly applied. That man must be exceedingly ignorant, or exceedingly careless, and in either case exceedingly guilty, who administers medicines without using the utmost caution to ascertain whether he is likely to make the patient better or worse.

I have treated but three cases of *acclimation fever*. One appeared to require little else than quinine, as there were no decided symptoms, and this remedy was quite effectual. The second came on rather suddenly, with giddiness and loss of strength. I administered a light emetic, followed by a mild purgative, rubbed the abdomen and spine with tincture of red pepper, and gave quinine. On the third day, the fever departed, and the patient was well with little loss of strength. The third patient was a robust, rich-blooded man, and the disease was acute. I gave seven grains of calomel, and prescribed the same again on the third day. He refused to take it. Two days after, he sent for a physician, and took calomel. He was soon well. In such cases, calomel is an unrivalled medicine. I have known a fever broken by one dose, worked off with epsom salts. If we say it must be used with caution, the same is true of all drugs whatever. Nothing should be used where it is not required, and calomel is not required in most African fevers. Blood letting is seldom admissible. In one of the Niger expeditions, there was great mortality, which the daily use of rum could not prevent. The general treatment of the patients, as recorded in the journal, may be expressed about thus, " Gave him calomel, bled him, shaved his head, and applied a blister—he died."

Large doses of calomel, such as we take in America, might prove dangerous in Africa, where the best treatment is that which spares the strength of the patient. In short, we should be guided by the favorite maxim of physicians, that nature cures the patient, or as Watson expresses it in his lectures, " The Lord healeth our diseases."

We have tried various remedies for dysentery, but there is one remedy which has never failed—the common gray powder or mercury and chalk of the shops.

The young leaves of the bene plant, which the natives call *yemmotee*, thrown into cold water, make a mucilaginous drink, which is very valuable in dysentery. The griping has always been relieved by cold water clysters. It should be remembered that dysentery and diarrhœa are totally distinct diseases. I knew a man treated for the former disease with brandy and the like, which endangered his life.

CHAPTER XXI.

GEOLOGY, PLANTS AND ANIMALS OF YORUBA.

ROCKS ON THE COAST — ORGANIC REMAINS — DRIFT — ROCKS IN THE
INTERIOR — GRANITE — ANCIENT SEA COAST — VEGETATION — TREES —
TIMBER — THE UPAS — POISONS — DRUGS — CLIMBERS — FLOWERS —
WEEDS OF CULTIVATION — FRUITS — BEASTS — BIRDS—REPTILES—ANTS.

No STONES are found near the coast. The first that I
saw on the road to the interior was a little *iron conglomerate*, about thirty miles from Badagry. The same rock
is found in various parts of Yóruba, and is particularly
abundant about Ilorrin. It is very similar to that used
in building at Freetown and Monrovia. *Sand stone,*
which appears in abundance at El Mina and Akra, is
found sparingly in Yóruba, and of inferior quality,
being soft and friable. Lime is not found in any form,
though marble is said to exist in the mountains back of
Dahomy. The German missionaries fifty miles in the
interior from Akra, informed me that lime stone is common there, and some has recently been discovered on
Sherbro Island.

Wherever I have been in Africa, I have searched dili-
gently for organic remains. No trace could be found,
unless an impression on a bit of sand-stone picked up in
the dry bottom of the lagoon, a mile east of Cape Coast
Castle, was made by a shell.

Water-worn stones or *drift*, are found in the east bank
of the river Ogun, about fifteen miles above Lagos, and
occasionally on the highest plains of Yóruba, sometimes
embedded in iron clay stone. Travelers have found them
on the desert west of Egypt, and in Mandara, south of
Kanikè. These stones in Yóruba are much weather-
beaten.

Impure quartz rock is found in all parts of the country. It is seldom crystalized, but some of the crystals
which I have collected, are of rare and curious forms.
The coarse granite at Abbeokuta presents fine crystals
of *feldspar*. *Trap rock* is found in the valley south of
Oke-Efo mountains, and a little *protogene* near that town.
In the granite of these mountains, I discovered small
quantities of *schorl*, a rare occurrence in Yóruba.

The only metal known to exist is *iron*, which in some
places appears to be abundant. Vast quantities appear
to have been smelted near Abberrekodo, but no one can
conjecture when or by whom it was done. The people
in Ilorrin assured me that *copper mines* are wrought six
days' journey east from that city. I have seen gold in
quartz rocks, and tested it both with acid and the blow
pipe. Lead mines are wrought beyond the Niger.

The most interesting feature in the geology of Yóruba,
is the granite. It frequently occurs in immense solid
masses, some of which, as Mt. Adó, are eight or ten
miles in circuit, and so high as to be seen from the hill
tops several days' journey distant.

The first granite occurs at Abbeokuta, where it is
quite coarse. As we proceed to the interior, the grain
becomes smaller, till at Oke-Efo we meet with granite
of decidedly fine grain, and capable of a high polish.

The usual color throughout the country is gray, but at Bíoku are traces of a fine rose color. In the deep ravine, north of the village, some of the usual gray stone is faced with a black material, which can not be distinguished from trap. Outside of the town wall, south east of Abbeokuta, are several blocks of granite faced with white.

There is a great rock in Abbeokuta, with two circular holes near each other, high up on the western side. They resemble two eyes, and the water which oozes from them during the rains has made two streaks down the side of the rock, suggesting the idea of tears. These holes are inaccessible to the examiner, but they appear to be a little more than a foot in diameter. In a bolder on top of the same hill, I found another hole, to which I clambered, not without some danger of a broken neck. Its depth was only about three times its diameter, and it tapered to a point at the bottom. There was nothing in it, but the sides appeared more quartose and crystalline than other parts of the rock. The two holes first mentioned, probably communicate with the interior of the rock by fissures through which the rain water trickles, impregnated with something which makes a whitish streak on the stone. I have seen similar holes in different parts of Yóruba, but none of them appear to form a passage for water, like the two at Abbeokuta. At Bi-olorrun-pellu, one rock is perforated by many little holes, two or three inches in diameter, and not very deep. But the most remarkable cavities of this kind that I have seen, are in a great rock of gneiss which rises in the palm-clad farms in front of the Baptist mission house at Ijaye. This rock may be four hundred yards in length, and fifty feet in- height. The eastern and western ends, which are perpendicular, are perforated by several holes three or four feet in diameter, which run into the rock horizontally to an unknown depth. Their sides are marked by longitudinal grooves. It is not improbable that such cavities were formed by the bursting out of steam and water, when the rock was in a state of partial fusion.

Nearly in a direct line between the Aké and Abaka road-stations at Abbeokuta, is a mass of granite hills, on the top of which is a crater-like basin surrounded by bolders. In the woods, on top of the mountain at Bi-olorrun-pellu, is a still larger crater, from which a bold ravine choked up with bolders, runs down the steep hill side to the plain. It has exactly the appearance that might have been produced by a stream of water gushing out of the crater when the rock was in a semi-fluid state. There are several other such crater-like basins among the granite hills of Yóruba, but the largest and most remarkable is on the summit of Imeggeh. This basin is large and deep, and a ravine full of bolders runs down the southern side of the hill. I could not resist the conclusion that these are true craters.

On some of the strong imperishable gneiss rocks a little to the east of Bi-olorrun-pellu, I observed certain erosions, which could hardly be attributed to the action of the weather. On the north side of the Awaye wall is a rock which is worn into gullies and prong-like points, some of which are a foot or more in hight. This strongly excited my curiosity. I looked in every direction for others, which I found, and finally became convinced that they must have been formed by the long-

continued dashing of waves, which rolled in from the
south-east. A few hundred yards north of Awaye there
is a mass of granite several hundred feet high. The
lower parts of this rock, for three fourths of its height,
are not water marked, but the upper part and the flat
top are distinctly worn. On the top, I picked up several
bits of granite which had been worn into an elliptical
form by sliding to and fro in the waves. Still further
west is another high rock, the perpendicular base of
which is much water-worn to the height of thirty feet,
but the top is not marked. The coarse granite at Abbeokuta has arisen from the deep places of the earth, since
the waves beat on the finer grained stone, three days'
journey further interior. The granite at Awaye has
arisen through sand-stone.

One of the first things that attracts the attention of
a new comer to Africa, is the greenness and density of
the vegetation. A person who has never been in the
tropics can form no just conception of its luxuriance.
The hill sides and the banks of streams often present
the appearance of solid walls of leaves and flowers.
The grass on the prairies is from eight to twelve feet
in height, and so thickly set as to be almost imper-
vious.

The forests of Africa are chiefly confined to the
western coast, and the banks of the great rivers. As
a general thing, the continent is destitute of large
trees. It is characterized by thorny bushes, which
grow on the desert and everywhere, and by low tide
spread scrubby trees, which flourish on the prairies or
grass fields. In most places it is impracticable to split
fence rails, or to build log cabins, the trees being too

short when of the proper thickness, and too large when sufficiently tall.

Some African trees are incredibly large. If we may trust our authorities, there are baobabs in the region of the Senegal, thirty feet in diameter. In Yóruba, the same tree scarcely attains one third of that thickness. The cotton tree (bombax) is frequently eight or ten feet in diameter. In Sierra Leone, it is a common thing to see canoes of a single piece sixty feet long, ten feet beam, and five feet deep, with a capacity of four or five tons. Such a vessel could cross the Atlantic to South America with perfect safety.

The African teak is one of the most valuable trees known for ship building. There are several other valu ble trees for coarse timber. One of these, the sassa-wood, called *iroko* in Yóruba, is regarded with super-stitious reverence on most parts of the coast. The Yórubas think there is a spirit in it, because doors and tables made of it have a singular habit of cracking or rapping, especially at night. Hence, the Yóruba man worships his own door when made, as it usually is, of this timber. Last spring, I came up the coast from Lagos, with a gentleman who had just shipped a cargo of wood from Old Calabar, which he believed to be mahogany. Some of the Yóruba chiefs had canes of ebony, which they say grows in the country, but I be-lieve that fine grained wood of every kind will prove to be scarce.

Cam wood, exported as a dye stuff, is common in the forests of Guinea, and appeared to be particularly abundant on the St. Paul's, where I saw it in Golah. The oil-palm is very abundant on the coast, and on the

rivers of the interior, especially of the Niger. It is
said to occur on lake Chad, but is unknown in the dry
sunny countries about the Benue. There is scarcely a
palm tree within twenty miles of Ilorrin. I have seen
four other species of palm in Yóruba ; the wine-palm,
erroneously called bamboo ; the fan-palm, a tall and
graceful tree ; the cocoa nut, and a palmetto ; somewhat
like that of the Southern States. The date-palm is
found in some of the gardens at Ilorrin. The prairies
of the interior are beautified by the butter tree and the
African locust, which are very valuable to the natives.
The seeds of the latter are much used in palaver sauce.
There are many species of fig tree, none of which bear
valuable fruit, though the small berries of some have a
pleasant taste. Some of these trees are occasionally
three feet in diameter, Others are remarkable for their
large and wide spreading branches, and are much used
for shade trees in towns. Another species has very
rough leaves, which are commonly used by the natives
for sand paper.

The natives have told me of a tree called *ashori*, which
is so poisonous that no plants grow under it, and birds
which fly too near it fall dead. The bark and wood of
this tree, which is commonly called *igginlá*, "the great
tree," are used for superstitious purposes, and sell for a
high price. They showed me a bit of the wood weighing perhaps half a dram, which was valued at two dollars. It was black and very heavy. The bark resembles that of the hemlock. When a man wishes to utter
a dreadful curse against his enemy, he puts some of this
bark into his mouth, from which I infer that the dried
bark, at least, is not very poisonous. Yet they pretend

that men sometimes lose their lives in attempting to detach it from the tree. There are several trees of this kind in the forests east of Yóruba, which is the only country where they are found. They are said to be large trees, and always green, except once a year, when the spiders denude them of leaves in a single night.

There is no doubt that the African forests produce virulent poisons. Some kinds produce speedy death. Others produce their effects more slowly by gradually destroying health and life. One reputed case of poisoning, which I saw, caused the whole abdomen to feel as hard as a board. The woman lived several months after this. All the natives are afraid of being poisoned by their enemies, and I suppose that such cases must be common, though I have never heard of more than two or three in Yóruba. The general introduction of fire arms has nearly superseded the use of poisoned arrows, but they are sometimes used and produce the most horrid effects. I was once called to visit a young man who had been wounded by a poisoned arrow, in the arm. His hand was gone, the bones of the lower arm were naked and dry almost to the elbow, and the inflamed stump was still rotting away.

Some of the medicinal drugs used by the natives are valuable, particularly the tonics and alteratives, in the use of which they exhibit considerable skill. Tonics are often used in the form of medicated baths. In some of the forests there is abundance of sarsaparilla, of the mealy variety, which has all the characteristics of the American roots. Cubebs are common but not abundant. The aloe plant flourishes on the prairies. The white pond lily here as elsewhere is used as a medicine. But most of the drugs, like the vegetation generally, are unknown in other countries.

The forests abound in climbers, many of which are as flexible and almost as strong as a hempen rope. They are used by the natives for tying all sorts of things. There are several kinds of reeds and ratans. The West India cane or bamboo is not found in the country, but has been introduced at Sierra Leone. I have sent some to Yóruba, where it will be invaluable on account of the great scarcity of poles for rafters.

None of the prairies, except about Ilorrin, are beautified by beds of bright flowers as in America. Herbaceous plants with showy flowers are remarkably scarce. Flowering trees and shrubs are very numerous. Gardenias and jasmins are seen everywhere.

The weeds of cultivation, as purslain, crab grass, Spanish needles, etc., are very similar to those of the Southern States. The trees, weeds and grasses of the forests and prairies are different. Oaks, pines, hickories, and the whole catalogue of trees with which we are familiar at home, are wholly unknown in Africa. The wild fruits are numerous, yet scarcely ever eatable except for monkeys. Blackberries, whortleberries, and the numerous other little fruits which flourish here are unknown there. Peaches, apples, plums, and other fruits of the temperate zone, will not grow in Africa, owing to the perpetual summer of the climate. None of the tropical fruits have been introduced into Yóruba, except plantains, limes and papaws.

The beasts, birds, fishes, etc., of Africa, like the plants, are mostly different from those of our own country. The principal beasts are elephants, rhinoceroses, hippopotami, lions, leopards, (no tigers,) panthers, two or three kinds of wild cats, civet cats, hyenas, wild dogs, (*ajako*, jackals ?) the casra (kollokolloh), coneys, rabbits, several species of squirrel, various antelopes, (no deer,) wild hogs (two species,) buffaloes, numerous rats and mice, bats, apes and monkeys. Among the birds we may enumerate eagles, several hawks, crows, two kinds of buzzards, herons, crested cranes, storks, two species of Guinea fowl, quails, the spurred partridge, the hen-tailed partridge (in the mountains,) various kinds of doves and pigeons, wild ducks, (no geese,) king-fishers, one species of which feeds on butterflies, swallows, mocking birds, the curious long-shafted goat-sucker, various other goat-suckers (whip-poor-wills,) parrots, paroquets, love-birds, cockatoos, horn-bills, creepers, larks, sparrows (some red and some black,) orioles, scarlet weavers, sun-birds and many other birds for which we have no names. Of fish, reptiles, and insects, we have perch, a sort of trout, catfish, torpedoes, and many other of strange forms ; huge snakes, fifteen or twenty feet in length, vipers, poisonous green snakes, and a few others, but no water snakes—guanoes, chameleons, various kinds of lizards, toads, frogs, tortoises, snails as large as a tea cup, crabs, muscles, some of which are like oysters ; spiders, centipedes, scorpions (yellow and black, the latter six inches long,) fleas, ticks, wasps, (no hornets,) bees, beetles, etc. House flies, fleas, musketoes and other troublesome insects are surprisingly scarce. Earth-worms of great size are innumerable. The natives deny that any of the spiders are poisonous.

Two species of the innumerable ants deserve a more

special notice. The white ant (wood louse) or large termites, commonly called bug-bug, builds hillocks to a height of eight or ten feet, which are usually surrounded by several picturesque spires or turrets. They feed entirely on dry vegetable matter, and are very destructive to cloth, books and most kinds of wood. Unless our rooms are well lighted by doors and windows, there is danger of their invading the house in such numbers as to do great mischief in a few days. Sometimes they will perforate a box and mar the contents before we are aware of their presence. They refuse to eat the iroko or sassa wood, and even pine boxes are safe if set on stones so as to be a few inches above the ground.

There are two species of ants, one black and the other red, appropriately called *drivers*. They march forth by the million and feed on nothing but flesh. No living creature can stand before them. When they invade a house, which is generally at night, we are obliged to retire, and every mouse, roach, cricket, scorpion, etc., which can not escape is sure to be devoured. On one occasion they killed a parrot in its cage. Their visits, though disagreeable, do not last more than an hour or two, unless they should find a piece of meat or the like to detain them, and they are useful and therefore welcome, because they clear the premises of rats and insects. The red drivers are particularly fond of feeding on the white ants, or bug-bugs, and in this way are often very useful.

The domestic animals in Yóruba are the same as our own, except that there are no geese or pea-fowls. Owing to the hotness of the climate, the sheep are covered with hair instead of wool. The bearded sheep is peculiar to Sudan. The common horse of the country is a compact sturdy pony, but the horses imported from the coast are fine animals, which sell at Ilorrin for three, four, or five hundred dollars, occasionally for one hundred bags of cowries, or one thousand dollars. None of the horses are gelded in Africa.

CHAPTER XXII.

ETHNOLOGICAL FACTS AND TRADITIONS.

ORIGIN OF THE NAME OF YORUBA — MEN CREATED AT IFEH — SIXTEEN
EMIGRANTS FROM THE EAST — DRYING UP OF THE WATERS — YORUBAS
ONCE LIVED IN NUFE — SIX YORUBA TRIBES — DESCENDED FROM NIM-
ROD — WHITE IMMIGRANTS TO SUDAN — AFFINITIES OF THE YORUBA
TONGUE — LIST OF YORUBA AND PULOH WORDS.

In several African languages, the syllable *ba* (cf. *aba*,
father) implies paternity, head-ship, greatness. Thus
in the Mandingo language, we have *ba*, *great*, and in the
Yóruba, *babba*, a *father*, *obba*, a *king*, and *baba*, a great
affair or matter. The Hebrew *yar*, a *river*, which has its
cognates in many languages, appears to be the same
word as the Puloh *goru*, a *river*, the *y* being hardened
into *g*. According to some travelers, the upper Niger
is called Jolliba, but the Mandingoes, whom I met in
Golah, called it Yolla Ba, the great Yolla.* By a very
customary interchange of letters, Yolla Ba becomes
Yorra Ba, Yaru Ba, Yari Ba and Yar Ba, which are the
various names by which our country of Yóruba is
known in different parts of Central Africa. We may
infer, then, that Yóruba, from Goru Ba, means literally

---

* The word *ba* (cf. *yar*) Arab *bahr*, signifies river, but in that sense
it precedes the name of the stream, as " Ba Fing," the river Fing.
It is a mistake to suppose that Jolliba means the river Jolli, for *jolli*
itself means river.

the "great river," and that the country derived its name from the Niger or Jolliba. It is worthy of remark, that the Yórubas, though very expert in tracing words of their language to their roots, never attempt to determine the etymology of their national name. We must admit, however, that the derivation of Yóruba from *Yar Ba* or *Goru Ba* is liable to one objection. In Africa as in America, the names of tribes are never derived from those of countries, but the contrary; and we are no more allowed to say Dahomans, Yórubans, etc.; than Cherokeeans or Choctawans. It is possible, then, that we must look to some other source for the origin of the name Yóruba. It is certainly a very ancient name in the traditions of the people, and may have been imported from the remote east. The resemblance between this and another very ancient traditional name, *Europa*, must be accidental.

According to one tradition of the Yórubas, their ancestors, and in fact, the original parents of the whole human race, were created at Ifeh, which still exists in the east of the Yóruba kingdom. They told Lander, and have told me, that Ifeh, where men were created, is several months' journey distant, and sometimes they speak of it as standing on the sea, although, of course, they are not ignorant of its true location. There seems to be a confused memory of another Ifeh, from which their ancestors emigrated to this country, and founded the present town of that name, which is universally regarded as the metropolis of all the Yóruba tribes.

According to another tradition, the Yórubas are derived from sixteen persons, who were sent out to form a colony by some personage whose name has not been preserved. Their leader took with him a hen and a piece of cloth, in which was tied up a palm nut and a quantity of dry earth. For a long time they waded through water, but at last their leader untied his cloth, and poured out the earth, which immediately became a small dry bank, and the palm nut sprang up into a tree of sixteen branches.* The hen then flew upon the bank and scratched the earth in every direction, which dried up the water.† The little colony settled at Ifeh, whence they spread abroad in the surrounding country.

Others relate that their ancestors once lived east of the Niger, and were driven into Yóruba by war, at a time when the water was very high. The language of Nufe still bears traces of its Yóruba origin, but most of the primitive roots and their derivations have been exchanged for other words.

We are told further, by another tradition, that the Yóruba tribes, Iketu, Egbá, Ijebu, Ifeh, Ibini (Benin) and Yóruba, are descended from six brothers of these names, who were the sons of one mother. Yóruba, the youngest son, became the ruler of the rest, and hence the Yóruba king was the sovereign of all these nations. After a while, Benin—(where the language at present has very little affinity to the Yóruba)—became independent, and in course of time, the other four tribes withdrew from the confederacy, leaving Yóruba alone. Still the Yóruba king was master of Effong or Kakanda and Kupa, and had Dahomy or Popo for a tributary.

---

* The hen and palm tree remind us of the dove and the olive branch.
† The North American Indians have a somewhat similar tradition, that the waters were dried up by means of a musk-rat.

All accounts agree that the Yórubas first lived at Ifeh. The next settlement was at Igboho, (Bohoo) which became the capital of Yóruba. The great mother of the six tribes is still worshipped at Ifeh and Abbeokuta, under the somewhat remarkable name of Iyommodeh— (*Iya ommoh oddeh*)—the mother of the hunter's children. We are not informed who this "mighty hunter" was.

But the most curious tradition is derived from another source. When Denham and Clapperton were in Central Africa thirty years ago, they obtained an abridgement of a work written in Arabic by the Puloh king, Bello of Sokoto, entitled "The Dissolver of difficulties in the history of the country of Takrour" (i. e., Central Africa) ; to which is added by the abridger, "Composed by the ornament of his time, and the unequalled among his cotemporaries, the Prince of the Faithful, and Defender of the Faith, Mohammed Bello, son of the Prodigy of his age, the noble Sheikh, Osman."* In this work, the writer refers familiarly to African chronicles written long ago anterior to the presence of the Arabs in Sudan, and he expressly says that the Copts, who settled Burnu, wrote a history of their transactions, though he does not say that these are the authorities which he uses.

After relating various particulars of other countries in Takrour, Bello gives the following account of Yóruba, which he calls Yarba:—"The inhabitants of this province, it is supposed, originated from the remnant of the children of Canaan, who were of the tribe of Nimrod. The cause of their establishment in the west

---

* See Appendix to Denham and Clapperton's Travels.

of Africa was, as it is stated, in consequence of their being driven by Yaarooba, (Yaruba,) son of Kahtan,* out of Arabia to the western coast between Egypt and Abyssinia. From that spot, they advanced into the interior of Africa, till they reached Yarba, where they fixed their residence. On their way, they left in every place where they stopped at, a tribe of their own people. Thus it is supposed that all the tribes of Sudan, who inhabit the mountains, are originated from them, as also the inhabitants of Yauri."

On this extract we may remark, 1. That Bello derives the Yórubas from Nimrod, while they themselves, who know nothing of Nimrod, claim to be descended from "the mother of the hunter's children." 2. Bello says they were *driven* from Arabia by Yaarooba, while they profess to have been *sent* from some remote country, and one of their first princes was named Yóruba. 3. If it is true that the kindred of the Yórubas in Sudan are now confined to the mountains, as Bello intimates, we may infer that they were forced into these positions by the encroachments of more powerful people. That there have been large immigrations of white people into Africa is proved by the fact that there are now millions of mulattoes in Sudan. Bello declares that a colony of Copts settled in Burnu. It is not improbable that the Psylli or Psulloi of Northern Africa were the ancestors of the Pulohs, who are now numer-

---

* "This," says the translator, "was a great sovereign of Arabia, who, according to an Arabian historian, was king of Yemen, in the days of the prophet Heber." Kahtan is said to have been the first who wrote the Arabic language.

ous on the south of Sahara. In addition to all this, that "giant race" of red-haired, hook-nosed men, who are affirmed to have figured so largely among the ancients of Europe, Asia, America, and the Pacific Islands, evidently came hither also; for we may find some negroes with Roman noses and some with a reddish tinge of hair and beard to this day. The fair-skinned, red-haired men who live in the Atlas mountains may be a remnant of the invaders.

It is now known that the affinities of the Yóruba language extend along the coast to Old Calabar, and far interior along the course of the Benue or Chadda. Some of the tribes in the latter locality, as the Jukus, are among the most degraded of all the Negro tribes ; whereas the language, arts, traditions and mythology of the Yórubas are good evidence that they themselves have always been somewhat civilized. The Jukus are probably a mixture of Yórubas and pure typical negroes, who have never yet been found in a state of society above that of deep barbarism.

Only four years ago, when Bishop Vidall wrote on this subject, the affinities of the Yóruba tongue were wholly unknown. It stood unclassified. Since that time the publication of Koelle's Polyglotta Africana, and the expedition up the Benue, and the researches of other travelers, have considerably extended our acquaintance with African languages.

I shall omit many things in relation to the affinities of the Yóruba language which I had marked for this chapter, but I can not forbear to give a few examples of words which appear to be widely diffused, not only in Western and Central Africa, but in other parts of the world. The Yóruba numeral *one*, is *eni* and *okkan* (or *kan*,) both of which are common in one form or another to various other languages. We can scarcely doubt that *eni* is the same word as the Greek *en*, Saxon *an*, French *un*, Spanish *uno*, Portuguese *hum*, Welsh *un*, Latin *unus*, English *one*. In Africa, we find in the Okam *weno*, Opandi *onyi*, Kupa *enyi*, and Nufe *weni*, corresponding with Yóruba *eni*. Some of the widely-spread cognates of *okkan* or *kan*, one, appear to be Sanscrit *eka*, Hebrew *ekhad*, Pelevi *jek*, Finnic *aku;* and in Africa, Uchaw *kan*, Isubu *yokkoh*, Ashantee *ekko*, Oloma *oggu*, and many others. In the Yóruba word *kan*, the *n* is a very slight nasal, almost silent, and the verb *ka* means to count.

Etta, *three*, corresponds with the Akra *etteh*, Kroo *ta*, Dahomy *aton*, Mahee *oton*, Opaddo *eta*, Puloh *tatti*, Ham *tat*, Mbariké *itar*, etc., and may be compared with the Sanscrit *tri*, Greek *treis*, Latin *tres*, Saxon *thri*, etc.

Babba, the Yóruba word for *father*, is found everywhere; Kanikè *aba*, Hausa *oba*, Mbe *mba*, Wolof *bai*, Mosé, Dey, and others *ba*, Shoa, etc. *aba*, Filham *papai*, Bullom *pua*, Mandingo, etc. *fa;* Portuguese *pai*, in the languages of Brazil *papa*, *papaio*, *paba*, *babi;* Java *ba*, *papa;* in some parts of India *baw* and *fa*, (see Balbi's Atlas,) Celebes *bapa*, Madagascar *baba*, Galla *abo* and *abai*.

The greater part of the Yóruba language has been derived according to definite rules from a little more than one hundred biliteral verbs, as *bo*, to cover, *fi*, to make, *wa*, to dig. Many, perhaps all of these verbs, can be shown to have a real, or at least, seeming and wonderful affinity to the ancient verbs of other languages, as for instance, *ri*, to see, Arabic *ray*, Hebrew *raah*, Greek *arao; loh*,* to grind, Greek *aleo*; *le*, to lay down, English *lay*; *de*, to bind, Greek *deo*, Saxon *tian*, English *tie*; *ti*, to shut, Hebrew *atar*. Making all due allowance for fancied and accidental resemblances, the Yóruba verbs, as the ground work for a primitive language, are exceedingly interesting to the philologist. They are still more so from the fact that they occasionally, or we might say frequently appear to contain the radicals of words which are primitives in other languages. To give an instance, *bi* means primarily to generate—hence to beget, to conceive, to bear. From this comes the noun, *bibi*, any thing which is born. In the Puloh language we have *bebi*, (pronounced baby) sometimes contracted to *bi*, meaning any young creature, man or brute. To *bibi* and *bebi* compare the English *baby*, German *bube*, a boy, and English *booby*, Irish *baban*, Syriac *babia*, Latin *pupa*, a girl, Arabic *babos*, the young of man or beast, Syriac *babosa*, a child, American Indian *pappoos*, a babe, all of which words may have been derived from *bi* or from some more ancient verb which *bi* represents.

In the Yóruba, we have *obi*, a parent, either father or mother. In Hausa, *oba*, a father, corresponding with *aba*, *baba*, etc., and probably from the same root, *bi*, to beget; the *i* being changed to *a* in *oba*, as it is *e* in *bebi*, to *u* in *bube*, and to *a* in the Syriac *babia*. The *o* in *obi* means (as it does in Yóruba and Nufe) *he*, and corresponds with the Greek *o, e, to*, Hebrew *ha*, English *he*. *Obi* means *he* or *she that begets;* and I suppose that *oba*, *baba*, etc., signify literally the begetter.

---

* The *h* is added merely to show that *o* is close, as in *lot*, *not*.

But there is another word for father, no less widely diffused than *baba* itself. The Dahomy word for father is *da;* Goali, *nda;* Opandi, *ada;* Bassa (of the interior), *ada;* Nufe, *nda* (*n* means *he*); Golah, *da;* Kupa, *dada;* Akra, *tatta;* Benin, *ita;* Isubu, *tete;* Melon, *ta;* Kakanda, *atta;* Eskimo Indians, *atta;* Basque, *aita;* in some of the Celtic languages, *athair;* Welsh, *tad;* Albanian, *ate* and *tatta;* Slavonic, *otdz* (*z*=terminal *s*) and *otac;* American Indian, *dadi;* English, *daddy*. In the Yóruba, we have *dadá*, which may mean either nature or creator, from *dá*, to create; and to this root I would refer all the above words for father. The Yórubas sometimes form a verb by uniting two others, and we could fancy that *bi dá*, to create, by begetting, may be the root of some of the words for father: as, Saxon, *feder;* Dutch, *vader;* Sanscrit, *pita;* Latin, *pater;* Danish, *fader;* Persian, *padar!* Then we could go further and fancy that *bi*, to beget, and *dá*, to create, are the radicals of the Swedish *foda*, and Danish *foder*, to beget, feed, etc.!

The Yóruba abounds in these curious coincidences, in regard to the sounds and meanings of words. Take the verb *sun*, to burn, and compare English *sun*, and by dropping *n*, or changing it to *l*, *so*, *sol*, *suli*, etc., in most of the Greco-Latin, Germanic and Slavonic languages and dialects. The Yóruba *orrun*, heaven; *orun*, sun; *oro*, one of their gods; may be compared with *ouranus*, heaven: with various words for day, as, Peruvian, *uru;* Phillipines, *arao;* Madagascar, *auru;* with Latin *aurora* and Yóruba *ouraw*, morning; with Hebrew, *aur*, light; Latin, *aurum;* and Yóruba, *wura*, gold; and with many other words in every part of the world. We have, in Yóruba, *akara*, bread; Hebrew, *akala*, food; *ataba*, a dove; Arabic, *hatafa*, to coo; German, *taube*, a dove. *Enni*, a personal pronoun, meaning one, any; *ehin*, the back; Arabic, *akhin*, last, hinderpart; *oko*, a farm; Coptic, *koi*, a field. But this may suffice for the present: at some future time I may enter more fully into this subject. The examples now given are only specimens of the various points in which the Yóruba language appears to be connected with those of Africa on the one hand, and of Europe and Asia on the other.

In some respects, the Yóruba language is very defective. It has no article. The plural of nouns is distinguished by prefixing *awon*, they. All the words used as adjectives, are either verbs or nouns. *Enia re,* means the person *is good;* the so-called adjective *re* being a verb, and conjugated like other verbs. *Enia rere,* a good person, means literally a person of goodness. The pronoun of the third person has no distinction of gender, *o* or *on* being used indiscriminately for *he, she,* or *it.* Verbs are conjugated by means of auxiliaries, and there is no variation for person and number. Finally, there is no passive voice. All the defects of the language, however, are ingeniously remedied by one contrivance or another, so that the Yóruba, after all, is no mean language. My vocabulary, which is nearly ready to copy, will probably contain twelve thousand words.

I may now conclude this chapter with some specimens of Yóruba and Puloh words.

English.	Puloh.	Yóruba.
Head,	Hore,	Ori, from ri, to see (?)
Hand,	Jungoh,	Awwáw, from wáw, to drag (?)

English.	*Puloh.*	*Yóruba.*
Hair,	Lebbeh,	Irun.
Heart,	Gabareh,	Okkan, from kan, to knock.
Heaven,	Itonda,	Orrun.
Hawk,	Chilál,	Awodi.
Hill,	Dun,	Oke.
Hoe,	Jaloh,	Okkaw, from kaw, to heap up.
Horn,	Waladu,	Iwo.
Horse,	Pochu,	Eshin, from shin, to run swiftly.
Face,	Yeso,	Ojú (the eye.)
Foot,	Koingal,	Esseh, from seh, to stumble.
Fever,	Háküa,	Iba.
Finger,	Kolè,	Iká, from ká, to bend.
Fire,	Hitè,	Ina, from na, to extend.
Fish,	Liko,	Ejja, from ja, to jerk.
Fog,	Shamaga,	Ikuku.
Food,	Nafa,	Onjeh, from jeh, to eat.
Friend,	Higo,	Orreh, from reh, to be friendly.
Fruit,	Biku,	Eso, from so, to bear.
Man,	Górrukaw,	Okkonri.
Mankind,	Adama,	Enia.
Woman,	Debbo,	Obiri.
Child,	Bingel,	Ommoh, from mu, to suck.
Mother,	Ina,	Iya.
Bow,	Biroga,	Orron.
Arrow,	Kodarh,	Offa, from fa, to draw.
Sword,	Lapbi,	Idah, from da, to bend.
Gun,	Bindegal,	Ibon.
Mouth,	Onuko,	Ennu.
Chin,	Neppi,	Agbon.
Tooth,	Nire,	Ehin, from yin, to shoot out.

English.	Puloh.	Yóruba.
Tongue,	Dengal,	Ahón.
Belly,	Bedu,	Innu.
Back,	Bao,	Ehhin.
Sack,	Zekkare,	Okkeh.
Bee,	Bubi,	Oyin.
Bell,	Jamga,	Agogo.
Bird,	Poli,	Eiyeh.
Bone,	Gierh,	Egugu.
Brass,	Zampdeh,	Odeh.
Camel,	Geoloba,	Ibakasië.
Cat,	Musuru,	Ologini.
Cloth,	Oderreh,	Ashaw, from shaw, to adorn.
Corpse,	Maide,	Oku, from ku, to die.
Desert,	Zari,	Aginju.
Moon,	Loru,	Oshu.
Sun,	Nange,	Orun.
Water,	Dian,	Omi.
Wood,	Legga,	Iggi.

Puloh verbs are varied to express the tenses, and the future is sometimes entirely different from the present, probably another root; but there is no variation for number and person. A few examples may serve to show the nature of the Puloh verb. *Mi yani,* I fall; *o yani,* he falls; *mi aha,* I will fall; *mi aili,* I go; *mi hoti,* I will go; *dilugo,* to go. Present tense, *hori,* carry; future, *hora;* imperative, *horu;* infinitive, *horugo.* The infinitive generally ends in *go,* but not always.

CHAPTER XXIII.

PHYSICAL, INTELLECTUAL AND MORAL CHARACTERISTICS OF THE SUDANESE.

TYPICAL NEGROES — MULATTOES — ORIGINAL SEATS OF THE NEGROES — THEIR MIGRATIONS IN SUDAN — WHITE IMMIGRANTS TO AFRICA — EFFECTS OF CLIMATE — PERMANENCE OF MULATTO RACES — BLACK MEN WITH EUROPEAN FEATURES — ACTIVITY OF NEGROES — INTELLECT — LANGUAGE — LAWS — RELIGION — COMMON SENSE — INVENTIVE FACULTY SCIENCE — MUSIC — LETTERS — POETRY — KINDNESS — INDUSTRY — COMMERCE NEEDED — IMMODESTY — COVETOUSNESS — PROVERBS.

THE people of Central Africa are of three classes, typical negroes, mulattoes, and black men with a European cast of countenance. Eastern and Southern Africa afford other varieties, as the Gallas, Caffers, Hottentots, etc., of whom it does not concern us at present to speak.

1. The true or typical negro, as every one knows, is distinguished by his low organism. His jaws are prognathous or monkey-shaped, his forehead retreating, his face larger than his hairy scalp, his feet broad and flat, his heels long, and his legs almost without calves. He is athletic, has a strong but harsh voice, is more capable of enduring fatigue and exposure to heat and moisture than other men, is more easily affected by certain drugs, and yet suffers less pain from blows, wounds, or surgical operations than others. His intellect, and

especially his reasoning faculties are weak, his moral perceptions low, and his animal feelings strong. He appears to be a stranger to modesty, doing and allowing things with brutal apathy, which other races can not tolerate. I doubt whether any negro of this class has ever felt disgust, or ever will. They are naturally incapable of refined feelings. This class is not confined to Guinea, but they are numerous in some of the finest districts of Sudan, where they are more degraded than they are on the sea coast, because the latter have been improved by intercourse with the whites.

2. Many of the Pulohs, and some other interior tribes, and a few of the Yórubas, Eboes, Nufes, Hausas, Kanikès, Mandingoes and Kroomen, are mulattoes, the descendants of typical negroes and white men. This is proved by several facts. 1. Their color varies from dark to very bright. Some of the Pulohs can not have more than one eighth of negro blood, if we judge by their color. 2. Their hair, though woolly, is long and bushy like that of other mulattoes. I have seen one woman, nearly black, with soft silky hair. Some have a sandy tint of beard and hair, as if their ancestors were red-headed. I have seen one with bright blue eyes. Lander saw one on the Niger. 3. Their features, noses, lips, skull, etc., are cast more or less in the European mould. Their hands and feet are frequently small and elegantly formed. 4. The language of the Pulohs, of which I have collected about three hundred phrases, containing one thousand words or more, is not African or Shemitic. 5. The Pulohs affirm that their ancestors were white. 6. And finally, we have evidence worthy of more or less confidence, that the white and

negro races have repeatedly come in contact under circumstances, which must have resulted in amalgamation.
On this point I may be permitted to enlarge by briefly
alluding to facts.

In the first place, I, at least, see no reason to doubt
the correctness of the opinion that the negroes originated in Northern India, or beyond it, whence they were
dispersed by three emigrations. One branch of the race
moved eastward, and retired before other tribes till they
became the Ainoes or hairy blacks of the eastern coast
of Asia. Another branch entered Southern India as
conquerors—the monkey conquerors of mythology—
whence perhaps the monkey worship of India and Africa.
Buddha is represented, and perhaps correctly, as a negro, and the existence of his religion certainly ante-
dates the era sometimes assigned to the warrior demi-
god. This branch of the negro race finally pushed on
to the Indian Archipelago, to the Pacific Islands, and
even to the western coast of America. The third stream
of migration flowed to the south-west, and passed over
into Africa. The name Ethiopia, like the black race,
was migratory, and passed from Asia to Arabia and
thence to the African continent. Now, if this view of
the case be in the main correct, we can not doubt that
negroes were intermixed with whites long before they
entered Africa, and that mulatto races may have existed in Sudan ever since it was peopled.

I have already noticed the migration of the Psulloi,
and Bello's account—perhaps a correct one—of a Coptic
colony in Burnu. Who can say how many such emigrations may have taken place from Northern Africa?
The usually tall and handsome Mandingo race are a

mixed people. The Saracens overran Sudan in the tenth century, and some of the tribes on the southern borders of the desert are still pure white men, as previously stated. In view of all these facts, it can not be unreasonable to believe that the red people of Africa are in fact mulattoes.

Here we may step aside to make two remarks. First, that the burning sun and dry air of the desert have not changed the color or the features of the whites, who have been there for three or four thousand years. Their children are still as white as any in the world. Secondly, the mulatto Pulohs must have been mulattoes many centuries ago, and they have intermarried among themselves, "hybrids with hybrids," all the time ; otherwise many of them could not still remain as bright-colored as quadroons or even brighter. But the Pulohs are physically and mentally a fine race. They show no symptoms of dying out.

3. The third of the classes above mentioned, are black people with European features. Some of them have a fine intelligent Grecian cast of countenance. Others present every degree of approximation to the typical negro. At Ilorrin I saw a few robust, handsome, heavily bearded men, who are called "Bature Dudu," black white men. They differ from the Grecian-faced men just mentioned, in being every way more manly in appearance, and they bear the reputation of being more learned than any other men in the country. One of them, a most noble looking man, "black but comely," is the chief alufá or doctor of divinity in Ilorrin. The home of these men appears to have been in Eastern Yóruba from time immemorial, though they are evident-

ly and reputedly another race. I suppose that all classes of these black men with European features are the
descendants of mulattoes and negroes, retaining the
features of the former and the skin of the latter. A
vast majority of negroes both in Guinea and Sudan belong to this class. In Sudan the mulatto people are
numerous, amounting, I suppose, to ten or twenty millions. The true or typical negroes are the least numerous class of the three, even if we include all the
most degraded nations of Guinea.

Whether it be the result of climate, or diet, or other
causes, the Africans of all classes are a healthy and
hardy race. The boys are unusually active. In the
towns of Yóruba I have frequently seen groups of boys
throwing summersets in the streets for their own amusement. The Nufe people are reputed to be the swiftest
runners in Sudan, and they are the only tribe who understand boxing. It is said that one Nufe will whip
four or five Yórubas if they do not close in and throw
him.

It is not easy, if possible, to ascertain a people's mental powers before they have been developed by exercise
and exhibited in the various pursuits of civilized life.
The Yórubas, Pulohs, etc., frequently have a good brain
and temperament, in some cases decidedly fine. Very
often the reflective faculties are equal to the perceptive,
or superior. The Yóruba language is remarkably rich
in abstract terms. To give one example : the various
relations commonly expressed by prepositions, have
names in Yóruba, as *abbe*, the beneath, *oke*, the above,
inu, the within, etc., whence the prepositions *labbe*, under,
loke, above, *ninu*, in. Very often there is both an abstract

and a concrete noun from the same verbal root. The existence and constant use of terms for the expression of thought, are certainly good evidence that the people think. The Yóruba language affords all the terms necessary for a full and clear declaration of the Gospel, as for instance a word for God, angel, heaven, hell, sin, guilt, atonement, mediation, repentance, faith, pardon, justification, sanctification, both objective and subjective, a distinct word for each, adoption, salvation, perdition, etc. The reason why they pay such deep attention to preaching as constantly reported by the missionaries, is that they understand what the Gospel teaches.

There are various other indications of the fact that the people are not deficient in intellect. One of these we find in their government and laws. The highest excellence of the best governments among white people consists in constitutional checks or limits to prevent abuses of power. Strange as it may seem, the Central Africans had studied out this balance of power and reduced it to practice, long before our fathers settled in America—before the barons of England had extorted the great charter from King John. The pure and correct theism, which rises far above the superstitions of the people, is another proof of their mental soundness. Even their idolatry, while it is substantially the same as that of Assyria, Greece and Rome, has not been loaded with such puerile fancies and debasing dogmas as were common at Corinth and Athens. These points will be further noticed under the heads of government and religion.

No one can live among the people and speak their language without being convinced that they have a good share of sober common sense. They are shrewd observers of character and motives. I have frequently been surprised at the readiness with which they form correct notions of the missionaries who go into their country. All of us would be surprised if we knew what they think and say of us.

In other respects, they are greatly deficient, and sometimes even stupid. Notwithstanding the various hereditary little arts which they practice, I am ready to doubt whether they have made a single invention in a thousand years. They have never thought of a plough, though their manner of cultivating the soil requires it to be well and deeply stirred. Sometimes their farms are ten or even twenty miles from town, yet they bring in their crops in baskets on their heads, and have never dreamed of such a thing as a cart, or even a slide or sledge. I have frequently seen cripples, but no one could invent a crutch. A pair which I had made for one of my boys, who was accidently crippled, filled them with astonishment Chairs, tables, bedsteads and the like were regarded with equal wonder.

They are almost as destitute of science as the Hottentots, having no weights or uniform measures, and in short, nothing pertaining to science of any kind. The Yórubas count days by fives, (from the five fingers ?) and have no names for days. The Pulohs, &c., count by sevens, and have a name for each day in the week. The Yórubas lay the ghosts of their dead seven days after death, which appears to be the only allusion to the seven days of the week with which they are acquainted. None of them can tell their age, but the Pulohs and others often can. The Yóruba astronomy extends to one name, the *dogstar*, which with them is Venus. They measure months by the moon, and years from one rainy season to another. Their *new year*, however, determined by their religious festivals, occurs in September or October. They believe the earth to be a circle, with the land in the centre, bounded by water. The Yórubas are exceedingly expert in multiplying and adding by the head, which arises from their constant use of cowries, in buying and selling. They and the negroes generally, display no talent for music, their best tunes being similar to the "corn songs" of the negroes in America. Their instruments are chiefly drums of various patterns, which they beat in excellent measure, so far as regards time. The Pulohs, on the contrary, compose and sing fine bold airs, which would be counted beautiful in any country. I was surprised to find the Puloh music totally different from the sad melodies of the Arabs. But in fact they are not Arabic, in any thing. Their guitar, or properly *banjo*, is a rude and primitive sweet-toned instrument of three strings, with the bass on the wrong side.

None of the negro nations and in fact, none of the white tribes in Africa, as the Azbens, Tuarics, Tibboos, Moors, &c., have ever invented an alphabet for their language, if we except the late syllabic alphabet of the Vies. The Moors now speak and write the Arabic language. The remaining tribes, white and black, write Arabic if they write at all. There are thousands of Pulohs, Mandingoes, and other negroes, who write Arabic, and their penmanship is often exceedingly beautiful, surpassing any printed page, but they never write their own language in Arabic characters. Indeed they could not do it, for the Arabic language has properly no letters out consonants, and the African languages abound in vowels.

Some of the Central Africans compose spirited verses, on war, love, natural phenomena, &c. The Hausas have a song beginning with, "Wheat grows on the hill, God gives it water," which strikes me as true poetry. The Yórubas scarcely attempt poetry, though they have their little songs. When I was refused admittance into Awaye, the women were soon singing about it, the first line of their song being, "The white man camped at the root of the tree." Some of the native stories display a good degree of fancy, often wild enough, as in the story of a murdered girl, who was changed into a mushroom, and another of a haughty belle, who was metamorphosed into the bush called *bujë*. They deal much in proverbs, and those of the Yórubas are among the most remarkable proverbs in the world.

When a man who is really acquainted with the Yóruba people reviews their moral character, he finds much to admire and much to condemn—strong virtues and strong vices. A transient visitor or a careless observer, might make them out an exceedingly good or an exceedingly bad people, by seizing on one half of the facts and overlooking the other. Among their good traits, we may notice first, their natural kindness and gentleness. There is little cruelty and little bloodshed among themselves. They are uniformly polite and courteous, fond of friendship, visits and conversation, and strongly attached to their country, countrymen and kindred. With very few exceptional variations, they have treated all the missionaries with the greatest kindness. Even in those cases where they shut their gates against me, and in some cases where they feared me as a spy, or as an evil genius, they never showed any disposition to treat me with violence. I feel as safe in person and property at Ijaye or Ogbomoshaw, as in Georgia. They are not treacherous; I never doubt their word when they have made a promise. They are not revengeful or unforgiving, but can fight and forget the quarrel almost as readily as children. They have several words for *honor*, and more proverbs against ingratitude than perhaps any other people.

The Yórubas and other tribes of Central Africa, are far from being a lazy people. In the farming season, they are always up and off to their work by daylight Their daily markets are well stocked with all the necessaries of life. Weavers and some others who work within doors, are seldom idle, but farmers usually rest in the heat of the day. In the dry season, when there is little farm work, we can hire any number of people to labor for reduced wages, and we can employ them to carry our loads from station to station on very moderate terms. It is true, that there are many days in the year when the people are comparatively idle, but this is not from unwillingness to labor. If they had a profitable market there would be more demand for labor, and more would be performed, but we can not expect men who have plenty of food, &c., to perform extra labor, in producing extra supplies which they can neither use nor sell. If direct trade were opened with Sudan, every man in the whole country would soon be in motion trying to make something which he could sell, to enable him to buy something. Of this fact I have been more and more convinced the longer I have remained in the country. Then with an increased demand for labor, I would advocate the introduction of ploughs and other improvements. But now, when there is no market for produce, I would strenuously oppose every labor saving expedient, because a diminution of labor would increase idleness and its consequences, vice and degradation.

Another virtue of these people is a reverential regard for their parents and rulers, for the aged, and in fact, for all superiors. This makes them easily governed and disposes them to receive instruction. They are naturally simple hearted, teachable and free from high estimates of themselves.

Finally, there is generally a strong current of public opinion against vice, and in favor of executing the laws. Hence they are remarkably free from adultery and theft, which we might presuppose would be very common. Although the women do not marry till they are eighteen or twenty years of age, I have never known a case of an illegitimate child. The law and public opinion are too strongly set in favor of virtue to allow the frequent occurrence of such things in Central Africa. It is very remarkable, that although there have been thousands of loads of goods and cowries for the missionaries, delivered to native carriers, to be conveyed from the coast to Abbeokuta, Ijaye, Ibadan, and other places, within the last ten years, yet scarcely one load has been robbed or stolen.

But now we turn to the other side of the question. The great defect of negroes is want of conscience. They believe in God, but have little notion of that justice which is revealed as a flaming fire against all manner of sin and transgression. They fear the penalties inflict-

ed on offenders by the laws of their country ; they can
not expose their good name to the withering condemna-
tion of public opinion, but I have seldom seen among
them that high and conscientious regard for honor which
we regard as indispensable to an honorable character.
This want of conscience is manifest in all the ten thousand details of every-day life, and generally impairs the
Christian character of converts.

They are almost, and in some things, altogether destitute of modesty. I have spoken of nude figures in
another place. Although females wear three wrappers,
two from the waist downward, and one over the shoulders, which might conceal the whole body, the upper one
is thrown off at will, without exciting either thought or
attention. As before said, the negro is incapable of
feeling disgust. Immodesty, however, visibly decreases
as we recede from the coast, till we arrive at Ilorrin,
where the Pulohs exhibit some degree of refined feeling.
Puloh women wear the upper wrapper.

I am not sure that the negroes are more covetous than
other people, though they are less careful to hide the
love of dishonest gain. If they swindle and lie, there are
thousands in our own country who are guilty of the same
practices. If fair dealing is one of the last things learned by the converts in the missions, honesty, both in
every day life, and in religious controversies, is one of
the rarer virtues among too many members and teachers
in the churches of civilized countries. It has not been
many years since a noble bishop declared that " he knew
nothing of moral obligation," in the use of certain revenues of the church. Custom was his authority for transactions which appeared to some members of Parliament

and to many Englishmen like swindling, and custom is the plea of the African when he cheats you in buying and selling. He will not steal, for that is disreputable, but he will defraud to the utmost of his power, and he will beg (from a white man) till you despise him, for these things are not branded with infamy by the public opinion of his country.

The numerous proverbs of the Yórubas are generally brief, clear and pointed, and sometimes highly poetical. Bishop Vidal, following out a hint of Mr. Venn, has discovered that they exhibit several kinds of parallelism, whence he thinks they are entitled to be considered true poetry.* We must not suppose, however, that this parallelism was studied or purposely employed by the makers of the Yóruba proverbs. I presume that even David had no definite idea of the parallelisms which have been discovered in his psalms. They arose spontaneously, like figures of speech, in obedience to the laws of the human mind. Shall we suppose that Paul deliberately framed parallelisms in certain passages of his epistles? or that the illiterate Christian in our own country is aware of it, when he utters them in his impassioned prayers? The various poetical features of the Yóruba proverbs are as free from art as the warblings of a bird.

Some of these proverbs, or proverbial sayings, are merely a play upon words, others are sprightly descriptions of natural phenomena and the like, but in general they are designed to convey moral truth. They constitute, in fact, the moral science of the nation, and being

---

* Introduction to Crowther's Grammar.

widely known and often quoted, have doubtless had a powerful effect in forming and preserving the character of the people.

I subjoin a number of these proverbs, as examples :—

" He that injures another injures himself."

" He who forgives is victor in the dispute."

" We should not treat others with contempt."

" An inmate that can not be tamed."   Said of fire.

" The sword does not know the head of the blacksmith "—(who made it.)

" When the day dawns the trader takes his goods,
The spinner takes her distaff, the soldier takes his shield,
The weaver bends over his loom,
The farmer awakes, he and his hoe,
The hunter awakes, with his quiver and bow."*

" Ojo pa, bàtta, bátta; bàtta, bátta,
Lori apatta, lode ajalubatta,
Báta li iggi, bàtta li awoh."

TRANSLATION.

" The rain beats patter, patter, patter, patter,
On the rock in the drummer's yard,
The drum is wood, the shoe is hide."

This, and various other proverbial sayings of the same nature, are a play upon words, not easily repeated with rapidity without a mistake.   I give another specimen:

" Ogidigbó pari ilu gbogbó,
Bi owe li alu ogidigbó,
Enni ti o ye ni ijó :
    Jbó, Ajagbó, gbó,
Obba gbó ; ki emi k, ó si gbó."

---

* This translation is literal.   In many cases a literal translation is impossible, owing to the great brevity with which thoughts may be expressed in the Yóruba language.

"The ogidigbó surpasses all drums,
The sound of the ogidigbó has a meaning,
Whoever understands it will dance:
 Grow old, Ajagbó, grow old.
O! king, grow old; may I also grow old."

Ajagbó was a king of Yóruba, who lived to a great age, and waged many successful wars.

Crowther's vocabulary contains many proverbs, which may depended on as genuine, as the author is a native. I will select a number at random, and translate them as literally as convenient.

" A mischief-maker will not do to tell secrets to."

" Smacking the lips precedes weeping;
 Mortification follows a difficulty.
 If the whole assembly of the town convene.
 They find no sacrifice to make against sorrow."

"The marsh (abata) stands aloof, as if it were not akin to the brook." Said of proud people. The " abata" is a little wet place in a dry prairie.

" The stocks never embrace the legs, except of him that does evil."

" The thread follows the path of the needle; " i. e., people seldom act independently.

" Let it be as you please; we should never laugh at the invalid: perhaps the disease that afflicts him to-day may afflict you to-morrow.

" When the farmer ties up bundles of corn he rejoices; by bundles of corn come bundles of money."

" Patching makes a garment last well; he who neglects patching, will find himself bereaved of clothing." Applied to economy in general.

" There is no market in which the plump-breasted dove (i. e. the cowry) has not traded."

"As the message is sent, so deliver it; if you vary it, the sin is your own."

"Though many guests be absent, it is the cheerful man we miss."

"He who harasses one, teaches him strength."

"We awake and find our hands marked (with black stripes),
We do not know who marked them;
We awake and find an old debt,
We do not know who contracted it."

(Children are obliged to pay the debts of their deceased parents, and hence this proverb.)

"A needle falls from a leper's hand (which is mutilated),
It requires consideration (how to pick it up);
A difficulty comes on the land,
It requires meditation." (A literal translation.)

"The pig has wallowed in the mire,
He is seeking a clean person to rub against." Said of disgraced persons who wish to keep good company.

"Open the cask of rum, open the cask of powder (if yours);
The carrier opens the cask." The fidelity of Yóruba carriers in this respect is almost incredible.

"A strong man without economy is the father of laziness."

"Help to the end, is the help we must give to a lazy man."

"A bribe puts the judge's eyes out, for a bribe never speaks the truth."

"If clothes remain long in the bog they rot;" i. e., do not neglect your business.

"One lock does not know the inside of another;" i. e. we do not know people's hearts.

"If we draw water and spill it, if the calabash is not broken, we can draw more." A man can repair his losses.

"The squash saves them (from starvation). They cut it for a water gourd (after it grows hard)." Said of ungrateful people.

"We find guests like the lower jaw, if you die in the morning it falls off in the evening."

"I know it perfectly prevents the wasp from learning to make honey."

"A stubborn man gets into trouble, a pliable man is imposed on."

"Every part of the butterfly praises God (by its beauty), and yet how frail it is!"

"If thirst would kill the lizard to-day or to-morrow, there will be rain."

"A dog with a man behind him will kill a baboon."

"Jerk it! shake it! who shakes a tree shakes himself."

"There is noise in the grave (made by the diggers); the vaulted tomb frightens old men."

"The partridge (seeing a cloth snare) cried, Why did the farmer bring his cloth here? The farmer replied, How could I come to the farm without my cloth (or wrapper)?"

"I am starving! cried the rabbit in the field; I am a spendthrift! cried the partridge on the corn stack."

"A witch, child of envy; she kills, but can't inherit."

"The loaf is the father of bread; he that eats loaf does not know there is a famine."

"A scorpion stings with his tail, a saucy servant with his eye."

"He fled from the sword and hid in the scabbard."

"The butcher never inquires what breed."

"The executioner never lets the sword come upon his own neck."

"Don't hang your troubles on my neck! was the quarrel between the warping-pin and the thread."

"The doer of a secret sin supposes it is him they are talking about."

"The whisperer looks suspiciously at the bush; the bush tells no tales. He that you speak to is the betrayer."

"He speaks of others' sins, and covers his own with a potsherd."

"Another's eye is not like our own; a faithful agent is hard to find.

"He who claps for a fool to dance is no better than a fool."

"A fool and an idiot met, and said they, We are friends."

"The man who is not thankful for a favor, will not be insulted if treated amiss."

"When a Mahometan is not hungry, he says, I never eat monkey."

"It may be long, but a lie will be detected."

"Ashes fly in the face of the thrower."

"As the yam-flour was once a green yam, so the slave was once a child in his father's house.

"Not keeping lip to lip brings trouble to the jaws."

"Special pleading makes a good cause."

"Ear, hear the other side."

"If the elephant may get angry so may the ant."

"A monkey having eaten to the full one day, he said, Come pull out my fore teeth."

"Anger does no one any good ; patience is the father of virtues. Anger draws arrows from the quiver; good words draw kola nuts from the bag." The kola, or goorah nut is eaten together as a mark of friendship.

The foregoing proverbs are merely specimens, selected almost at random, from a multitude of others. There is probably no sin, or virtue, or human relation which is not described and forbidden, or enforced, by some Yóruba proverb.

CHAPTER XXIV.

SOCIAL LIFE IN YORUBA.

TOWNS — WALLS — STREETS — MARKETS — HOUSES — DRESS — FOOD — AMUSEMENTS — DANCING — RELIGIOUS PROCESSIONS — SALUTATIONS — MARRIAGE — POLYGAMY — DIVORCE — INHERITANCE — WIDOWS — CHILDREN — BURIAL — GHOSTS — OCCUPATIONS OF THE PEOPLE — FARM-ING — TRAFFIC — ARTS — TOOLS — GLASS MANUFACTURE.

ALL the Africans in this region live in towns, and cultivate the surrounding country. Several of the Yóruba towns are surprisingly large and populous. The congregating of people into large cities modifies their character in various ways, and among the rest, by giv-ing their barbarism a sort of polish, which we should hardly expect to find in the depths of Africa. It also compels many people to go several miles to cultivate their farms, and greatly increases the labor of gathering in their crops, which of course are brought into the city for use. By this means they are made more industrious, and consequently more virtuous, or in other words, less addicted to vice, the offspring of idleness.

In consequence of frequent wars, all the towns, large and small, are surrounded by clay walls about five feet high, and sufficiently thick to be a good defence, in a country where they are happily destitute of cannon. A ditch three or four feet wide and several feet deep, runs around the town at the outer foot of the wall. At various convenient distances, the wall is perforated with gates eight or ten feet wide, which are closed at night with heavy shutters. On the inner side of the gate, there is usually a house which we must pass through in entering the town; and here reside the men who remain at the gate day and night, to guard the entrance and to take toll of caravans and other traders. The walls being made of mortar, which dries hard in the sun, endure for a long time with trifling annual repairs in the dry season. An African town, with its thousands of low broad grass-thatched houses, peeping above the wall and sweltering in the torrid sun, presents to the approaching traveler a unique appearance which he will not easily forget.

The streets of the best and largest cities are generally very narrow, crooked and intricate. You pass on with rough solid clay walls close by on each side, and the eaves of the low thatched roofs almost brushing you in the face, till at last, weary of monotony and filth, you turn about to retrace your steps, and discover that you are lost in a net work of interminable alleys. There is generally, however, a tolerably broad, though seldom straight street, running from each gate to the market-place, and these wide streets, as the market-place itself, are commonly shaded with beautiful wide spreading trees.

African towns have no public buildings, except shabby little temples and *oboni* houses, so rude in appearance as to attract no attention. Architecture, monuments, &c., are unknown. The house of the king differs from others only in size, and in high sharp gables called *kobbi*, which are weather-boarded with grass thatch.

The houses of governors and other nobles, are in the same unimposing style as those of the common people.

The most attractive object next to the curious old town itself—and it is always old—is the market. This is not a building, but a large area, shaded with trees, and surrounded and sometimes sprinkled over with little open sheds, consisting of a very low thatched roof surmounted on rude posts. Here the women sit and chat all day, from early morn till 9 o'clock at night, to sell their various merchandize. Some of the sheds, however, are occupied by barbers, who shave people's heads and faces, and by leather dressers, who make charms like Jewish phylacteries, and bridle reins, shoes, sandals, &c., and by dozens or scores of men who earn an honest living by dressing calabashes and ornamenting them with various neat engravings.

The principal marketing hour, and the proper time to see all the wonders, is in the evening. At half an hour before sunset, all sorts of people, men, women, girls, travelers lately arrived in the caravans, farmers from the fields, and artizans from their houses, are pouring in from all directions to buy and sell, and talk. At the distance of half a mile their united voices roar like the waves of the sea. The women, especially, always noisy, are then in their glory, bawling out salutations, cheapening and higgling, conversing, laughing, and sometimes quarreling, with a shrillness and compass of voice which indicates both their determination and their ability to make themselves heard. As the shades of evening deepen, if the weather allows the market to continue, and there is no moon, every woman lights her little lamp, and presently the market presents to the distant observer, the beautiful appearance of innumerable bright stars.

The commodities sold in market are too tedious to mention even if all could be remembered. Besides home productions there are frequently imported articles from the four quarters of the globe. Various kinds of meat, fowls, sheep, goats, dogs, rats, tortoises, eggs, fish, snails, yams, Indian corn, Guinea corn, sweet potatoes, sugar cane, ground peas onions, pepper, various vegetables, palm nuts, oil, tree butter, seeds, fruits, fire-wood, cotton in the seed, spun cotton, domestic cloth, imported cloth, as calico, shirting, velvets, etc., gunpowder, guns, flints, knives, swords, paper, raw silk, Turkey-red thread, beads, needles, ready made clothing, as trousers, breeches, caps, shirts without sleeves, baskets, brooms, and no one knows what all.

Every fifth day there is a " large market," when the few thousand people who attend daily are increased to a multitude, and the noise and glee are proportionately increased. The larger towns have small markets near to each gate for the sale of provisions; and some towns, as Ilorrin, are so large that there are several markets for the sale of general commodities. In the afternoon, when only a few hundred are sauntering about, and the traffic has not fully set in, we often go out and preach to the people under the trees, and here we meet with men from all parts of the country, who have come to remain in the town a few days or weeks to traffic.

All the houses in Yóruba, etc., are built of clay or mortar and covered with grass in the manner which I have described in chapter sixteen. In Nufe, as also in Futa as I have heard, they sometimes build of sun-dried bricks. But this plan is more expensive and not so good as the solid clay walls. People from the interior have informed me that the houses in Sokoto are built of mortar two stories high and covered with *canoes*, which they explained to be troughs open at each end. First a sufficient number of troughs are laid across the building side by side, with their mouths up, and then other similar ones are turned mouth down upon these, so as to break joints. Yóruba houses are only one story high, and that one is so low that the ceiling over head is only from six to eight feet above the floor. The rooms are from ten to fifteen feet long, and seven or eight wide, without windows, and having only one door, which is scarcely four feet in height. Of course, the room is very dark. This, however, is of little consequence since it is only used for storing—they have little to store—and for sleeping when the weather is too bad to sleep in the piazza or the yard. The house itself consists of ten, twenty, or may be fifty, of such rooms, so disposed as to enclose a quadrangular court or area which is open to the sky. The court is entered from the streets by a single large door or gate, and the little doors of the rooms open inward into a piazza which runs entirely around the court. The gate of the house is prudently furnished with charms or amulets, among which is sometimes seen the curved or horseshoe formed iron, and which are affirmed to have the power of defending the premises against the "ghaists, sprites, and divils," who used to give so much trouble to our own forefathers. The interior court is ornamented with sundry large earthen pots, which are the roosting places of the poultry, and bristled over with short stakes to which

the women tie their goats and sheep every evening.
Instead of chimneys, there are little fire places in the
piazza against the wall, where the women cook their
food in earthen pots.

The simple habits of the people require little furniture.
They sit and sleep on mats spread on the earthen floor
of their piazzas and rooms, and they eat with their
fingers from coarse earthen plates, every one, like the
brethren of Joseph, having his own mess to himself, or
if they are equal in rank, all dipping into the dish together. The women do not eat from the same dish with
the men. The furniture of the rooms consist of earthen
pots and grass bags to hold clothing, cowries and other
valuables, and perhaps you may see a gun and shot-
pouch, or more rarely those venerable weapons, the
sword and the bow.

The usual dress on the coast is a breech-cloth and a
wrapper. In the interior, both Mahometans and heathens dress in a very different manner. The men have
various garments, as long trowsers and short breeches,
of several styles, tunics, tobes, or large flowing gowns,
wrappers, palm-hats, cloth caps, turbans, and, if not
barefoot, sandals, shoes, or moccasins, with or without
soles, and boots. None of their garments are fastened
by buttons. The trowsers and breeches are secured
around the loins by a draw-string. Little boys sometimes wear nothing but an apron, but usually they are
clad in breeches and tunic, or breeches alone. The men,
except among the Mahometans, generally shave their
beards and heads. Women never wear frocks or tunics,
but are clad in three wrappers, two around the middle,
and one, often laid aside, thrown over the shoulders.

Their head-dress is a piece of cloth, or handkerchief. They never shave their heads, except as a mark of mourning for the loss of friends.

Most of the negroes, and especially those of the interior, are remarkably cleanly, often washing their clothes, and bathing or rather scrubbing their bodies with soap and water almost daily. Hence they seldom have the odor which is so disagreeable in the negroes of the Southern States. Both men and women are fond of ornaments, as rings on the fingers, toes, arms and ankles. The women wear beads on their necks and wrists, and girls, who often (in the low country) appear without clothing, wear them around their loins.

The usual articles of food are the flesh of goats, sheep, fowls, hogs and cows, and various roots and grains, as yams, sweet potatoes, tania, Indian corn, millet, or Guinea corn, cow peas, etc. They also eat rats and snails, and the meaner people feed on the flesh of horses which have died of disease. Fish are abundant in the large streams, and dried fish from the Ogun, Niger, and other rivers, are commonly sold in the markets.

Their manner of cooking is quite different from ours. They bake nothing, but all their food is boiled or fried in earthen pots. Various kinds of bread of corn and peas are fried in palm oil or tree-butter. Sometimes they cook Indian corn in whole grains, like our "big hominy," but the usual preparation of corn is the *ek-kaw*, described in another place. Meat is always cut fine to be cooked. Sometimes it is stewed, but it is usually made into palaver sauce, which the Yórubas call *obbeh*, by stewing up a small quantity of flesh or fish with a large proportion of vegetables, highly seasoned with onions and red pepper. Obbeh, with ekkaw or boiled yam, pounded or unpounded, is the customary diet of all classes, from the king to the slave. They take three meals a day, breakfast a little after sunrise, dinner about twelve, and supper after dark. No people are so much in the habit of eating in the streets, where women are always engaged in preparing all sorts of dishes for sale to passers by. Their usual drink is water. Tea and coffee are unknown, but hot ekkaw, diluted to the consistence of gruel, is much used as a morning beverage. The women make beautiful malt, and passably good beer, of Indian corn and millet. In many parts of the interior, palm-wine is very scarce and highly prized. Rum seldom finds its way into Yóruba, and never without being well diluted with water.

The Yórubas are eminently social in their feelings and habits, fond of visiting each other, of eating together, and of sitting together of evenings under shady trees, engaged in conversation, or in playing little games for amusement. One of their games is a sort of draughts, in which the men are not caught, but checked, and thus driven from the board, or rather from the field, for the board is marked out on the ground. The game of *ayo* or *wari* is played by throwing small balls or seeds into twelve holes, six in a row, in a board or block of wood. Gambling, it is said, is prohibited by law. The boys amuse themselves with a sort of hulgul, by whipping tops, and by wrestling and turning summersets. Young people often amuse themselves with riddles and by dancing to the sound of noisy drums. One of the favorite dances is called *babbika*. There gestures are never improper, and never graceful. It would seem that he who can throw his feet, hands, head and body about in the most awkward and grotesque manner is considered the best dancer.

All classes are very fond of religious festivals and processions, chiefly, I think, for the sake of amusement. The theatrical performances which Lander saw at Katunga, and misdescribes, were a religious ceremony. Some parts of their worship are funny and clownish enough. The Mahometan feast, which succeeds their thirty days' fast, is a great holiday, not only to them but to the heathens. They also have torchlight processions, which afford them no small amusement. Our own Christmas, and the saints' days of Catholic countries, celebrated with the firing of guns, gluttony, drunkerness and debauchery, are only remnants of European heathenism, and here, as in Africa, the beloved formalisms of unsanctified religion rise up among the strongest barriers against the conversion of men to the Gospel.

The Yórubas, Nufes, etc., like other orientals, are unreasonably ceremonious. To shake hands on meeting a friend is not enough. If equals, both often kneel, and inferiors frequently prostrate themselves flat on the ground before superiors. On entering a house, they leave their sandals at the door, if they wear any, but never uncover their heads as a mark of respect. When a visitor retires, he simply arises and says, "I am going," whereupon the host follows him to the door, and bids him farewell.

The Yórubans have a profusion of salutations. In the morning it is *O ji re?* "did you wake well?" and the person replies, "God be thanked." On taking leave at

night, they often say, "May you sleep well." When a
visitor retires, and frequently when you meet him in
the street you say *wo' leh*, "look at the ground," that is,
to prevent stumbling. "Be careful" is often a salutation on passing a person in the road. But the word
most used by every body, is *okú* or *akú*, properly *aikú*
"may you not die!" or more exactly "immortality."
When you visit a man who wishes to pay you particular
respect he will salute you *akú! akú!* perhaps twenty
times, and you must invariably answer, *O*, to each salutation. This word *O* expresses assent. If you say to
your servant, do so and so, he replies *O*, and if you
perform any little incidental act of politeness, as picking
up a thing that has dropped for a person, he may say *O*,
instead of "thank you." The word *akú* is compounded
with many others, so as to form an appropriate salutation for every situation in life. When they meet a man
traveling, they often say *akúrin*, because *rin* means to
walk or travel. So we have *akúale*, good evening,
akúoro, good morning, *akúassan*, good day, *akúle*, to one
in a house, *akú joko*, to one sitting down, *akúshe*, to one
at work, and so on, to a hundred examples. To all
these you reply *O*, and if you make no reply, it is considered a gross insult.

Courtship is generally carried on by means of female
relatives, and either sex has a right to make a proposition. Very often, however, courtship is prevented by
early betrothment, either by contract between the parents of children, or between a man and the parents of
a little girl. In such cases, a dowry or price of some
forty dollars or more, is paid by the expected husband
to the mother of the girl. A betrothed woman is so

far a wife, thut her unfaithfulness would be adultery, yet conventional modesty forbids her to speak to her husband, or even to see him if it can be avoided. If she meets any of his previous wives in the street, she salutes them by falling on her knees. After all, it sometimes happens that she prefers some other man, and absolutely refuses to fulfil her engagement. Then she is either teased and worried into submission, or else the husband agrees to receive back her dowry and release her.

Before a couple are married, they must go separately to a priest of Ifa and make sacrifices and offer prayers. On the nuptial night, the bride is taken to the bridegroom's house, just after dark, by several virgins, and the friends of the parties are regaled with a feast. The virgins remain with the bride for several days, and sleep with her at night. After the days are fulfilled, they conduct her to the bridegroom's room. On the following morning, if his bride is worthy, he dismisses her attendants with presents, and sends some beautiful white cowries to her mother. If his bride is not worthy, he drives her attendants from the house with blows and abuses, and sends some dirty old cowries to her mother as an emblem of impurity.

Polygamy is universal in Africa. Kings, nobles and rich men, have large numbers of wives, and even the common people sometimes have two or three. No woman, pretty or ugly, rich or poor, is obliged to go unmarried. Men, of course, have the privilege of divorcing their wives, and the matter is all the easier, from the fact that every woman is a free dealer, who labors for herself and supports herself, and has no claim on her husband's property. If divorced without a cause, she takes up all that is her's and returns to her relatives and friends. If divorced for adultery, she or her family are obliged to refund the dowry to the husband. Further than this he has no claim on her property. Even during the continuance of the marriage relation, the woman is sole owner of her property and her earnings. She is not obliged to work for her husband, and has no claim on him for support, either for herself or her children. In this way the man escapes the burden of supporting his wives and children, except that he is obliged to furnish them with house room.

When a man dies, the eldest son inherits the house, and all the wives except his own mother. Incest is never allowed except in conformity to this law of inheritance—the reason of which appears to be, that the women may not be left widows and houseless. I am told that both son and wives are very well contented with the arrangement.

Yóruba women are not prolific, and entire barrenness is not uncommon. Though not a crime, it is regarded as a great disgrace to be without children. In their quarrels they may call each other fools, liars, thieves, or anything ; but "agan," *barren,* is a word which the most malignant and enraged person scarcely ever presumes to address to a childless woman.

Children are much beloved by both parents. I once asked a woman how much she would take for her child ? "What !" she exclaimed, pulling her child towards her with evident indignation, "sell you the child that I bore ? " From some cause the mortality of children appears to be greater in Yóruba than at home. One reason may be that they are so much exposed to the sun, slung, as they are, on the mother's back in a cloth. Such exposure would certainly kill most white children. People who die at home, are generally buried in the piazza of the house. Just before a respectable man is interred, the corpse is carried about the town on a litter, with discharges of guns, which collect a crowd of people. The bodies of infants are sometimes thrown away behind the wall, because it is thought they died through the influence of an evil spirit. The clothing and implements of hunters and warriors are thrown out by the side of the road, not far from the gate, to prevent their ghost from entering the town and disturbing the people. Even the ghosts of quiet citizens have to be laid on the seventh day after death. For this purpose, the friends of the deceased go out at the gate of the city, a little after dark, and call the dead man's name three times, telling him that he is now done with the world, and must not come back to haunt them. Women who have lost their husbands, howl and lament together at day break, for several days after the burial. When the days of mourning are ended, they give a public entertainment. In other respects, the mourning of the people has nothing absurd or unusual.

Most of the Yórubas are farmers. Their only implement is the hoe, and they have no carts or wagons, but they cultivate the ground well, and raise abundant crops of everything needed in the country. The principal and most valued crops are Indian corn and yams. Next to these, are Guinea corn and cotton, which they spin and weave into cloth. The common crop of corn is from fifteen to twenty-five bushels to the acre, and it sells in the country from twenty to fifty or even seventy-five cents a bushel. Both upland and sea-island cotton are planted, but neither produces very well, owing to the extreme and constant heat of the climate. For the same reason, wheat, oats, &c., as also apples, peaches and the like, can not be raised. Among the other things commonly planted, we may enumerate cassava, sweet potatoes, tania, Lima beans, peas, ground peas of two kinds, bene or sesame, a kind of uneatable watermelon planted for the sake of its oily seeds, telfaria, onions, okra, and other vegetables. Turnips, radishes, &c., will not flourish.

Every man has his own farm, but there is no property in land. When a farm is abandoned, it becomes common property, that is, any one who chooses may plant it. The farms are not fenced, because there are few cattle, and these are kept near the town, and constantly watched by the servants of the owners. Sheep and goats are fed chiefly in the towns, and but few hogs are raised.

A good many men, and still more women, are engaged in traffic. Some are engaged in exchanging the commodities of the interior, chiefly ivory and carbonate of soda from the desert, for the productions and imports of the low country, as salt, tobacco, cotton cloth, beads, guns, &c., and others in trading from town to town, in the various productions of their own country. All these commodities being carried on peoples' heads, in loads of sixty or seventy pounds weight, give employment to great numbers of carriers. Two years ago, when the caravans passed between Ogbomoshaw and Ilorrin, every five days there were sometimes two or three thousand persons on the road at a time, and I calculated that one hundred yoke of oxen would be required to convey all their merchandize.

For the most part, men and women have their own occupations, and it is worthy of particular remark, that women never cultivate the soil as they do in Guinea. All the arts are in a rude state, yet they are sufficient to supply the wants of the people. The iron smelters furnish the iron, which the smiths manufacture into hoes, axes, knives, nails, &c. The carpenter, as he is called, splits trees into boards, and makes doors for the houses. The leather dresser prepares morocco leather from sheep and goat skins, and makes bridle reins, and a sort of shoes. The saddle maker exhibits his skill in saddles, which, like the bridle-bit used in the country, is almost identical with that made in Mexico. The women spin cotton and sell the thread to the weavers, who are men, and men are the tailors who make garments. The women again make earthen pots, cook, wash, dye with indigo, and buy and sell most of the provisions which pass through the market. Some of the men find good employment in the barber's profession, and a few are professed hunters and fishers. Every one is perfectly free to choose, follow, or change his occupation at pleasure.

The tools and implements used by the people, are generally contemptible. The axe is little more than two inches wide, and is always inserted into the helve, which is large and clumsy. The only tools of the carpenter are his little axe, an adze of the same character, and an iron spindle, to burn holes in his timber. The blacksmith has a stone for an anvil, and an iron cudgel for a hammer. His bellows is a couple of goat skins stretched over two wooden bowls, into which are inserted two air pipes which run into one. The weaver's loom, though constructed on precisely the same principle as ours, is so small that his cloth is only six inches wide, but he can weave forty yards a day.

So far as I could ascertain, the peculiar glass manufacture of Central Africa, is confined to three towns in Nufe, one of which is situated on the west of the Niger. The art is kept a profound secret. The porcelain-like appearance of the glass would indicate that the feldspar which abounds in the country, enters into its composition. The singular mineral described by Lander, was a conglomeration of melted African beads of different colors.

CHAPTER XXV.

RELIGION AND GOVERNMENT.

MONOTHEISM — IDOLATRY — MEDIATORS — SYMBOLS — SACRIFICES —
PRIESTS — THREE PRINCIPAL IDOLS — OBATALLA — SHANGO — IFA —
GOVERNMENT — WAR — CAPTIVES.

No MAN has ever believed in two gods, or that the
Jupiters and Astartes which he worshipped, were really
gods at all. To some they were merely personifications,
to others real persons, but all have looked beyond these
to THE GOD, the Unknown, the Cause and Preserver of
all things. Polytheism has no existence in Sudan, nor
yet in Guinea. The objects which they worship are
not regarded as God ; they are not even called gods,
but by other names to distinguish them from God. In
Yóruba many of the notions which the people entertain
of God are remarkably correct. They make him the
efficient, though not always the instrumental, Creator.
They have some notion of his justice and holiness, and
they talk much of his goodness, knowledge, power and
providence. " Who," said I to some heathens, " is like
God ? " and they replied, "There is none." They may
extol the power and defend the worship of their idols,
whom they regard as mighty beings, but they will not
compare the greatest idol to God.

Practical idolatry is no less natural to man than a belief in one God. The Israelites had felt an inward religious yearning for the idols of Egypt, before Aaron, with hearty good feelings, made the golden calf and exclaimed, "This is thy god, O Israel." For many ages the twelve tribes were never satisfied with the sole worship of Jehovah, the boundless, formless, incomprehensible I AM; though they knew, as the Egyptians and Canaanites knew, that their idols were not the very God. To this day the nations of Europe have not been converted from the idolatry of their ancestors. The Jews always called their idol worship the worship of Jehovah. So do the negroes of Africa, so do the Catholics ; and the Roman priest who invokes the saints is no less a heathen than the Jewish woman who made cakes to the queen of heaven.

Belief in one God is the result of *reason ;* the worship of idols arises from man's ineradicable *feeling* or sense of guilt and feebleness. The instincts of his soul compel him to seek a mediator, as a means of communication between himself and the infinite, invisible God. This is precisely the view which the negroes take of their idols. In Yóruba, the *órisha* (idol) is esteemed and called an *alaybawi,* intercessor, literally one who receives petitions from man and offers them to God. It is precisely the same as the Roman saints, who stand between God and the Catholic ; and the feelings which actuate the worshippers are radically identical with those which lead so many Protestants to believe that the prayers of a minister are more effectual than their own. Nothing but correct views of the mediation of Christ can correct this natural obliquity of the human heart. Could we convince the heathens that Jesus is a better mediator than their idols, they would be converted. But the difficulty of producing this conviction is illustrated by the fact that Catholics will cling to their saints, that Puseyites inwardly groan for a restoration of Catholicism, and that many Protestants make mediators, that is, idols, of their religious teachers. It is very difficult to bring the sense-bound, sin-defiled heart of man to apprehend Christ ; and still more difficult to prevent its apprehending some other refuge, when it can not rest in Christ as the sole and all-sufficient mediator.

The devil-worship of the Africans, of which we have heard so much, is nothing more nor less than the idolatry, or trust in false mediators, just mentioned. Their fetishism is precisely the same system of superstition which leads Mahometans and Catholics and many Protestants, to employ charms and amulets as a means of averting evil. The noble duke who fastened a horseshoe to the marble steps of his palace, believed in the power of the fetish as well as the negro king who hangs amulets and charms in his house to prevent the entrance of witches and devils. But the fetish is not *worshipped*, either in Europe or Africa. It is not a mediator, but a "medicine," as the Indians and Africans call it, which preserves the superstitious from spiritual ills, as drugs avert bodily maladies. The Guinea man who bows before idols, and trusts in the amulet called a fetish, is certainly very stupid, but he does nothing which is not imitated by half the people in Christendom.

The images made by the negroes are only symbols. No one supposes that they are endowed with spirit, intelligence or power. They are precisely analagous to the images, pictures, and crosses of the Catholics. It is surprising to me how Europeans, who have worshipped images and worn amulets all their lives, should so far have misunderstood and misrepresented the religion and superstition of the Africans.

There is one respect, however, in which the negro differs from the Catholic. The latter worships to escape the pains of purgatory or the perdition of hell. The former gives himself little trouble about the future. He believes in hell, or at least, has a notion of the place called by the Yórubas, *orrun-akpadi*, "the furnace-world," but he has no fears that he is in danger of being lost ; and hence, all his sacrifices and prayers, and religious hopes and fears, have reference to the good and evil things of this world. Both his idol and his fetish, like the white man's amulet, are wholly for the body.

The desire to offer sacrifices is instinctive and inseparable from the notion of mediation. The priest is the living representative of the two ideas, mediation and sacrifice. In Yóruba, every idol has its priests, who offer sacrifices of goats, sheep, hens, pigeons, &c. Sometimes, though very rarely, they sacrifice men, as the most valuable sacrifice that can be offered. No sacrifices are offered to God. Sometimes they pray to Him. They thank Him often for the blessings of life ; and they speak daily of His providence over the world ; but they never approach Him with gifts and offerings.

The idols of Yóruba amount to three or four hundred ; most of which are of little note. Some of them are spiritual creatures, superior to men, and different from angels ; others are ancient heroes, or heads of families. They are often symbolized by trees, rivers, and other natural objects, but the symbol is not the idol. Once, before I understood their doctrines, I objected to the stupid materialism of their idolatry. A young man stepped forward, and inquired : " Did you ever see God?" I replied : " No." " Neither can you see órisha," he continued, " but there is an órisha there." It is not usual, however, for the common people to distinguish so clearly between the idol and the symbol. Most of them confound the symbol with the thing symbolized.

When I asked an intelligent man : "How many great órishas are there ?" he replied : " Three." The greatest of these is *Obbatalla*, who is the reputed maker of the human body ; whence he is called *Alamohrere*, the owner of the good clay. After the body had been made, God himself imbued it with life, for this was more than Obbatalla could do

The Yórubas never attempt to reconcile their contradictory opinions and traditions. Notwithstanding all they say about the creative work of Obbatalla, they also affirm that God himself made heaven, and earth, and man. The name of the first man was *Okikishi* and *Obbalufoh*, and the name of his wife was *Iye*.* They came from heaven, and had many children on earth. The first sin was war. They have no tradition of the flood; but the ship, called in Yóruba *Okkoh* is one of

---

* These names are, at least, curious. *Okiki* means *"fame."* I suspect that *shi, si, isi* and *s*, at the end of words in many languages, are from *si*, to be, [Latin *esse*] and signify being, person. *Obbalufoh* means the king or lord of speech, because the first man was the first speaker. *Iye*, from *ye*, to live, signifies *life*, cf. Heb. *khavah*, (Eve) life, Arab. *Hawa ;* cf. Yóruba *wa*, to be, to be alive, to live

their sacred symbols, they know not why. The first settlement of Yóruba was at Ifeh; the next at Ikoso, a town lately destroyed; the third at Igboho, (Lander's Bohoo); the fourth at Awyaw (Eyeo or Katanga,) which was destroyed by the Pulohs soon after the visit of the Landers. By some, Obbatalla is made a descendant of the ancient Yóruba kings. The etymology of the word appears to be *obba ti nlá*, "the great king." He is often called *Orishanlá*, the great órisha, and *Orishapopo*, the órisha of the gate, because his temples, or houses, are sometimes placed just without the gate of the city, to which he acts as a guardian spirit. He is sometimes represented by images, as an armed male on horseback, and sometimes as a female suckling a child;* but, in fact, is an androgyne, representing the productive power of nature, the great father and mother of all things material. The reader will scarcely be surprised, then, when I inform him that the mysterious serpent-symbol, and the *partes genitales in coitu*, are sculptured on the temple doors of this idol. Sometimes there are additional symbols, as a leopard, a tortoise, and a fish. In one place only, I have seen a woman with one hand and one foot, (a half Obbatalla, the feminine principle of nature?) and long hair tied into a cue with a ball on the end. Who can believe that this long-haired goddess originated among the woolly-headed negroes?

The next great órisha is Shangó, the ".Jupiter Tonans" of the Yórubas. He is often called Jakuta, the stone-

---

* In this form, she is called *Iyangba*, "the receiving mother," and is reckoned the wife of Obbatalla, the horseman. Qr. *Ob-buddhanla* the great Buddh?

caster, and certain old stone hatchets, (leather dressers?)
like those found in America, are picked up in the fields
and venerated as thunder-bolts; or shall we say that
these stones, wherever found, were symbolical thunder-
bolts from the beginning? Shangó is the son of Or-
rungan (mid-day), and the grandson of Agunju* (the
desert), and a descendant of Okikishi, the first man.
His mother is Iyemojja, a river in Yóruba. His elder
brother is Dada (nature, from *da*, to create), who is one
of the Yóruba idols. His younger brother is the river
Ogun, which is the symbol of war and blacksmithing,
and bears the name of the warriors' and blacksmiths'
god. His wives are Awya (the Niger), and the rivers
Ossun and Obba. His friend, or associate, is Orishako,
the god of farms, whose symbol is an iron bar, by
means of which people are mesmerized to make them
strong and healthy.† His slave is Biri, darkness, and
his priest is Magba, the receiver. Notwithstanding his
high relations, Shangó was a mortal man, who was born
at Ifeh, and reigned at Ikoso, whence he was translated alive to heaven, and made immortal. He is a
hunter, fisher, and warrior. The gates of his palace are
of brass; the number of his horses 10,000. The righteous are favored of Shangó, but he kills the wicked with
thunderbolts, and sends them to hell.

The sun and moon are not worshipped in any part of
Yóruba, except at Ifeh, where there are said to be large

---

* I rather think that *Agunju* here means the empty expanse of the
sky.

† Want of time forbids me to describe the various religious ceremonies.

brazen images of these objects, and a brazen chain, which fell down from heaven. But there are traces of sun-worship in many parts of Africa. Oro, the executive god of the Egbás, and Purrah, the oppressor of nations, on the Mendi Coast, are of this nature, (cf. *Pharaoh, pur,* fire, *uro,* to burn, and many other cognate words in all parts of the world.)

The next and last órisha which I shall notice, is the great and universal honored *Ifa,* the revealer of secrets, and the guardian of marriage and child-birth. This god is consulted by means of sixteen palm nuts. The reason of this is not assigned, but sixteen persons founded Yóruba; the palm nut which they brought produced a tree with sixteen branches ; and there is said to be a palm tree with sixteen branches on Mt. Adó, which is the residence of the chief priest of Ifa. The worship of Ifa is a mystery into which none but men are initiated. Neither have I been able to collect much information in regard to the nature of the idol or the ceremonies of his worship. Hence I am not able to affirm what I suspect, that Ifa corresponds with the Restorer of other mythological systems. According to some traditions, it would seem that Obbalufoh, or Adam, was the founder of Ifa.

In addition to all their other idols, usually called devils by the Englishmen on the coast, the Yórubas worship Satan himself, under the name of *Eshu,* which appears to mean "the ejected" from *shu,* to cast out. He is not worshipped like the idols as a mediator, nor yet because they suppose he will hereafter attain to power and dominion; but simply as a malignant being whom they think it best to conciliate. His altar is a rough conglomerate stone of clay and pebbles, cemented with iron, upon which they pour oil, as if to mollify the devil's evil disposition.

The civil officers are the king at Awyaw, and his counselors, and the governors and their counselors, in the various towns. At present, the towns are nearly independent of the king, and manage their affairs very much in their own way. The military officers are generals, and others of various inferior ranks. Laws are made in each town by the chief and his counselors, but sometimes they call a public meeting of the people. Neither the king, nor any governor or chief in the country, is arbitrary or above law. The ruler can do nothing without the assent of his council, and the ruler and council together can not violate the ancient traditional laws of the country. Whatever despotic acts may be witnessed in Africa, they are all performed according to "the common law" of the land, the origin of which is lost in the immeasurable depths of antiquity.

The only tax of which I have heard, is the toll paid in cowries for merchandise which enters the town, and sometimes a small tax on corn, which is paid in kind to the gate keepers, as the farmers bring in their crops. Public labors, as the building of town walls, are performed by the people without remuneration.

Judicial proceedings are of two kinds: First, before the ruler of the town and his council, according to law and testimony; and Secondly, before the *oboni* lodge, a sort of Freemason institution, who are connected with the government on one hand, and with the religion of the country on the other. The *oboni* house has three courts, into the interior, or third of which, no uninitiated person may enter under penalty of death. When a person is initiated, he has to kneel down and drink a mixture of blood and water from a hole in the earth; but what else he is required to do I am not informed. The business of the *obonies* being transacted in secret, I have no knowledge of their method of trying cases when they sit as a court. They are feared by the mightiest men in the country.

Criminals are executed by beheading, or strangling with a rope. At Ilorrin, they break their necks with a mace or iron cudgel. The capital offences are murder, treason, and house burning; in some places, theft, robbery, and adultery. Minor offences are punished by fine and imprisonment, rarely by whipping.

The Dahomies and some other heathens, make war for the purpose of catching slaves. The Mahometans do so both for this purpose, and to convert the heathens. But in general, African wars arise as wars in other countries, about any great or little matter which the rulers can not settle by negotiation. A campaign is a grand spree full of noise and confusion, and is soon over. A single battle often terminates the war; but in some cases there are long sieges. The soldiers provide their own rations, by foraging in large or small companies, and receive no pay except what they can steal or rob during the expedition. At present, most of the people have inferior smooth-bored guns, which are sold to the Guinea negroes by European traders, and sent off to be sold again in the interior. Their powder, chiefly from Boston, is very coarse, and their rough iron balls are made by their own blacksmiths.

All prisoners taken in war are slaves; and if not redeemed by their countrymen, are set to work by the captors, or sold to dealers. The price varies from thirty to sixty dollars, according to age and quality. I have never known them cruelly treated in Yóruba. Home-born slaves are seldom sold to the slavers. At least *four fifths* of the people are free.

CHAPTER XXVI.

ON THE MEANS OF REGENERATING AFRICA.

SAVAGES MAY BE CONVERTED — THEY CAN NOT SUSTAIN THE GOSPEL —
THEY MUST BE CIVILIZED — THE DIVINE METHOD OF DEALING WITH
MAN — THE FORMER STATE OF AFRICA — ITS PRESENT STATE — WHAT
TYPE OF CIVILIZATION SUITS IT — THE DUTY OF MISSIONARIES — IM-
PORTANCE OF COMMERCE — COMMERCIAL RESOURCES OF CENTRAL AFRICA
— INDUSTRY OF THE PEOPLE — NAVIGATION OF THE NIGER.

The barbarous negro of Africa, and the enlightened
white man of America, are endowed with a common
human nature. Although in different degrees of development, they both have the same good and evil propensities, the same hopes and fears, the same instinctive
religious yearnings, and the same capabilities. It follows, then, that the Gospel is adapted to both. The
veriest savage on earth is not too unhuman to be capable of conversion. If à priori reasoning on this point
were not sufficient to convince us, the fact is manifest in
the success of missionaries among the Hottentots. No
Christian will deny that men may be converted without
civilization, or that whole communities of barbarians
might become at least nominally Christian, like the civilized nations of Europe and America.

But our designs and hopes in regard to Africa, are

not simply to bring as many individuals as possible to the knowledge of Christ. We desire to establish the Gospel in the hearts and minds and social life of the people, so that truth and righteousness may remain and flourish among them, without the instrumentality of foreign missionaries. This can not be done without civilization. To establish the Gospel among any people, they must have Bibles, and therefore must have the art to make them, or the money to buy them. They must read the Bible, and this implies instruction. They must have competent native pastors, and this implies several things which can not exist without a degree of civilization.

Suppose, now, that all the people of Africa were converted to-day, and left to-morrow to perpetuate their Christianity without foreign assistance. In a few generations they would sink to a level with the Christians of Abyssinia, as unconverted, as superstitious, and as vicious as the very heathens themselves. The great Roman apostacy was only the natural result of that superstition, and that ignorance of the Bible, which were inevitably connected with the social state of the people in the first ages of Christianity. While it is the glory of the Gospel that the weakest reasonable creature can perceive its essential truths sufficiently to be sanctified and saved, it is nevertheless true that the Gospel can not be divorced from the written word, as it must be among illiterate barbarians. To diffuse a good degree of mental culture among the people, though a secondary object, is really and necessarily one part of the missionary work in Africa; and he that expects to evangelize the country without civilization, will find, like Xavier in the East, and the Jesuits in South America, and the priests in Congo, that his labors will end in disappointment. It has, indeed, an appearance of simple energetic faith, to affirm that the Gospel alone is sufficient to evangelize the barbarous nations. So it had an appearance of great piety when the cynic saints of antiquity abjured society in order to spend their days in desert ravines, or mountain caves, or on the tops of pillars. But the experience and the sober sense of mankind, will always decide that true faith and true piety are inseparable from a due regard both to the body and the soul, and to the mental as well as the moral nature of man. The Gospel was never intended to feed and clothe us, or to instruct us in reading, writing and printing, or in grammar, history, geography, and other things necessary to a correct understanding of the Bible. Yet without food and clothing, and several branches of secular knowledge, the Bible and the Gospel can not exist in any country.

It is not the fact that the Gospel exists, nor yet the mere preaching of the Gospel, that converts the soul. In the parable of the sower, the good-ground hearer, the only one who is saved, is "he that heareth the word and understandeth it." Now in all countries, if the influence of friends, or the influence of false religion, if mental pride or mental barbarism, or any thing else, should seal up a man's heart and prevent his understanding the Gospel, that man will be lost. One of the great reasons why the Gospel has so little effect in barbarous countries, is found in the fact that the barbarism of the people seals up their hearts and prevents their understanding the necessity and fitness of Christ as the only Sacrifice, and the only Mediator by whom they must be saved. The savage may be converted if he can be brought to understand these truths. Yet we have always found, that comparatively very few can be brought to understand the Gospel, and the conversion of these partakes of the general imbecility of their barbarous souls. The duty of preparing the hearts of individuals, and, of course, of communities, as a discreet farmer prepares his soil by the removal of stones and thorns, is taught in the parable of the sower just mentioned. The preaching of the Word is one, and a chief, means of preparing the heart, but every bodily and mental advantage which enables a man to understand the Gospel, is an auxiliary. Since God is pleased to work by consistent means, it is doubtless owing in part to natural causes, that some whole families in our own country are religious, from generation to generation, while not a single member of other families has ever been known to be a Christian. In like manner it is owing in part to natural causes, that Christianity flourishes wherever it is planted in its purity, in civilized countries, while it either degenerates into contemptible superstition or becomes extinct among barbarous tribes.

We may learn a great practical lesson, by observing God's own method of proceeding. All his providences from Adam until now, have been ordered not only to secure the salvation of individual souls, but to prepare the minds of men for the establishment and perpetuation of the pure Gospel throughout the earth. It was not without a cause deeply laid in the nature of things, that the coming of Christ was delayed for four or five thousand years. This delay was necessary to the establishment of the Gospel, unless God should choose to dissolve the connection which he had established between the human intellect and affections, and the means which he had ordained to impress and govern the human race. To state the whole matter briefly, the promises of a Saviour to Adam and to Abraham; the patriarchal doctrines of sacrifices and mediation; the doctrines and rites of the Mosaic dispensation; the varied fortunes of the Israelites and Jews; the wide diffusion of the Greek language by the mad adventures of Alexander ; the wars and conquests of Rome, and in short, the history of the whole world, were only one harmonious scheme of divine providence moving irresistibly forward to make ready a people prepared for the Lord Jesus, when at last in " the fullness of time," he should make his appearance on earth. The preaching of John was a necessary precedent to the ministry of Christ, and his ministry laid the foundation of the great success which attended the preaching of the Apostles. But the work of preparation, consistently with the laws of the human mind, was not yet accomplished. Without abandoning the plan of divine government over man, the Gospel could not yet eradicate superstition and establish itself in its purity over the earth. The great Apostacy, the long conflict between the true Church and Antichrist ; the revival of letters and science; the great but still defective reformation of the sixteenth century; the extension of geographical knowledge ; the American revolution ; the recent going forth of the missionary spirit, and the labors which we are now performing, are all indispensable links in that chain of providence which is to fill the whole earth with the knowledge of God. Observe then that in every step of these providences, the Almighty and All-wise himself has proceeded in exact accordance with the whole nature of man, and let us learn that we too must proceed in the same manner, if we desire to be good ministers of Jesus Christ. Evangelization is our great first object, because the soul is more than the body; but evangelization involves civilization, both as cause and effect, because the body, the intellect, and the affections of man, are so inseparably united, as to act and react upon each other, both for good and for evil.

We return now and say, that if the twelve apostles had gone into tropical Africa, and labored there and there only, their success would have been limited, not only in regard to the conversion of souls, but especially in regard to the establishment and perpetuation of the Gospel; unless indeed God had been pleased to reverse his long-established plan of government, and to work such a change in human nature as would amount to an unmanning of man. For at that time, far more than at present, Africa was covered with her primeval forests which generate barbarism as naturally as the mangrove swamps on her sea coast generate malaria, and the removal of these forests, as already stated, was a condition of African civilization. As yet, also, Africa had not felt the influence of that mighty scheme of providence which had long been preparing the civilized world for the reception of Christ. Still further, she sustained no such relations to the rest of the world as united her to the great community of man, and would compel her to move with the progress of human society. But if the apostles could not have established the Gospel in Africa, any attempt of their successors during the first, mid dle and latter ages, would have been still less successful.

We have too often condemned the supineness of our predecessors in the missionary work, by our not remembering that the providential fullness of time had not yet come. The conversion of the world was then naturally and absolutely impossible. Our hated and persecuted predecessors "in the kingdom and patience of Jesus Christ," had their own appropriate toils and duties, and for the most part they performed them well. Our duties are different. To us Africa presents a new and hopeful aspect, one which she has never before presented since the foundation of the world. Her primeval forests are gone, and with them her savage state has perished forever. The new condition of the country has produced a new condition of the people. New wants, new hopes and new ideas are forcing her tribes upward in the scale of humanity. Almost the whole continent is agitated by the events of a transition state ; the eyes of the world are upon her; the hearts and the hands of the world are drawing her into the great confraternity of man; the heralds of Christ are there, pushing forward into the unknown depths of her interior nations ; and now it requires no prophet to declare the natural result of all these potent forces, " Ethiopia shall soon stretch forth her hands unto God."

What, then, shall Christians of this favored age attempt to do for Africa ? The same as we are now attempting. Give the people missionaries, give them Bibles, give them the power to perpetuate the Gospel amongst them, or, in one word—civilization. It is not wise, however, to commit the too common mistake of

supposing that our form of civilization is the exemplar
for the whole earth. It is not the best form for ourselves, and is not adapted to Africa at all. The climate
and the moral and mental constitution of the people
are unanimous in demanding an African civilization for
Africa, such as that which the people of the interior
have already originated, and which only needs to be
developed on its own basis, in conjunction with pure
Christianity. Too many persons seem to regard the
English language as a sort of second gospel to mankind,
and in some parts of Africa they have absolutely cursed
the people by means of English schools. Too many appear to think that African civilization ought to leap
into full grown existence, as if by miracle, and they are
not willing for the negroes to grow up into civilization,
as other people have done, by the natural and slow development of civilizing forces. Hence, they either deny
that the present gradual progress of the Africans will
ever elevate them to the estate of civilized men, or
else they become careless in their labors for Africa,
because they shall not live to see the final result. To
be the true friends of Africa, we must agree to labor
patiently, and almost unrequited. Every attempt to force
our full-grown civilization upon barbarians, serves only to
stupefy and paralyze them by exhibitions of skill which
they can neither understand nor imitate. By this means
they are not stimulated to action, but become discouraged.
The wise instructor of Africa is content to begin with the
elements of knowledge, both religious and secular, and
he continues his course by attempting a diffusion of such
principles of Christianity, science, art and social improvement as the people can appreciate and reduce to practice.

The missionary work, and the only duty of missionaries, as such, is the preaching of the Gospel, and the planting and training of churches. The duties of this single calling are sufficient to fill the hands of any laborer. After all, the missionary is a man, no less than a minister, and, as a man, he can not avoid feeling an interest in everything pertaining to the physical, mental, or moral improvement of mankind. He must not be a schoolmaster for the heathen, but, if he is wise, he will do all that he consistently can for the promotion of such schools as are adapted to the condition and wants of the people. He can not instruct them in the arts of the blacksmith, the carpenter, the mason, &c., but he will desire them to have that degree of instruction in every art which is necessary to their present improvement. He may not turn merchant among them, but he will rejoice at the extension of commerce, as one of the great means of civilization. In like manner, missionary societies can not become the patrons and supporters of anything which is not directly a part of the missionaries' work ; but, if need be, they may render any kind of assistance to school teachers, mechanics, and traders, which may be consistent with the design for which missionary societies were created.

No one denies that schools and the industrial arts would be useful to Africa, and helpful to the establishment of the Gospel, but the greatest of all these secondary means for the extension of the Gospel, is commerce with Christian countries. Of course, I make no allusion to the slave trade, which is supported by the most demoralizing species of war, and causes the death of two or three persons, on an average, for every slave that is brought to the market. Like many other things in human history, the slave trade was a mixture of good and evil ; but the great cycle of human events has passed it by, never to return. Already "lawful commerce," as it is usually and significantly called, has taken fast hold on most of the old stations of the slave trade, as at the mouth of the Gambia, at Sierra Leone, in Liberia, on the Gold Coast, and lastly, at Lagos. This is the traffic which we regard as a powerful auxiliary of the Gospel, and upon the steady advances of which we look as an evidence that our missionary labors shall not cease till Africa has been added to the civilized world. That the men who are engaged in this work feel intense interest in the progress of present events is not to be wondered at, when we consider that as preachers, school teachers, mechanics and traders, they are creating nations and founding empires. Never before have the benevolence, the wisdom, the wealth and the might of men been devoted and pledged to such a work as this, of which Africa is now the object. However much it may be delayed, the ultimate success of the undertaking is no less certain than the principles of nature upon which it is founded.

While we remember that African commerce is yet feeble, we are not discouraged in our hopes that it is destined to become a powerful instrumentality in the civilization and conversion of the continent. The commercial importance of the country is beginning to be recognized. The scores of French and English vessels constantly engaged in navigating the Senegal and Gambia rivers, and the rapidly-increasing traffic of several nations with the Western Coast generally, are proof of this. But the present trade is probably not a tithe of what it might be, even with the present population. The single article of palm oil—to say nothing of all sorts of tropical productions—has no assignable limit, as regards either the production or the consumption. The little palm nut is the greatest enemy that has ever reared its head against the slave trade; for civilized nations will soon find negroes too valuable in Africa to suffer their exportation to other countries. Hereafter every war in Western Africa will be an injury to Europe and America, and we rejoice to see so strong an advocate of peace arising to power and immortality on the shores of that hitherto wretched country. We thank God for that emblem of peace, the palm tree.

But the internal wealth of all countries, and especially of so broad and rich a continent as Africa, must always be vastly superior to that of the Coast. In every thing except rice and palm oil, Sudan has the advantage of Guinea. The air is more salubrious; at present, the people are more civilized, and are superior as to race; and the soil and climate are better adapted to most of the tropical productions which are accounted so valuable to other hot countries. Here at the present moment, are millions of people, every one of whom may have something to sell, and desires something to buy. The caravan trade across a thousand miles of desert, is computed at several millions of pounds sterling, even now, although it is expensive and unnatural, owing to the character and length of the road. The negro caravans of the interior, which travel from one market to another, often consist of hundreds, and sometimes of two or three thousand people, laden with home productions, with salt and carbonate of soda from the desert, and with numerous articles from civilized countries, which by some long and expensive route have reached the heart of the continent. From what I saw and learned at Ilorrin, I suppose the weekly arrival of such traders at that town can not be much, if any, less than ten thousand, and the same is going on in every part of the country. There is not a town without its market, and not a market without some European goods, and a desire for more ; and yet all this vast, populous and productive region, is cut off from all direct and convenient intercourse with the civilized world. How much, and how many valuable commodities are there wasted annually for want of a market, or else not produced, or but little produced, we are not able to say. The present trade of the country is of course almost nothing to what it might be.

So far as the productions of Central Africa depend on the willingness of the people to labor, there is no doubt as to their abundance. The industry of these people is one of the most remarkable and unexpected facts which have been brought to light by our acquaintance with the country. It is a land without vagrants. The black smith, the weaver, the farmer, in short every body, male and female, has something to do, and their markets are always abundantly supplied with every home production for which there is a demand. No argument is needed to show how probable it is that such a people would labor still more, if stimulated by the demand of a good foreign market.

For what now, does the majestic Niger, the Mississippi of Africa, flow through the heart of Sudan, except

to form a great highway for a great traffic with foreign
countries ? But the civilized world is still unacquainted with the Niger. Strange, indeed, that the great and
enterprising commercial nations of the world, should
not know whether the Niger is or is not navigable for
steamers ! But this fact has arisen partly from our
mistakes in regard to the character of the country and
people, and partly from some mistakes which have been
made in attempts to explore the stream. The manner
in which several travelers have pushed through the
country, as if traveling against time and reason, has
brought more reproach on the climate of Africa than it
ever deserved. Travelers would be likely to lose their
lives in any country if they should hasten on, as did
Park, without shoes, or as the younger Park, with no
clothing but a calico wrapper, or as Clapperton and
others, exposed to sun and rain, wading streams, lying
on the wet ground, and too often endeavoring to counteract these imprudences by an imprudent use of brandy.

Mungo Park lost his life by the mistake of firing on the
kind-hearted people of Busa, who meant him no harm.
and thus throwing them into the mistake that his canoe
was the advance of the Fellatah army. Lander floated
down the river from Yauri to the sea, but forgot to observe whether there was any real impediment to navigation by steamers.

Laird and Oldfield, who reached Raba, were not provided with boats of sufficient power and lightness for
the service.

They lost many men, partly from imprudent exposure,
partly from the constant use of rum, and partly by purging, bleeding, and blistering the heads of men whose

cases required an opposite treatment. In the lower part of the river, they were troubled with sand bars, because they were not acquainted with the rules by which the eye may determine the course of the channel. Finally they made no money. This expedition discouraged the English for several years, during which time Captain Beecroft, late Consul at Fernando Po, ascended the river on his own account to a point some distance above Raba.

The recent expedition, (in 1854,) ascended the Benue to 11° east longitude, and returned at the end of six weeks without the loss of a single man. This result had been predicted by Mr. Hutchinson, (see his journal) provided the men would live prudently and make free use of quinine. The boat returned professedly for want of wood, but really, some were dissatisfied, and unfortunately, among the several personages on board, there was no one invested with authority to control the movements of the expedition. It still remains for England or some other power, to make a well-ordered, persevering effort to explore the Niger and its tributaries. The matter would be very easy to our own government.

Our present knowledge of the Niger is rather extensive than definite. The delta is sickly, but may be passed in a short time by a good steamer, after which. the climate is probably as good as in other tropical rivers The sand bars would give little trouble to an experienced river pilot. There are "rapids" at Busa, but the river is several hundred yards wide, and canoes are paddled up and down it daily. The broad river above Busa, is full of shoals and islands, but is navigable for canoes, and we can scarcely doubt that some of the wide channels are sufficiently deep for steamers. The proper season to enter the river would be about the end of April, so as to allow ample time for interview with chiefs, and to reach Busa in June. One error of the English explorers has been too much haste to return, and another, too much desire to traffic. According to Caille, who descended in a canoe, the river above Timbuctu is broad and deep, and it probably retains this character for several hundred miles. Below Yauri there is no danger to be apprehended from the natives. The Moors about Timbuctu, might or might not be hostile, but it is most probable that they would receive the explorers with friendship. Prudence would suggest that the steamer or steamers should be adequately provided with means of defence.

One serious mistake has been committed by commercial adventurers on the Niger. They have expected, very wrongly, that if the country were rich they should find abundance of valuable commodities, ready to be purchased, and brought aboard the steamers. Because they have not found this, they have been discouraged. Even McGregor Laird, so lately as last year, complains that the expedition up the Benue was not remunerative. How could he expect that any first or second expedition of this kind could be very profitable ? I presume he did not expect it ; but his remark was made to induce the British government to relieve him of the expense of another expedition ; whereas they ought to have taken the affair into their own hands at first, and have put the expedition in command of some man who would have finished the work.

The navigation of the Niger is not a lottery, in which

men may draw a fortune, but a matter-of-fact work, in which they may earn it. If trading houses were established at suitable points on the river, the people would soon come to buy and sell, first by hundreds, and then by thousands, and the productions of the country could be laid up ready for the steamers. Before many years, the centres of trade would remove from their present locations to the banks of the river ; the caravan trade across the desert and to the distant coast of Guinea would be broken up ; wagon roads would be opened ; new articles of export would come into notice, and the production of old ones would be increased ; and, at last, the traffic which would not pay the expenses of the first expedition would be an object of importance to the civilized world.

Possibly this commerce might need some protection, either by forts, with a few civilized negro soldiers, or by armed steamers, which is the method adopted by the French on the Senegal. We, who have lived for several years in the country, however, can scarcely believe that any protection would be needed, except good behavior. All our supplies and cowries, to the amount of several tons, have been brought into the interior to us by native carriers. We have lived in unlocked houses, and have traveled .far and wide through the country, and have ever felt as secure in our persons and property as if at home in America. For my own part, if I were a trader on the Niger, I should have no fears of the people.

I need not attempt to say how much the interests of Central African commerce might be favored by treaties with the kings and chiefs of the country. The extension of commerce is professedly an object of national importance ; and there is probably no uncivilized country which is more worthy of the attention of governments, than Sudan. Why should it be too much to hope that our own government may explore the Niger, and establish commercial relations with the adjacent nations ? By this measure, another wide field of enterprize would be thrown open to our citizens. The influence of civilization and Christianity would be brought to bear upon twenty or thirty millions of people, who are now prepared to receive them ; and there would arise a necessity for laborers in Sudan which would put a natural and effectual stop to the North African slave trade, and to the wars by which it is supported. Neither is it too much to say that the diffusion of civilization, prosperity, and happiness, is an appropriate work of Christian governments. Philanthropy, no less than good policy, is worthy of the attention of nations ; and especially when good policy and philanthropy are inseparably united, we must say that the preservation of a nation, as in Turkey, or the creation of nations, by the reciprocal benefits of commerce, as in Sudan, is legitimately a national work. In our own nation, raised up by Providence for the exposition and vindication of principles which are destined to govern the world, such a work would be particularly consistent. When we look back upon the long train of heaven-directed events which have conducted us to our present position—the ancient civilization of Assyria and Egypt, its transference to the republics of Greece and Rome, its victorious conflicts with the barbarous tribes of Central and Northern Europe, its union with the elements of true liberty in England, its toils, battles, and victories in the name of the living God, here in America, its reflection in purer form upon Europe, its late expansion to Africa, its constant advances to higher and higher purity—when we contemplate all this, who could be surprised if America, the exponent of civil and religious truth, should invade the dominions of sin and degradation, in new and surprising ways, with results never before realized or even expected?

The extension of civilized commerce to Central Africa, attended, as it would be, by the pure Gospel, could not fail to have a powerful effect on the minds and institutions of the people. The various branches of business called into existence by commerce would require education ; and the people would be anxious to obtain it. Then the philanthropic supporter of schools could teach the youth of the country, without standing exposed to the charge of performing the absurd labor of cramming their minds with learning for which they have no use, and consequently, no appreciation of. Soon, also, as now in Sierra Leone, the natives would sustain their own schools, esteeming education far more valuable than the time and money expended in obtaining it. As a consequence, missionaries would no longer preach to illiterate barbarians who will never be able to perpetuate the Gospel among them, but to men who can learn their duty by reading the Bible, and, of course, would be able to sustain their churches and pastors from generation to generation, like other Bible-reading people.

Another advantage of commerce would be an increase of industry, which, in all climates and states of society, is indispensable to the existence of virtue. No people will labor merely for the sake of toil. The Central

Africans at present, produce abundance of every thing necessary to their existence as barbarians, but there is no market to draw off surplus produce, if it existed, and the supply is very naturally limited by the extent of the demand. Under these circumstances, an increase of industry, and consequently of virtue and of civilization, is impossible. We might introduce ploughs, wagons, and other labor-saving appliances ; but without a greater demand for produce, these apparent steps toward civilization would be a curse instead of a blessing, because every hour saved from labor is only so much added to idleness, and consequently to immorality and degradation. But create a demand for all that they are able to produce, or in other words, give them commerce with the civilized world, and then the introduction of plows, wagons, &c., and the opening of roads, would be a work of real benevolence. The demands of the foreign market would stimulate industry ; the supplies brought into the country by foreign traffic, together with education and the Gospel, would create new wants and new aspirations, which would naturally and inevitably lead to the regeneration of society.

No matter by what means the people of different countries may be civilized, the principles upon which civilization is founded, are everywhere the same. Thus far in the history of man, there has been no civilization which has not been cemented and sustained in existence by a division of the people into higher, lower and middle classes. We may affirm, indeed, that this constant attendant upon human society—gradation of classes—is indispensable to civilization, in any form, however low or high. Take our own country and social state as an

example. The highest class, which with all its various
component parts is a unit, consists of our eminent scientific men, of our great merchants and mechanics (whose
ships, engines, etc., are at once the substance and
the expression of our civilization,) of our wealthy citizens, and political leaders and rulers, and in short
of all who are truly eminent in any department. The
middle class is composed of all whose attainments in
science, art, wealth, etc., are of secondary order and
importance, though some of this class approach near to
the maximum or first class. The lowest class consists
of the millions whose attainments, though not contemptible, are neither great in themselves nor controlling in their individual influence. This is the laboring
class, or the peasant class, which always has existed
and ever must exist in the very highest states of society,
so long as the earth and man retain their identity.
Now remove the highest class from our society, and the
eminence of our science, art, wealth, and skill in social
or political problems, would be gone. Enlightened
America would sink down to a state of bare civilization. If we proceed further, and remove the second
class, our country would be only half civilized, without
the power of self-government or self-defence. If we
still proceed to remove the upper strata of the lowest
class, the remainder would be barbarism, and this
brings us precisely to the state of society in Central
Africa. In those nations we find no class of eminent
men whose attainments may give unity, force and direction to society; no middle class who are prepared
by their attainments to receive impulses of knowledge,
wisdom and power from their superiors, and communi-

cate it to the millions of the common people. With the single exception of political chiefs, themselves barbarians, the whole society of Sudan rests and stagnates on a dead level, and the people remain poor, ignorant, and wretched, because they have no superiors. I need not say that a second and a third higher class must be added before we can regenerate African society ; but I plead for commerce in Sudan as one of the most powerful means for the creation of that wealth, science, and art, which are indispensable to civilization.

I will specify yet another advantage which commerce would bring to Sudan. Much as the people trade, they have no other currency than the cowry, of which two thousand shells, weighing from five to seven pounds, are worth only one dollar. Since the recent expansion of traffic in that country, the cowry currency is already becoming an almost intolerable burden, which operates as a powerful check to the prosperity of the people. Direct trade would soon necessitate a better currency, and this would give impetus to a new branch of industry, the exploration of the gold mines which extend over a vast tract of country, west of the Niger. The present merchants on the Slave Coast might easily introduce specie currency in the purchase of palm oil, and this would be a great benefit to the people ; but self-interest is one of the ruling forces of the world, and it seldom hesitates to do evil or to prevent good for its own gratification. So long as the merchants can sell several ship-loads of cowries a year, at a profit of fifty per cent., they will not agree to introduce a specie currency. But direct commerce with Sudan would soon outstrip the paltry supplies of shells from the Indies and

Zanzibar, and after lingering for a few generations as the medium of petty traffic, the cowries would disap pear.

A very little acquaintance with Africa is sufficient t) convince us that the conversion of the people to Christianity, involves a change of their whole social existence. Polygamy, interwoven as it is with the whole fabric of society, is one of the greatest difficulties with which the Gospel has to contend. Many persons perceive the excellency of the Christian religion, and they can easily give up their idols, as some have declared ; but to relinquish their wives, the number of whom is the measure of their respectability, is more than they have strength to do. The general extension of commerce would erect new standards of respectability, and thus remove one of the strongest props of polygamy. Another practical reason for the continuance of polygamy is found in the form of the African houses, a gloomy square of twenty, thirty, or fifty rooms, one or two of which is assigned to each of a man's wives. Should these be dismissed and sent away, their rooms must be given up to the rats and scorpions, and a large part of the great polygamist house would soon go to ruin. Besides this, there is no place to which the women could go, except to other houses of the same form. The effects of commerce would be a widening and straightening of streets for the passage of vehicles, and a remodeling of houses to suit the altered circumstances of the people. In the meantime, the abundance of employment and better wages would enable all the poor bachelors to take wives, even if the expenses of marriage should continue as at present, and all these circumstances would

favor the efforts of missionaries to break down polygamy. Finally, in the present state of society, every
wife is a free dealer, who has her own property and supports her own children. There is no family unity, and
little desire to provide for children. The increase of
wealth, knowledge, refinement of feeling, and respect
for family, which would result from commerce, would
operate with other causes to revolutionize the present
relations of husband and parents and children, and this
would remove another and almost the last support of
polygamy. In the end it would fall of itself, and the
influence of the Gospel would hasten its overthrow.
This is only one case of many in which commerce would
be a powerful auxiliary of the Gospel. We might extend our remarks to the government and all the social
relations of the people, but we forbear to argue further
on a point which is too manifest to be denied or under-
valued.

We may remark in conclusion, that although the
Gospel, science, art, commerce, treaties, and all the influences which can be brought to bear upon Africa can
not regenerate society in two or three generations, yet
we have no reason to be discouraged by the delay of
final success. No great moral or social revolution has
ever been suddenly brought into maturity. There is
always a gradual preparation of the public mind, re-
sulting from a gradual development of public necessity
which grows broader and deeper till the whole soul of
the community is strongly imbued with some prominent
idea, and then a trivial event may produce a sudden,
perhaps unexpected out-burst of humanity, in which
the work of ages appears to be done in a day. We

have mentioned the long and gradual preparation of
the human mind for the success of the Gospel under the
apostles. Our own great revolution was not begun in
1776. It was working strongly when the sturdy barons
surrounded King John and extorted the Great Charter
of England and the world's liberty. It brought the
chevaliers of the South and the pilgrims of New England to America. It was struggling in France long
before the earthquake of the French revolution, and
still unsatisfied because unsuccessful, it struggled on
in Europe till its next premature and abortive attempt
in 1848. Its work is not done. In America it succeeded
more fully than elsewhere, because as a work of providence it took God for its guide, and amounted, in fact,
to a great religious revolution, bursting the shackles of
state and setting the Church free. It failed in Europe
because it acted prematurely during the controlling
prevalence of infidelity and Romanism, which tore it
away from dependence on God. But whether in Europe
or America, it is still preparing for a future crisis, to
which all preceding events were only preparatory steps.

It has not struggled and grown stronger, and shaken
the nations for so many centuries, to end at last in
failure. Its motions are as irresistible as the course of
the planets, and its triumph is as certain as the rising
of the sun.

The extension of this great movement to Africa occurred in the mad irruption of the Saracens in the tenth
century. The character of its results was fixed by the
slave trade ; and it is now advancing to completion in
the events of African colonization, African missions and
African commerce. At present, its effects are small,

but Guinea, and even Sudan, feel its approaching change. The missionaries see it, and have expressed wonder that far off Nufe and Hausa are impressed by the mighty and mysterious influence which is moving the whole world. Verily, if God lives in the history of the past, he lives in the onward events of the present. As time advances, and the influence of the Gospel and civilization are brought more and more to bear upon Africa, the effects will deepen and deepen, till at last, in some critical outburst of social energy, a nation will be born in a day.

CHAPTER XXVII.

AN APPEAL FOR MISSIONARIES.

THE GREAT COMMISSION — OUR MISSIONS TO CENTRAL AFRICA — MEN NEED-
ED — WHO SHOULD GO — OUR PROPOSED LINE OF STATIONS — A WAGON
ROAD TO BE OPENED — LOVE TO THE SOULS OF MEN A MOTIVE — THE
HEATHENS NOT SAVED — THE APPOINTED TIME FOR THE CONVERSION OF
AFRICA — A WIDE FIELD OF LABOR — LIBERALITY OF THE CHURCHES.

In this concluding chapter, I propose to state some
of the considerations which should impel us to send a
large reinforcement of missionaries to Africa. The first
one is, that Africa is included in the terms of the great
commission which Christ gave to his apostles—"All
power is given unto me in heaven and in earth. Go ye,
therefore, and teach all nations, baptizing them in the
name of the Father, and of the Son, and of the Holy
Ghost ; teaching them to observe all things whatso-
ever I have commanded you ; and lo, I am with you
always, even unto the end of the world." Matt. xxviii.
18, 19, 20. Or as Mark records it—"Go ye into all the
world, and preach the Gospel to every creature. He
that believeth and is baptized shall be saved ; but he
that believeth not shall be damned." Mark xvi. 15, 16.
This commission is universal, extending to all the world,
and to every nation under heaven, Jews and Gentiles,
Asiatics, Europeans, Americans and Africans. It is
perpetual, including every creature, always to the end

of the world. It grants no permission to pass by any country, because the people are barbarous, but it makes us "a debtor both to the Greeks and to the Barbarians, both to the wise and to the unwise." Rom. i. 14. The wisdom of man may decide that the barbarous African tribes are incapable of receiving Christianity. The wisdom of God decides otherwise, for it predicates success on omnipotence : all power is given to Christ ; go, therefore, and he will be with you always, in all countries, and in all states of society ; sanctifying means to his own purposes, working supernaturally by his Spirit, and accomplishing all things which the preaching of the Gospel has been appointed to do.

Although it is more than eighteen hundred years since the commission was given, it is not yet ten years since the first missionaries were sent forth to Central Africa. The Mahometans had been there for centuries, and whole nations had received the religion of the false prophet, but the Christian stood aloof, and the name of Christ was, and yet is, unknown to the millions of Sudan. But now, at last, the Christians of England and America have been aroused from their long indifference, and there can be no doubt that every part of Central Africa will soon hear the Gospel. So far as the Baptists of the Southern States are concerned, we have made a good beginning. The first attempt to establish missions in Central Africa, and the first exploration of interior countries for this purpose, was committed to us by the Head of the Church. Our first station was founded in October, 1853, at Ijaye, which is about one hundred and twenty miles from Lagos, on the sea coast, if we travel by land, or one hundred and fifty miles if we ascend the Ogun river to Abbeokuta. In 1855, we planted a second station at Lagos, and a third at Ogbomoshaw, which is fifty miles further interior than Ijaye. The four missionaries, already in the country, have just been reinforced by three others. Another and still larger reinforcement is needed immediately. Not only private individuals, but the governors of cities and provinces, and the kings of countries, have repeatedly asked for missionaries to come and live with them ; and we have been obliged to inform them that our force is not yet sufficient to grant their request. When the people are crying, Come, and Christ in his word, is saying Go, we must not and dare not refuse.

About three months ago, speaking of these things in a public address, I said " we *must* have more missionaries ! " After the address, a brother remarked : " You say we must have missionaries ; but what if God has not called them ? " I replied, " God never does half-handed work. The desire of the people to hear the Gospel is not an accident ; this is the hand of the Lord. If God has stirred up the people of Africa to desire missionaries, He has doubtless provided the men who will go and preach to them. When the time had come for Israel to crown a king, he was not to be found ; but the old prophet declared, 'He hath hid himself among the stuff,' and there they found him. Many a valuable missionary is hid among the 'stuff,' but God will draw him out." We shall yet see that some who now are laying plans for earthly greatness, will spend their days as humble and successful missionaries. " Seekest thou great things for thyself ? Seek them not." (Jer. xlv. 5.) The time has come to do great things for God ; and if He has touched *your* heart, saying, " Son, go work to-day in my vineyard," beware how you refuse Him who speaketh from heaven. What will it matter a hundred years from to-day, whether you have risen to distinction among your countrymen or not ? for then you and they will all be dead—some in heaven and some in hell, and your ambition will have departed like the dew of the morning. And what would you answer, in the day of judgment, if Christ should ask you, " Why did you stifle your convictions and refuse to preach the Gospel ? " How small the greatness of earth will then appear to your spirit !

I am far from saying that it is the duty of every Christian to go forth as a missionary. Neither is it the duty of every missionary to preach in Central Africa. On this point, as on all others, men should exercise sound discretion. If a man desires to be a missionary, and finds the way open before him, let him go. If his heart glows with love to God and to man, and he can not become a missionary, let him induce others to go, and let him contribute liberally of his substance to the support of missions.

Some men who would do well in other fields, are not adapted to Africa. The physical and mental qualifications of a good African missionary, may be stated briefly, as follows : He should have a sound and vigorous body, without any disposition to chronic disease ; an active temperament, a buoyancy of constitution, which enables him to recover readily from sickness ; and finally, he should be lean and tough of fibre, because fleshiness and softness of muscles are not well adapted to a hot climate. Although a classical education is desirable, it is by no means indispensable. But no man should be a missionary in any country, unless he has a large share of practical common sense, industrious habits, a good knowledge of every day business, a thorough acquaintance with the Bible, and considerable experience in human nature. The Scriptures and history should be the constant study of every missionary, be- .cause by this means he will become more and more acquainted with the nature and destiny of man, and with the moral and social forces or motives which govern both individuals and nations.

In the preceding pages, I have repeatedly noticed the interesting fact, that the people of Sudan are more civilized and every way superior to those on the western coast. Dr. Livingston, who has just returned to England, from a long exploring tour, reports that the same is true on the south of the equator, and that the barbarous tribes will not permit their more civilized neighbors to visit the coast to traffic with Europeans. The heavily wooded countries of Western Africa, more- over, are far more unhealthy than the open and eleva- ted plains of the interior. These circumstances have materially modified our plan of missionary operations. We propose to run a line of stations from Lagos on the coast, directly to the remote interior, and there to spread abroad our operations on all sides, in a healthy country, among semi-civilized people, just as a miner runs his shaft directly down to the material for which he is seek- ing, and then extends his explorations on every side of the mine. It is most convenient to locate our stations at distances of fifty or sixty miles apart, so that mission- aries' supplies, and our mails, may conveniently proceed from one to another. The physical characteristics of Sudan, as distinguished from Guinea, or the low country, begin a short distance below Abbeokuta, but are not fully developed till we reach a point a few miles north of Awyaw. Our line of stations when completed, will probably include Lagos, Abbeokuta, Ijaye, Awyaw, and Ogbomoshaw. Hence we may properly spread abroad to Iwo, Idoko, Ofa, Ishakki, Igboho, Ikishi, Kaiama, &c. But still we propose to push forward to Sokoto and Kano. We have no doubts as to the willingness of the people to receive us. Nothing is wanting but men and money, and both of these God has given to our churches in abundance.

We can generally proceed from Lagos to Abbeokuta in canoes, with less expense and fatigue than by land ; and this is a happy circumstance, since the greater part of the way is through a forest country, where the opening of wagon roads would be very expensive. By straightening the road from Abbeokuta to Ijaye, the distance would not exceed fifty miles, almost wholly through the grass fields, where the trees are neither large nor numerous. Thence to Ogbomoshaw, by the most direct route through Awyaw, the distance would be about forty-five miles, thus making the whole road from the canoe landing below Abbeokuta, to Ogbomoshaw, about one hundred miles. We propose to open this road and to introduce vehicles as soon as possible This step would be attended with several advantages. 1. It would diminish the expense of transporting our supplies, which are now carried on people's heads along narrow and crooked paths. 2. Riding in a carriage would very much diminish the fatigue of traveling, and thus might save the lives of missionaries, who are now obliged to ride through the sun on ponies. 3. A road would give the people better facilities of trade with the coast, which would stimulate their industry and promote their civilization. I should be ashamed to live and die in the country without bursting away from the shackles of barbarism in which we, in common with the people, are now bound in this roadless country.

But the opening of our proposed road will incur expense. The natives having no carriages, and seeing no utility in a road, will not perform the labor of opening it without remuneration. The missionaries have commenced raising a road fund, by contributing from fifty to one hundred heads of cowries each, a head of cowries being nominally one dollar. All the profits of the present volume, which may accrue to the author, have been turned over to the same fund. There will still be a deficiency. The Foreign Mission Board can not appropriate Mission funds to open roads, but we hope that liberal friends, of enlarged views, will not permit our road to fail for want of money. Any contribution forwarded to the Treasurer of the Board, at Richmond, would soon reach its destination in Africa.

Having thus urged the command of the Saviour to go and preach, and having shown what we are attempting to do for Central Africa, I proceed to say that *love to the souls of men*, is another consideration which should induce our brethren to come over and help us. I will not insist on the pleasure with which every generous-hearted man contemplates the conversion of barbarous tribes into civilized and Christian nations. I will not enlarge on the millions of substantial wealth with which

Africa will annually repay her civilizers ; but I will look forward to the final home of the sanctified, into which no sin, and consequently no unpardoned sinner, can possibly enter. The heathens and the Mahometans of Africa, like the sinners of America, have no hope of heaven, and still more they have no means of attaining that faith which purifies the heart, (Acts xv. 9.) " Faith cometh by hearing, and hearing by the word of God," which they have never heard. No Christian can fail to rejoice when he hears that the heathens are being converted. No Christian would declare himself unwilling to do every thing in his power to send the Gospel into all the benighted regions of the earth But my present remarks are addressed principally to the man who feels an impulse of conscience to preach the Gospel in Central Africa, and yet stifles his convictions in consequence of some selfish consideration. It is very unlike the spirit of a Christian, to prefer our own bodily and earthly good to the spiritual and eternal good of our fellow men. Jesus Christ was a missionary, for the Father sent him to preach and to establish the Gospel on earth. Though richer than the richest, and greater than the greatest, he became poor for our sakes, and submitted to death among felons on the cross, that we might hear the Gospel. The servant is not above his master, nor the disciple above his Lord. None of us are too rich, or too honorable, or too wise, to be missionaries, and woe to that man who scorns the missionary work in consequence of exalted opinions of himself. Or, if attachment to worldly comfort and ease deters us, how easily God can turn our sweetest pleasures into gall, and strip us of our idols ! After all, the sacrifice of becoming a missionary is next to nothing, if the heart is full of love. There are comforts and peace and joy in Central Africa, also ; and I can testify that the greatest sacrifice I have made in this work, was leaving my field of labor for a short period when I departed for America. More than all this, the happiness attendant on the missionary work is an overflowing compensation for all its toils and troubles. The man who is hesitating over his duty to-day, may yet be the happy instrument of conversion to persons in Sudan, whose heads are already hoary with age, and who have approached thus near to the grave without hearing of a Saviour. He may meet with men in the judgment who will rise up and call him blessed, declaring in the face of an assembled world, "If you had consulted your own ease by remaining at home, we had never heard of Jesus our Redeemer."

If a man should decide on the future state of the heathen according to the impulses of his natural feelings, he would probably say, they are saved. But the natural feelings of man are enmity against God (Rom. viii. 7)—not against his mercy; but precisely against his justice, by which sinners are condemned. The heathen and ourselves are lost by nature, polluted, unfit for the society of heaven ; and he that believeth not will be condemned in the last day, not merely for rejecting the Saviour of whom they have heard, but because they have failed to hear and to attain that faith by which we may be justified. It is a great mistake to suppose that all the punishment of lost souls is retributive. Perdition follows from pollution as a natural and inevitable consequence. Philosophers have told us that the universe is governed by immutable laws ; but they have not generally troubled themselves with the most important of these laws—one which is eternal in its existence and consequences, viz. : That sin and misery are inseparable. Angels are happy because they are pure. Devils are miserable because they are wicked ; and if any sinner in America or Africa escapes from this sequential misery, he must first be purified by the atoning blood of Christ.

The Bible teaches that the heathen are lost. "They that have sinned without the law shall also perish without the law."—(Rom. ii. 12.) Paul declares that the Ephesians, before their conversion through faith " were children of wrath."—(Eph. ii. 3 ; cf. verse 8.) In short, if the heathens of Africa are saved without the Gospel we might be saved in the same manner ; and hence it would follow that men are not " saved through faith"— ͺEph. ii : 8,) and that the preaching of the Gospel is not the power of God unto salvation. I will not pretend to say what will be the final destiny of a virtuous heathen. Some heathens are practically better than others ; but if any of them are pure and good I have not seen them in Africa. It is affirmed that Socrates, the most admired of the ancient heathens, was guilty of crimes, which it would be a shame to mention. The Saviour declares that " he that believeth not shall be damned," and the Spirit of Christ which dwells in the hearts of Christians will not permit them to rest supinely in the expectation that the heathen will be saved without faith.

As a third consideration, to fill Central Africa with missionaries, I will glance at the grand scheme of providence which is now ripening for the conversion of

Africa and of the whole world. That scheme includes the Gospel and civilization, as a condition of its power and perpetuity. Noah and his sons were civilized men, otherwise they had never built a ship four hundred and fifty feet in length, and strong enough to ride out the storms of the deluge. While the tribes of mankind were growing more and more barbarous in consequence of their dispersion to wide and thinly-peopled countries, the God of providence preserved and developed the ancient civilization on the banks of the Euphrates and the Nile. At the proper time he transferred it to Greece and Rome, then to Middle and Northern Europe, and finally to America. At last in our own day, he is converging its rays upon the African continent.

While God was nourishing civilization as a blessing for the whole earth, he was engaged in preparing and bringing forward the infinitely greater blessing of the Gospel. The first promise of a Saviour to our fallen race, was made in Eden, "The seed of the woman shall bruise the serpent's head," and that seed was Jesus, the Christ. This promise was afterwards repeated and more fully explained to Abraham, to Moses and to the subsequent prophets. As the appointed time drew near, the extension of the Greek language, the enlargement of the Roman empire, and the wide dispersion of the Jews and the Jewish scriptures, prepared the way for the spread of the Gospel. When the great Roman Apostacy arose as a natural consequence from the remaining barbarism of the nations—when this corrupt religion, which Gibbon has mistaken for the Gospel, was extending, as he has shown with needless subtlety, by the inevitable force of natural circumstances, then

God raised up a succession of faithful witnesses, the Donatists, Novatianists, Paulicians and Waldenses, who preserved the body of truth for a future resurrection. The revival of letters, of commerce, and of the feeling of personal individuality in the affairs of religion and of government, resulted in Luther's great reformation, which prepared the way for one still greater and yet future. The revival of religion under Wesley and Whitfield, and the outburst of the missionary spirit under Carey and his cotemporaries, were important steps toward the consummation, the civilization and con. version of the world. Finally, when commerce and civilization are drawing Africa into their embraces, Christianity also is there to point her to God, her Sovereign and Redeemer. With or without missions, Africa is sure to be civilized before the passing away of many generations, for the forces which are urging her onward have never yet failed in the case of any nation to which they have extended, and they cannot fail consistently with their own nature.

Since commerce and civilization are such powerful auxiliaries of the Gospel, now is the very time, and the first time since the foundation of the world, for the herald of righteousness to claim the country for God, in the name of His Son and the Gospel. If we are remiss in this work, others will not be. If Protestants do not extend the dominion of Christ over the continent, Romanists will extend the dominion of the Pope, and the conversion of the people will be delayed for indefinite years. I call, then, on every man, and every denomination, who loves the truth, to direct a part of their missionary zeal to Central Africa, as the proper place for the commencement of their work. I would not have any other African mission weakened, but Central Africa is large enough for us all, Methodists, Baptists, Presbyterians, Episcopalians, and all others who hold the pure doctrines of grace. We may differ at present, on some points of importance, but the fundamental doctrines of brotherhood are common to us all ; and the day is not very distant when a mutual renunciation of all human errors will bind us into one body somewhat different from any of our present organizations. Now is the time to fight with sin, and not with one another.

So soon as health and other Providential dispensations will permit, I expect to resume my labors in Africa, with my companion, who, if possible, is more ardent than myself—a woman who has never faltered at any difficulty, or uttered a word of complaint against any of the troubles which we have encountered in that country. I do not expect to return alone. Some of my brethren will transfer their hopes of glory and of happiness to a better and surer state of existence than this ; and they will be missionaries, some in Africa, and some in other parts of the world. Our brethren who can not go, and whose duty requires them to remain at home, have never yet refused to contribute according to the wants of the faithful missionaries in the field. They never will refuse, for the work is of God. We ask nothing but the necessaries of life ; and I, for one, have never entertained the least transient fear that these will not be supplied by the liberalities of the churches. The number of Baptists in the Southern States only, are nearly, or quite six hundred thousand. Their contributions at present average five or six cents to each member, and this has been sufficient to sustain our infant missions. I feel the utmost confidence that our contributions will increase with the increase of our missions. Strange as it may seem, it is only a few weeks since I saw anti-missionary Baptists contribute publicly, boldly. and freely to the Central African mission. Here is an object which lays hold on our hearts. The people to whom we are sending the Gospel are negroes, in whose welfare we take so deep an interest at home. The missionaries are our own people, brought up, as it were, by our own firesides—whose history and former prospects in life we know. Their wives are our own daughters, or the daughters of our neighbors—the graduates of our Female Colleges ; reared, as the world would say, in the lap of luxury ; who have everything earthly to lose, and nothing to gain, by becoming missionaries. These are facts which tell upon our feelings, and we must and will have a part in this great Gospel work. Fifty cents a year, for each of our members would raise a Foreign Mission Fund of three hundred thousand dollars, which would sustain six HUNDRED missionaries, at our rates of support. Give us the men, and we shall find the money. That sum is nothing for us. We give ten times fifty cents a year for coffee or tobacco. Give us twelve hundred missionaries, and we will contribute an average of a dollar a year for their support. God has blessed us with abundance, and to spare, and we will freely give for the CONVERSION OF THE WORLD.

THE END.